TENAX   IN   FIDE

Lord Carrington.

BEYOND THE SUNSET

Charles Villiers

BEYOND
THE SUNSET

Charles Villiers

Thomas Harmsworth Publishing
Company,
Stoke Abbott

British Library Cataloguing in Publication Data
Villiers, Charles
Beyond the Sunset
I. Title
941.082092

ISBN 0948807-16-4

The publishers wish to thank British Steel
for allowing the use of copyright photography
and other (unidentified) copyright holders.

Printed and bound in Great Britain by
Bookcraft [Bath] Ltd.

From ULYSSES

by, Alfred, Lord Tennyson

'Tis not too late to seek a newer world.
... My purpose holds
To sail beyond the sunset, and the baths
Of all the western stars, until I die.

...Tho' much is taken, much abides; and tho'
We are not now that strength which in old days
Moved earth and heaven; that which we are, we are;
One equal temper of heroic hearts,
Made weak by time and fate, but strong in will
To strive, to seek, to find, and not to yield.

TRIBUTE MADE BY LORD CARRINGTON AT THE SERVICE OF THANKSGIVING FOR THE LIFE OF SIR CHARLES VILLIERS ON THURSDAY 12TH MARCH 1992 AT THE LONDON BROMPTON ORATORY

Charles Villiers' life was a full life - full of work, full of enthusiasms, full of a sense of duty and obligation and, perhaps above all, full of friends, as the congregation here this morning so clearly bears witness. Indeed, his life was so varied and he did so many different things that there can be no one, with the exception of José, who can know at first hand everything he did in the many different areas of his life.

He was in fact a most unorthodox man, in the sense that he did not always think or behave in the way which one would expect of someone of his background. He started off conventionally enough at Eton, where he rowed and played football and sang, and no doubt showed, as he did throughout the rest of his life, a determined spirit of independence.

There is an apocryphal story about how he was being particularly tiresome to one of the masters, who happened to be in Holy Orders and who got very annoyed with him. Steeling himself, he said, 'Villiers, just because I am a Parson you think I can't swear - but I can! Damn you, Villiers, and damn you again!' I don't suppose he minded very much.

But after Eton he did the unexpected. He became Assistant to Tubby Clayton at Toc H and deeply involved in the work of Toynbee Hall. I suspect that this experience developed one of his most dominant characteristics - a deep and abiding social conscience which motivated the rest of his life and career.

I first knew him at the beginning of the War when we were in the Grenadiers together and was present on that tragic occasion on Salisbury Plain when he, among others, was very seriously wounded at a flying demonstration. This left him physically scarred, but in no way weakened his resolution to take an active and proper part in the War. When he recovered from his wounds he joined the SOE, parachuting into Austria and Yugoslavia, and was decorated for conspicuous bravery. It seems very fitting that Charles should marry José, whose courage and determination and patriotism matched his and with whom he spent the happiest married life.

As we all of us remember, he had a distinguished and successful career in the City as a merchant banker, but there was always an imperative in his make-up to take part in public service of one kind or another. In fact, he was for a time a member of the Chelsea Borough Council. I don't believe that partisan politics suited him all that well. He was in a way far too individualistic and non-conformist. He made up his own mind about things. But his chance for public service came when he was asked to become Managing Director of the Industrial Reorganisation Corporation under the chairmanship of Lord Kearton. I asked charles not very long ago what was the most satisfactory period of his life and what had he enjoyed most. He replied that it was the IRC because it gave him the opportunity to put into practice some of those ideas which he had developed in his period in the City and which he believed to be vital for the regeneration of Britain.

He strongly believed in the rationalisation of British industry. He saw clearly that we were falling behind our European competitors, and increasingly so, and wanted to do something about it. The IRC gave him that opportunity. To say that the IRC was politically controversial would be to understate the case. There were those who believed that quasi-Government interference of this kind was unacceptable and that those who practised it were pretty unacceptable too. On the other hand, there were those who thought it did not go nearly far enough and that the policy of rationalisation should have been pursued much more vigorously.

One of Charles' greatest strengths was that he believed implicitly in what he was doing and, though he found some of the things that were said about him pretty wounding, he was not afraid of unpopularity, nor of being the odd man out amongst so many of his friends who, in the nature of things, were not wholly convinced in what he was doing. In other words, he had not just physical courage but great moral courage which supported him and sustained him in a difficult period, and indeed in an even more difficult period when he became Chairman of British Steel. This moral courage and his conversion to the Roman Catholic Church gave him the strength to do things which lesser men would not have even attempted.

I don't think his chairmanship of British Steel can have been a very happy period of his life. He had to take decisions which were not only difficult but quite contrary to his own instincts.

British Steel was in a desperate situation and, in order to ensure its survival, he had to make redundant somewhere in the region of 70,000 people. He tried with the best will in the world to do it with the collaboration of all concerned. It was an almost impossible task. His successors would agree that he laid the foundations on which the re-birth of British Steel took place.

As usual, he did it with the resolution which was so characteristic of him.

And what was also characteristic of him was that he set up a company to help the re-settlement of those who had lost their jobs and to help the economic recovery of the areas of former steelworks. He remained Chairman of that company until two or three years ago. A large number of new enterprises were born and with great success. No one could have worked harder or been more deeply involved than was Charles.

But business and industry were only a part of his life. He had countless enthusiasms and occupations. Anyone who visited his garden at Blacknest knows at first hand the zest, skill and knowledge of gardening which he showed, and, unlike some gardeners, we were more often than not the recipients of shrubs and trees which he thought would look well in our own gardens.

He was an enthusiastic lover of the arts. He was at one time a Trustee of Covent Garden but, more particularly, he was the most active and devoted Chairman of the Theatre Royal at Windsor.

He was a keen golfer with his old friend, Brian Johnston, who used to refer to him as 'a Second World War Golfer - out in 39 and back in 45!'

Over and above all this multitude of activity, both work and play, he was most particularly a patriot - someone who wanted this country to succeed, who was disappointed at its relative lack of success in the post-War years, who felt he had something to contribute towards putting things right and who worked doggedly to do so, regardless of opposition and personal criticisms. He looked at things with a fresh eye and, as somebody said, he was cultivated, communicative and active.

He was a lively companion, a good friend, the centre of a happy family. I went to see him shortly before he died. He faced what he knew was inevitable with his usual courage; serene, calm and optimistic. I suppose that some might say that the trouble with Charles was that he always thought that everyone was as principled and as good and as nice as he was. What a pity they are not.

CHAPTER 1

'CHERRY'

Everyone is, of course, the product of the seeds of heredity and the culture of environment; which comes out on top is anyone's guess, but in my own case I know that the earliest and strongest influence was my father, the much loved 'Algy,' who was killed in action in France during the British offensive at Cambrai, in the battle of the Bourlon Wood, on 23rd November 1917. He had given up his Captaincy in the Lothian and Border Horse to get into action in France, and had transferred to the newly formed Machine Gun Corps, in charge of a section. On that day the Bourlon Wood was an essential objective in the British assault by 381 tanks, which had to be covered by the MGC. His Commanding Officer wrote - 'I went to his guns just after dawn and found him sitting under a bank - asleep. I woke him and we talked over the orders, which he had received some hours before. We both knew he had a dangerous task to perform. He was extraordinarily happy and as keen as a boy, and I thought at the time how ready he was for whatever might come.' A sniper's bullet got him early on in the battle and he died instantly. He was just 31 years of age.

His life had been full of promise; after a scholarship at Wellington College and a demyship at Magdalene College, Oxford, my father went into James Capel - then, as now, a prime city firm. He married my mother in 1911 and in the following year (when I was born) he took a partnership in Govett, now amalgamated with 'Kit' Hoare's firm on the

Stock Exchange. Then came the first World War and exit.

What a waste! He was clever, original, artistic and very religious. His brother-in-law, Harry Graham (the lyricist), wrote of him 'there was something extremely infectious about his zeal, his wholehearted and eager absorption in whatever work lay to his hand, and no one could be in his company for long without unconsciously reflecting the glow of his enthusiasm. His views were always unconventional, often very original, and to doubt their sincerity was as impossible as to doubt his own conviction of their truth. Though essentially critical, he was broad-minded and tolerant enough to listen patiently. He was a redoubtable, but most charming, antagonist.' Brother officers wrote, 'It is no exaggeration to say that officers and men adored him.'

My father became my hero and without him I realised that I was on my own, to paddle my own canoe as best I could, in fair weather and foul.

My mother was left with sister Theresa (born 2 months before my father was killed) and me, and very few resources. We were poor, very 'pi,' but everything had to be 'done proper.' We lived with my mother's parents near Ashdown Forest in Sussex in a house called Cherry Orchard - always 'Cherry' to us. My mother was beautiful, dutiful, young and rather shy, and devastated by my father's death. Theresa and I when referring to our father, always added sotto-voce 'which art in Heaven.'

So much, for the moment, for my immediate, small family. Looking further afield, however, I must say a word about not only my father's family, but about my mother's relatives, the Pauls and the Ritchies and about the family to whom we were later to become related by the re-marriage of my mother, the Gibbs.

First, then, my mother's parents; her father, my grandfather, Herbert Paul, after Eton and Oxford (where he got a First in Greats and was President of the Union) became Member of Parliament, first for Edinburgh South and then for Northampton. He was a friend and admirer of Mr Asquith, the Liberal Prime Minister; for this his very Tory family never forgave him. He was also, for a time, the leader writer of the *Daily News*, absorbed later into the *News Chronicle*. In 1910 he became a Civil Service Commissioner. His literary efforts were prodigious; he wrote a classic History of Modern England (in 5 volumes) which that fine historian, Professor Lord Asa Briggs, told me that he found invaluable. Grandfather also wrote the standard life of Queen Anne and a profound study of Mr Gladstone, who was his hero.

His family had been squires and parsons - 'Squarsons' - of the village of Finedon, near Kettering, for hundreds of years; indeed, his father and grandfather had between them been that for over one hundred years. But when his mind began to get clouded, no doubt through overwork, he retired to 'Cherry,' where he spent the rest of his days, till he was 82, reading and walking in Ashdown Forest. My grandmother was embarrassed by his habit of saying out loud what he was thinking privately. When there were visitors he would walk into the room and say loudly 'I wonder when these dreadful people are going to leave.'

I was myself puzzled when walking with Grandfather in Ashdown Forest and he kept on saying 'God butter my soul;' my mother told me to mind my own business!

Later, when I was at Eton, I asked him to explain 'the Eastern Question;' he sent me a note which amazed the Eton 'beaks' by its clarity. When he died Lord Crewe wrote in *The Times*, 'It is sad that he left a slighter mark on his age than those who could not claim a tithe of his ability or his achievements.'

My mother in her sorrow at the death of my father went off on her bicycle most days to Wych Cross Place, 3 miles up the hill, where Uncle Douglas Freshfield had turned his mansion into a hospital. She worked there as a nurse in the Voluntary Aid Detachment and that helped her to recover her balance.

I was left much in the care of Grandmother, Herbert Paul's

wife, who was a most splendid lady, both in appearance and in intellect. She was one of the eight children of William Ritchie, whose family had been successful farmers in Aberdeenshire. William, after Eton and Oxford, (where he earned the name 'Gentleman Ritchie') went to India, where he had strong connections. His mother was born Thackeray (a sister, I believe, of the writer W M Thackeray), and the family had given long service to the Indian army and administration. William was a barrister and soon rose to be the leader of the Calcutta bar and a member of the Viceroy's Council. My grandmother, as a girl, stayed with him in Calcutta during the Indian Mutiny, when he wrote home, 'Nearly all our friends are safe, but we are anxious to hear of the two young Macnaghtens, one of whom was at Allahabad, where there has been a dreadful massacre, and one at Cawnpore, where they have been besieged. Poor Tom's (his cousin's) regiment, the 22nd, has been hitherto considered a crack corps, but now, I fear, is not to be trusted any more than the rest.' William's bust and memorial tablet stand in Calcutta Cathedral, commemorating his good work and fine character. He died in 1862, in his 46th year.

Of William's daughters, Augusta (Gussie) married Douglas Freshfield, who climbed Mount Kanchenjunga and another, Elinor (Nellie) married Herbert Paul. She was one of the first women to attend a university in England, and every day she read the New Testament in Greek, making notes, as she read, on the blank page opposite. She became what was then called a 'blue stocking' and was much sought after in intellectual and literary circles, especially in Chelsea.

Unfortunately, she also became stone deaf and my sister and I used to listen in amazement when she shouted into her hearing aid, whose batteries were always 'down,' phrases such as, 'Can you hear me now?' She had to spend much time in bed as she suffered from what was then called a 'dropped stomach.' But she was wonderful to me and taught me to read and write at a very early age. I learned a lot of poetry from her and got deep into Tennyson and Kipling - where I have stayed! She coped with her disabilities and, during the difficult war years, held the whole family together. I am glad to say that she lived to a ripe old age, retaining all her mental faculties.

Great-grandmother, Herbert Paul's mother, came to live with us at 'Cherry,' together with her unmarried daughter, Helena. The old lady was the widow of Canon Paul, who had been vicar of Finedon. She lived to the age of 97 and always had a little whisky in her afternoon tea, a habit I have copied after an afternoon's work out of doors. My mother's brother, Humphrey Paul, often came to stay. He was a perfect example of the 'clever fool:' he tried his hand at many things - barrister, parliamentary candidate, parliamentary draughtsman, solicitor, all sorts of legal activities, but he could never hold a job. My grandmother spoilt him, always giving him more money, and my mother made him 'take the pledge,' but it was no good and he died penniless in the Charterhouse.

Looking back on those years, the first seven of my life, I see a vivid picture of a family crouching together in misfortune. Their intellectual, literary, and Parliamentary life had caved in. They had very little money and the war made everything more difficult. They were lucky to have Ada Benson to look after them. She came from Finedon with Great-grandmother and did everything in the house at 'Cherry;' she followed my mother and worked for us till well after World War Two. She was part of the family and lived till she was 100 years old, or so she said, but she was never quite sure of the year she was born.

Then there was Jeanie, who looked after my sister and me. She had come to us when my father was in the Lothian and Border Horse at Haddington, just over the border in Scotland. We adored her and she fell for an artillery man in the army camp on Ashdown Forest, near to 'Cherry.' After the war they married and, as the story goes, lived happily ever after. Mr Pook was the gardener - a man straight out of 'Puck of Pook's Hill,' with a large spade beard and a tall hat which we never saw him remove. Between them these wonderful people did the hard work and enabled us to be what we felt we were, and were generally seen to be - gentry, living in reduced circumstances.

'Cherry' had no electric light, only oil lamps, and no telephone; we had no car or carriage. Forest Row was 3 miles away and food, coal and other supplies were delivered once a week; we never visited shops, but the catalogue of the Army and Navy Stores was endlessly pored over. The postman called twice a day and he was our main contact with the outside world. Communication was by postcard or letter. There were no near neighbours and not many people came to call, being rather frightened by grandfather. We could never get to Church, but my grandmother gave me a lot of religious instruction.

Our most regular visitor was Uncle Douglas Freshfield, who had married grandmother's sister, by then deceased. He was very rich and had commissioned his son-in-law, Edwin Fisher, to build him an Edwardian mansion on the South Downs, Wych Cross Place, later owned and lived in by Lord Samuel. He lived there with his two unmarried daughters, who were dedicated to good works. He was always called 'Gompy' because he was so 'gompitious,' whatever that may mean. He bought 'Cherry' for my grandparents to live in when grandfather retired from Parliament. I don't suppose we paid any rent. Anyway, he was devoted to grandmother and took her for drives in his splendid motor car, with no hard top and a glass wind shield pulled up in front of the back seat. They wore caps and dust coats and wrapped up in rugs. The chauffeur was similarly equipped and they drove round the Sussex countryside, very slowly but in fine style.

As a small boy I cannot of course be sure what these older people were thinking, but I listened carefully to what they said and I became much too old for my age. I gathered that the Pauls and the Ritchies had been rather important people in

6

the previous century and, indeed, they remained so up to about 1910, when grandfather retired from Parliament, due to his unreliable memory. They had a number of strong convictions. They believed in the Monarchy, Parliament, the Church of England, the Empire (especially India), the public schools (especially Eton), Oxford and Cambridge (especially Oxford), Mr Gladstone, free trade and the Reform Club. They took for granted England's world leadership, their own intrinsic superiority, an income from somewhere, domestic servants and the Grace of God. They accepted the leadership of Mr Asquith, but they distrusted Mr Lloyd George, (Ll.G) and Mr Winston Churchill. They detested the German Kaiser.

The Americans were, for them, an unknown quantity. France, Italy and Switzerland were for the Grand Tour. We were, in fact, though none of us knew it, at the fag end of the great British era, the 100 years which followed the Battle of Waterloo.

At 'Cherry' we lived in a closed little world, looking after each other; we did not have much fun, but I was not unhappy. We lived in the past. I did not feel restless, because I knew nothing else. I was certainly ready to break out, which I was able to do when what we called the 'Great War' came to an end. I took with me from 'Cherry,' and I have always been grateful for it, a strong sense of Christianity, a love of England and its countryside, and of books and learning, fear of poverty and a desire to be worthy of my father, who remains my hero.

At the end of the Great War the soldiers were singing to a catchy tune, 'When this bloody war is over, oh how happy we shall be,' and there is no doubt that the peace was welcomed in Britain and the other allied countries with unrestrained relief, happiness and even joy - with pride too, because we had fought throughout and endured a million Empire soldiers dead and double that number wounded. Some said that a million would have emigrated anyway during the 4-years of war, but the losses fell heaviest on the junior officers, who would have been the leaders in peacetime, instead of the older generation which 'stayed obstinately alive.' We young people took it in our stride, but we were undoubtedly deeply affected by the changed attitude of the 'grown-ups' and by their sincere sorrow at the loss of so many loved ones.

This is not a history book. My aim is to recount not only what happened to me, but also the hopes and worries of the older people to whom I listened, and how these changed with the events of the next three score years and ten - a normal life span. These older people were in my case parliamentary, professional and business people at the upper end of the middle class, who considered themselves part of the ruling class of Britain at that time. Later I found myself deeply involved with middle management and the working class, with whom I worked. I was brought up on Liberal principles, to which I still adhere, but as the Liberal party faded away from political leadership I found myself drifting into the Tory party - part of its radical left wing.

In 1921 the grown-ups in my life were rejuvenated by the peace. They saw England (as they had always called Britain) enhanced in their own and, indeed, in the world's view by the dogged and successful fight against Germany, a fight for liberty and against aggression. The German, Austrian, Russian and Turkish empires had been destroyed and broken up. Two new countries - Czechoslovakia and Jugoslavia - had been created and self-determination was the order of the day. Of course, it was very sad that Russia had gone communist, but then it had never been a democratic country and it seemed that they had just exchanged one autocracy for another, equally difficult to understand, trust or do business with.

It was, of course, regrettable that Lloyd George, our Prime Minister, had said that the German lemon must be squeezed till the pips squeaked, but the French Premier, Clemenceau, was tougher still on German reparations and in his insistence that Germany must admit guilt for having caused the war. Reparations at 10 billion gold marks were agreed, but were unpayable and the occupation of the Rhineland by allied troops did not seem unreasonable under the circumstances, nor did the limitation of the Germany Army to 100,000 soldiers and no airforce. The Germany Navy had scuttled itself at Scapa Flow. I do not remember that we felt sorry for the Germans, but we were not as vengeful as the French, who had earlier scores to pay off, and part of whose country had been occupied or even devastated for much of the war.

Amazingly, England found itself able to recover its financial, industrial and commercial wealth quite quickly, or so we thought. It was not long before taxation was reduced and the talk was all about getting back to 1914 conditions. The National Debt had grown colossally, which was a worry, but it was also an excuse for not increasing social insurance schemes, on which Ll.G had been so keen. We were short of housing, but that could be solved in time. The social structure appeared to be intact (especially domestic servants) and although the coal miners and the railway men were badly paid, their efforts to get more by striking failed ignominiously and the miners went back to work on terms worse than what they could have got before the strike began. The postwar boom was followed by the inevitable slump and unemployment went up to 2 million, but politicians still talked of 'homes for heroes' and 'a country fit for heroes to live in.'

Ll.G remained Prime Minister, but was distrusted even by Liberals like the Paul family, who remained loyal to Asquith, who had been bundled out of the way by Ll.G, and to the memory of the great Mr Gladstone. However, in 1922 the Tories withdrew from wartime coalition and dumped Lloyd George. Bonar Law led the Tories with a small majority in Parliament, but Labour won many seats - mainly at the expense of the exhausted and divided Liberals - and the result was a stalemate. There was soon another election and Labour formed a minority government, which lasted for only a short while. In 1924 Stanley Baldwin, leading the Tories, won a substantial majority and settled down to form a more permanent government, which included Winston Churchill, who had returned to the Tories after his flirtation with the Liberals.

There were, of course, some worries. Ll.G had said, 'We shall have to fight another war in 25 years time, all over again and at 3 times the cost.' The American Congress had refused to ratify the Peace Treaty or join the League of Nations invented by Lord Robert Cecil, one of our few neighbours at Cherry. But US President Wilson had launched the League and it was a terrible shock when the US Congress turned aside from it. Who then was this Corporal Adolf Hitler, who had formed a National Socialist party in Germany, demanding a revision of the Treaty of Versailles, and what about this fellow Mussolini, who strutted about Italy calling himself 'Il Duce,' and was it significant that Hirohito had taken over as Regent of Japan? These were the questions being asked.

At home, writers such as Siegfred Sassoon and Osbert Sitwell, who had become radicals during the war, were saying things the ruling class did not want to hear. Maynard Keynes wrote 'The Economic Consequences of the Peace,' in which he prophesied that Europe could only recover when Germany was restored to her old economic strength. Labour elected Ramsay Macdonald as leader; he said, 'We can have no truck with tranquillity,' and advanced a social reform ticket. The unions were ineffective over the miners' strike, but insisted that unemployment relief was too low.

But on balance the mood was confident and optimistic. Britain was still 'great' and rich. The Americans had opted out. The rival empires had been broken up. We and the French ruled the roost and Ll.G, for all his faults, usually seemed to get the better of Clemenceau. Complacency ruled the day. We had won, hadn't we? - as we always did. And if there were problems, well, there have always been problems. By 1924 the Parliament was moving from Liberal to Tory and the Labour Party had only 142 seats. We had had a boom and a slump, which was in the natural order of things. One or two million people unemployed should keep wages down, thought some. In short, God was in his Heaven and all was well with the world.'

Looking back on the immediate post-Great War years one can now see what was then invisible - that they were the last years of the Adam Smith political economy, when taxes were low, Government intervention was minimal, trade was as free as possible and 'laissez faire' was the answer to economic problems, plus a little conciliation here and there. It was, of course, true that Ll.G's social insurance schemes clashed with this philosophy, but fair-minded people thought that these were necessary to conciliate the working class. We did not have to wait many years for Maynard Keynes' economic policy to change all that: in fact, the Welfare State was even then coming to birth.

The change in attitudes which came with the end of the war affected even the little world of my childhood. The hospital at Wych Cross, no longer needed, was closed down; the house was turned into a school for the nephews and nieces of Gompy, and I went to live there.

Then my grandfather Villiers came back from Le Havre in France, where the Belgian Government had established itself. He was the British Minister, soon to be appointed first British Ambassador to the King of the Belgians, Albert I. He and Granny Villiers became very interested in my sister and myself, whom they had never seen before. It was exciting too, to meet my father's brothers and sisters and their children, of whom we became very fond.

And then my mother married again, to everyone's delight. He was tall, dark and handsome - Walter Gibbs, heir-pre-sumptive to the head of that rich family of landed gentry, who had their own private merchant bank in the City of London. He was a kind, gentle, clever, rather shy man, who did his best to integrate two fatherless little Villiers into his own family, whose culture was very different.

Everywhere my sister and I met a wave of kindness and involvement, which carried us into an entirely new ambience, but I believe I was never detached for long from beliefs and attitudes absorbed at Cherry. Expectations did alter with unfolding opportunities, but I am still the same person. I know that because I have in front of me as I write a letter from my own father to my prospective housemaster at Eton, in which he wrote, 'My small boy seems likely to be a perfectly healthy, normal person of sharp wits and moderate industry.' This I have remained, but with duller wits.

CHAPTER 2

'STANSTEAD'

Wych Cross was a wonderful place for a private school. A dozen children could stay there without being noticed by Gompy, whose quarters were at the end of a long gallery, where he was looked after by his Dutch butler, whose name was Zuchler - or that is what it sounded like. His daughter Katia (Kok) was a large, gaunt, toothy woman had never married, but who had a heart of gold. Her friend, Miss Prynne, Pin to us, was a breezy no-nonsense teacher. We were well taught to a high standard while still very young, and the fun was that we were all cousins - Fishers, Ritchies, Thackerays and us.

I never found difficulty in learning. (That's not quite right, because I nearly quit on a word processor course at the age of 76!) But I preferred romping around in the vast gardens of Wych Cross. There was an ornamental pond, where we sailed our boats.

There were huge Ali Baba pots in which we hid, until we broke one of them! There was a kitchen garden we could raid for strawberries, raspberries and cherries. There were ponies in the stables, where the groom, Fred, taught us how to ride and to look after horses. There was a stream at the bottom of the Sussex Down on which Wych Cross stood, with a waterfall under an enormous beech tree, which we called the Royal George, a great place for picnics. There were huge trees of every sort where we got to know squirrels - red ones - and badgers, weasels, stoats and of course hundreds of rabbits and occasional roe and fallow deer.

We were all country people and we throve in these circumstances, but our natural inquisitiveness about each others' bodies was sternly suppressed. It was, indeed, an idyllic life in the age of innocence and when I went from time to time to see Gompy, I always was drawn back into the magic of those childhood days.

Of course, it was too good to last and in 1921 Walter Gibbs turned up at Cherry in his large Minerva car. He was recently married to my mother and had come to take my sister and myself away to his home, Stanstead Lodge, (always Stanstead to us) near Ware, in Hertfordshire. Stanstead was on his father's large estate called 'Briggens,' and was to be our new home. At about the same time I went to a preparatory school called Saint Cyprians, at Eastbourne. Everything was new and I remember the shock to this day. The people were kind, the new home was fine and the school was welcoming, but it was all different.

To take the people first. Walter, my new stepfather, was devoted to his own parents, who lived at 'Briggens,' as big as Wych Cross, just up the hill and through the park from Stanstead, and he used to go and see them every day. Five days a week he went doggedly by train to the City to run the family Merchant Bank, Antony Gibbs and Sons (AG&S), which he was determined to keep going in just the same way as his father had intended. His other great interests were shooting and fishing, at which he excelled, and gardening. He had not much time for books or music, and was a very good but rather limited man, with traditional City interests.

AG&S had been started by Antony Gibbs, who, with his brother Vicary, had come up to London at the end of the eighteenth century from their property near Exeter, which had the romantic name of Clyst St George. They were a bright pair; Antony founded the business and Vicary was knighted as Chief Justice of Common Pleas. Their family can be traced back to the 15th century, always living in Devon, usually near

14

Exeter, where they are mentioned in many historical rolls and documents. But the Gibbs really took off under Antony in London. His portrait hangs in the Royal Exchange and his trade was with South America, chiefly Chile and Peru, importing nitrate, iodine and guano. Needless to say, the City being what it is, the versifiers said:

'And now we come to Messrs Gibbs,
Who made their dibs
By selling turds
Of foreign birds.'

Antony's grandson bought a fine property at Aldenham in Hertfordshire, just north of London, and in due course became the first Lord Aldenham. His son, known to me as Uncle Alban, was a famous gardener and gave his name to many varieties of flowering shrubs. He had complained bitterly when the Great War broke out and he had to reduce the number of his gardeners to 70! At an early stage in his life he stood for parliament as a Tory. His platform was that if the voters thought that his Liberal opponent was the better man, they had better vote for him, and that is exactly what they did. He became quite literally a sleeping partner in AG&S and I remember him snoozing on a sofa in the partners' room with *The Times* over his head. He lived to a great age and was succeeded by his son Gerald, who had no children.

Alban's brother Herbert became head of the firm, 'Prior,' as they quaintly called it. Herbert was the father of Walter, my stepfather, who thus became the heir-presumptive to the Aldenham title, but before that happened Herbert was made a peer, as the chairman of the City Conservative Association, and because during the Great War AG&S had taken no commission on the nitrate they had imported for munitions. Herbert became Lord Hunsdon, a title which died out when Walter succeeded Gerald as Lord Aldenham. My mother was styled successively Miss Paul, Mrs Villiers, Mrs Gibbs, Lady Hunsdon and Lady Aldenham. Sometimes she got a bit muddled and I remember her writing 'from Lady Villiers' on the back of a Wartime letter she wrote me. Walter was very amused on taking his seat in the House of Lords and the official said 'the blood has sat.'

Walter's father, Herbert, and his mother Anna ran the whole family. They had 6 children of whom the eldest was Winifred, who married Charles Ponsonby, MP for Sevenoaks; he was created a Baronet for being Parliamentary Private Secretary to Anthony Eden, when Foreign Secretary. Then came Walter. Next was Geoffrey, who had a fine City career and was knighted for service to Export Credits. He and his wife Helen had a large family and they inherited the Manor House and thatched village of Clifton Hamden in Oxfordshire. They turned out to be my best friends among the Gibbs family. The third son, Humphrey, was a farmer, who went to Southern Rhodesia and married Molly, a courageous South African lady, who presented him with 5 sons. They farmed near Bulawayo and he was knighted as the last Governor of Southern Rhodesia. Walter had two sisters who never married and stayed at home looking after their parents, and were dedicated to good works.

This was a formidable array by any standard and there was more to it... There was cousin George, who, after a political career, became Lord Wraxall and lived in an immense Victorian mansion at Tyntesfield near Bristol. Herbert always referred to those Gibbs's as the 'Barrow lot' - a reference, I suppose, to a property once owned by them.

Walter was very loyal to his family and called his two sons by my mother Antony and Vicary, thus going back to the 18th century pair who came up to London from Devon. They were my half brothers. Vicary was killed in action in 1944. Antony, who loved being in the Navy, brought his wardroom tastes and habits to AG&S after the war was over.

Through the Gibbs family ran a very strong and tenacious conservative trait. For example, Uncle Alban Gibbs referred to my grandfather, Herbert Paul, as 'a dangerous radical.' Herbert Gibbs got into trouble during the General Strike of

1926 when he wrote to *The Times* saying he thought the strikers were as much the enemies of the country as the Germans had been during the Great War, and should be dealt with in the same way! Anna tried, but failed, to stop the postman before he got back to the Post Office in Ware. The letter was published and evoked much comment. High Tories were confirmed in their view; those of a Liberal outlook were scandalised.

Walter's conservatism came out when, as he sometimes did, he quoted the verse of the hymn which runs:

'Change and decay in all around I see,
Oh Thou who changest not abide with me.'

Conservative they may have been, but the Gibbs family had many endearing features. As far as my sister and I were concerned Briggens, later to be our home, was a beautiful place. It was a big house of some 20 bedrooms and very much a Gibbs family centre. Herbert had built an immense garden of flowering shrubs on the side of a hill, sloping down from the house to the valley of the River Lea and a railway connecting London and Cambridge. There were farms and woods, which made a good pheasant shoot, and a valley over which partridges were driven to the guns. Two lakes below the house were created by a previous owner, as was the ice house, where ice used to be stored for much of the year in straw. There was a big staff run by the housekeeper, Annie Hearn and the butler, Mr Woolard. The chauffeur, Mr Ford, drove Herbert to the station or to the office in the City in a Sunbeam car. There was a head keeper and a head gardener, and I should think at least another seven people, working in the garden. 'Upstairs, downstairs' could have been written about them.

Stanstead was modest in comparison. Its name on the Ordnance Survey map was 'Buggs Farm.' However it had been improved and became home for us until Herbert died, just before World War Two began, when we trekked up to Briggens. A great deal of money was needed to support all this, which was always gentlemanly, and never ostentatious. The Gibbs family were what Galsworthy would have called 'warm men.' Indeed, I often thought that the Forsyte Saga had been modelled on them. They had all inherited or accumulated money, which came from participation in AG&S, which had done very well in the City and was highly regarded, along with Barings, Rothschilds, Morgans and the other 'accepting' houses. They accepted bills of exchange drawn on them by their customers, who could cash the bill by discounting it in the money market.

It was understood that the Bank of England would never let an acceptance house fail. Nevertheless, AG&S did fall upon hard times after the Great War. Herbert went on importing nitrate long after the demand for munitions had fallen away. When my mother married Walter in 1920, her new mother-in-law said, 'My dear, you will never want for money.' Famous last words, because from then on Walter, who soon became 'Prior,' always thought himself strapped for cash and although he struggled on for the next 40 years the firm went down and down and disappeared altogether in the eighties. Walter and Geoffrey, who always sat next to him, probably got more satisfaction from their 'outside' directorships.

Walter became chairman of the Westminster Bank (now NatWest) and Geoffrey was Chairman of an Australian bank in the City, where they were both liked and respected for their experience and for their conservative and prudent views.

I had an interesting and enjoyable life with the Gibbs family, who were amazingly kind and thoughtful to me - even though I did become an 'enfant terrible,' struggling with their sporting and commercial culture for which I had inherited neither taste nor aptitude. I did try, most unsuccessfully, to shoot and fish properly and to 'pursue a guinea with undimmed zeal' and I came to enjoy this life on grouse moor, river, field and woodland. I know well all the inhabitants of these delightful areas, but I have no wish to kill any of them, not even the rabbits which infest our garden at Blacknest, on the edge of Windsor Great Park, which we bought in 1960.

The Gibbs always intended that I, like them, should work in the City of London and so I did. They gave me a good start, for which I am grateful but I was always really aiming in other directions.

These years, the early 1920s, were both enhanced and complicated for me by making contact with my father's family, the Villiers, who were entirely different from the Gibbs; the two families regarded each other with some suspicion, perhaps even dislike. The Villiers were very grand people, and had a long historical tradition.

Alexander de Villers (a French or Norman colonist) who died in 1242, had married the heiress of the village of Brooksby, near Melton Mowbray in Leicestershire, where he became feudal Lord of the Manor. His grandson was knighted as Sir John and is recorded as being alive in 1276. He changed the spelling of his name to Villiers, but to this day the pronunciation has remained Villers. There the family lived, without any special distinction, until Sir George, who died in 1606. By his first wife he had Sir Edward, who was the grandfather of the first Earl of Jersey, and the uncle of the notorious Barbara, mistress of Charles II and Duchess of Cleveland. By his second and very beautiful wife, Mary Beaumont, he had George, who became the first Duke of Buckingham and whose astounding career, till he was murdered by Felton, in Portsmouth in 1628, has been fully recorded elsewhere.

Young George was an outstandingly handsome - even beautiful - man, and he was introduced by a faction at the Court of King James I as Groom of the Bedchamber, to gain influence over the susceptible and homosexual monarch. The King almost certainly had George at Farnham Castle in August 1615. Later George, now Duke of Buckingham, wrote to the King, 'Do you love me now better than at the time at Farnham when the bed's head could not be found between the master and his dog?'

From then on James could refuse Steenie (as he called our George) nothing and he became, in effect, the deputy sovereign of England. The strange thing is that George was also adored by James' son Charles, later King Charles I, with whom he went on a number of diplomatic and, as they were both womanisers, probably amorous adventures. Buckingham's strength lay in the large connection he formed to support himself, based on jobs, titles and land granted under royal patronage. Buckingham's line fizzled out when his two grandchildren died, one of the pox and the other in a skirmish at Richmond.

The Jersey line, however, took firm root. In 1776 Thomas Villiers, the second son of the 2nd Earl, married Charlotte who was the heiress of Edward Hyde, first Earl of Clarendon. After the execution of Charles I, this extremely able person went into exile with Charles II and at the Restoration became Lord High Chancellor, the actual managing director of England. His volumes, 'The Great Rebellion,' remain English classics. His elder daughter married King James II and thus was the mother of both Queen Mary, who married William of Orange, and of Queen Anne. It was through Clarendon's second daughter, Jane, that his properties came to Charlotte and so to Thomas Villiers, when she married him. Thomas was a successful diplomatist and when he was first raised to the peerage took the title of Lord Hyde and, on further promotion, the Earldom of Clarendon, as a compliment to his wife's family and to preserve a famous name. The two Villiers earldoms continue to this day, The Clarendons are usually named 'Hyde' and the Jerseys 'Child,' following the 5th Earl's marriage to the daughter of the banker, Robert Child of Osterley, where his grand house stands today.

The Clarendon family produced a series of public servants - particularly George, the fourth Earl, of what the College of

Heralds calls 'the second creation.' He was successively Ambassador in Madrid, Lord Privy Seal, President of the Board of Trade and Viceroy of Ireland. In Ireland he had to deal with the potato famine of the late 1840s and subsequent revolution, but he was able to invite Queen Victoria and Prince Albert to stay in Dublin Castle in the following year. The visit was a great success, but the compositor in the *Irish Times* got his own back the next day by printing, 'a great crowd gathered and cheered vociferously as the Queen and Prince Albert pissed over the bridge.' In such circumstances who would not? But George's real triumphs lay in diplomacy. He was Foreign Secretary to Palmerston, Lord John Russell and to Gladstone - always a Whig. He died in 1870 and the next year his daughter found herself sitting next to Bismark at dinner. Bismark in his rough, teutonic way said to her, 'I was delighted to hear news of your father's death.' When she shrank away, Bismark explained, 'While he was alive I would never have dared to attack France.'

The Foreign Secretary, as we referred to him, had a brother Charles, after whom I was named. He was an active Liberal member of Parliament and regularly proposed the repeal of the Corn Laws, which propped up the price of corn to protect the farmers and the landed gentry. In 1848 he, along with Cobden and Bright, was successful in getting repeal through Parliament. Charles never married. He was member for Wolverhampton for 60 years, Father of the House of Commons and died at the age of 96. It was his elder brother Edward who succeeded to the title and became Lord Chamberlain to King Edward VII. He was succeeded by his son, Bertie, who became Chairman of the BBC and then Governor General of South Africa, where I served him as a sort of temporary, volunteer ADC in 1936. He also became Lord Chamberlain. Bertie's eldest son George was killed in a shooting accident in South Africa and his grandson is now 8th Earl of the 'second creation.' My dear wife, coming from Belgium to marry me, was very confused by the 'born again' condition of the head of my family.

My grandfather was the Foreign Secretary's youngest son and not unsurprisingly went into the Foreign Office, where he prospered and became Minister and then Ambassador to the King of the Belgians. He was covered with the most senior decorations, of which the most prized was his membership of the Privy Council.

His best remembered remark was made to Brand Whitlock, the American Minister to Belgium. On the day the Great War broke out, Grandfather went round to the American legation in Brussels and asked Whitlock to look after the British legation 'for the duration.' Whitlock said he would do so and Grandfather replied, 'It's all a most frightful bore. I shall lunch quietly at the office and then go down to Antwerp' - a typical English response to a cataclysm. Brand Whitlock, together with the Spanish Ambassador, were to remain in Belgium for the duration of the war, assisting most capably in the distribution of food relief. The King of the Belgians stayed at La Panne, on Belgian soil throughout the war, but his Government and the diplomatic corps stayed at Le Havre in France where grandfather had a visit from my father, on local leave, just before he was killed.

After the war Grandfather reassembled his family in Brussels, where as the first British Ambassador he was a VIP, a very important person. He had married Virginia Smith, sister of Lindsay Smith of Ashfold. Granny Villiers had a little money of her own but Grandfather, as the youngest son, had virtually none. Their eldest son Eric won a DSO with the Highland Light Infantry in the Great War and became a partner of Madame Martel: he was inevitably known as 'Brandy' Villiers. His brother Gerald went into the Foreign Office but refused to go abroad except on one occasion during World War II when he was sent by the Ministry of Economic Warfare to Stockholm (a neutral capital) to persuade SKF, the Swedish ball-bearing manufacturers, to supply Britain equally with the Germans. Gerry, by then no chicken, was packed into the bomb bay of a Mosquito (wood and aluminium frame bomber) and was flown by night to Sweden.

Gerry is supposed to have addressed Jacob Wallenberg, SKF's chairman as follows; 'I am sure, Sir, that it keeps you awake at night to realise that you yourself are one of the very few people who are deliberately prolonging the course of the war, by refusing to supply Britain with a specified range of ball bearings; which as a neutral you should do.'

'Ach, Mr Villiers, you have travelled far, as an old man, in an uncomfortable vehicle to tell me that, which I greatly resent. But if we were able to supply, we could not deliver, because the Skagerrak and the Kattegat exit to the North Sea is mined both by the Germans and yourselves.'

'Mr. Wallenberg, if you can supply, the Royal Navy can deliver.'

'Go home, Mr. Villiers, you have won!'

Jacob Wallenberg was as good as his word and the Royal Navy delivered, but he never forgot and I had a sharp brush with him twenty-five years later when, as Managing Director of the Industrial Reorganisation Corporation, I frustrated his attempt to make SKF the sole ball-bearings manufacturer in the UK.

All these good Villiers relations, including especially my father's two married sisters, were most kind and affectionate to my sister and me, mainly, I believe, because of my father, who was mourned by them all. We stayed in their houses and spent holidays with their children. Indeed, returning from Dunkirk in 1940 I arrived out of the blue at Eric's house near Oswestry, where he entertained me and my family nobly. Best of all they did not mind when Granny Villiers left her much-diminished fortune to be divided between Gerald and me.

To this day I recall the confusion in my mind caused by the different cultures and circumstances of the three families which contributed to my upbringing. The Pauls were basically poor, intellectual, Liberal and Christian. The Gibbs were non-intellectual, commercial, sporting, rich and Tory. The

Villiers were public servants with Royal collections, Whig/Liberal and lofty, but their great estates had largely been sold off. I know, because I was the last Clarendon trustee to be appointed, the first having been Lord Mansefield in 1660, whose portrait I have on loan from the family collection.

I could not help being overwhelmed by this formidable background and for a time I was torn this way and that, but in a strange way, by the time I went to Eton, I knew that I had to be my own man and make my way, probably without much help from anyone else. I doubt if anyone, except perhaps my father, would think I had made much of a fist of it.

CHAPTER 3

SCHOOL AND TOC H

In September 1921 my mother and Walter deposited me at the door of St Cyprian's private preparatory school at Eastbourne - selected by my prospective housemaster at Eton. I was terrified; at Wych Cross everybody was 'family' and I knew them all already. St Cyprian's was an unknown world, but the welcome by a genial bespectacled Vaughan Wilkes and his broad-beamed, wide-faced, grinning wife, known to all as 'Flip,' was genuine enough and their private quarters, where we had tea, looked familiar territory - large sofas, armchairs, cushions, books, dogs and a smell of wood smoke. I sat silent except when asked embarrassing questions about work and games, of which I knew nothing. Then matron came in and my mother gave her an account of my teeth and bowels. Eventually another new boy's family arrived and, after rather desperate signals from Walter, my parents departed.

I had never been left on my own before and I felt awful. The dormitory, exhibited by matron, looked as bleak as a hospital ward, with which I was familiar. The class rooms were, as I had expected, desks and a blackboard. The chapel was homely, the indoor swimming pool looked petrifying as I could not swim, and the playing fields were so enormous that I could not even imagine crossing them - and anyway, I could not play any game. But the red-brick, white-gabled school building looked friendly enough.

And then, all of a sudden, a small boy ran out, and then another and another. 'We're new boys,' they said. 'So am I,' said I, and at once was happy and felt at home. This little band, of course, soon expanded and was integrated into the whole school of some 100 boys, whose parents were aiming at the bigger public schools, Eton and Harrow in particular. We were taught very well, professionally and imaginatively in the then classical manner. The masters (I only remember one mistress) were qualified university men who enjoyed teaching, loved sport and made the most of the long holidays. The head master's son, John, was later an Eton housemaster and then headmaster of Radley - a nice, good, clever man whose friendship I valued. The oldest was Mr Sellars, a scholar, whose most remembered contribution was a presentation of Dickens' 'Christmas Carol,' with slides projected by a magic lantern. Learning by heart was then much in vogue and every Sunday in term time we had to learn and recite by heart to our form master the collect for that Sunday from the Book of Common Prayer. That had a triple effect; we came to appreciate the exquisite language of the English liturgy, we became familiar with Christian practice and we became practised at learning by heart; I remember also the day when with a great flourish the decimal point was first chalked on the blackboard.

I was happiest when rehearsing for the school plays, which were a great feature. The Wilkes' loved Gilbert and Sullivan and for many years I could recite and sing every line of The Mikado and the Pirates of Penzance. Acting and singing in chorus released something in me and I got great satisfaction from it, but unfortunately I always sang a bit flat when singing solo, so I developed a sort of talk and sing, which went over quite well. The games were always a great problem for me because I could never co-ordinate hand and eye and foot. When I was eight, Walter found that I was shortsighted and I have worn almost the same strength of glasses ever since. Strangely, my son and eldest daughter can swap spectacles with me without noticing the difference. The other thing I got into trouble with was the difference between left and right. We had at St. Cyprians a rather ridiculous sort of OTC, drilled by the swimming instructor, Sergeant Barnes, and he made me put a white band on my right arm, but even then I constantly got it wrong. Later, in the Grenadiers, I used to panic when I could not remember which was which!

The school revolved around the famous 'Flip.' She inspired the whole place with her energy, her invention and her favouritism. If you were not 'in favour' everything went wrong for you; you were left out of all the special events and 'Flip' was apt to make cutting remarks about you when the whole school was together - at lunch time, for example. People used to cringe as she got going. But if you were 'in favour' every-thing was fun; there were early morning swims in the sea, followed by a special breakfast; there were teas in 'Flip's' study with older, interesting people; there were flattering references in front of the whole school, and such like. I was one of the lucky ones. I don't know why; perhaps because of the singing thing or, worse, because my parents were 'The Hon...' There is no doubt that 'Flip' and therefore the ethos of the school was snob, mainly social class snob, but also brains, sport and art snob. I managed to stay on the right side, and when I left 'Flip' said I was 'a perfect gentleman - shades of 'gentleman Ritchie'! But others suffered: George Orwell (of 'Animal Farm' fame) was there just before me and he hated it. Of course, he hated everything and said so and would never have been 'in favour' with 'Flip.' Others have complained about the teaching, the food and homosexuality. I was totally inno-cent, completely naive and I enjoyed and benefitted from the school immensely.

I had been a lonely boy at Cherry and at school there were boys of the same age with whom one could rag and find out the minimum level of work which one could do without being found out. We were scared of being caught and of being punished; we worked as hard as was necessary to avoid those two undesirable situations. I have always had difficulty in getting out of this very English attitude, which accounts for much of our national performance. As the fear of punishment decreases, so does the standard of performance.

During my last year at 'prep school' my mother came down and we had a rather secretive conversation about Walter's father, Herbert Gibbs, becoming a peer, Lord Hunsdon. This meant nothing to me, but it had a very positive effect upon 'Flip,' which did me no harm. At the same time my prospective housemaster at Eton, 'Blacker' Blakiston, left to become Headmaster at Lancing College, and his successor, 'Cyrus' Kerry, said I must come at once or not at all.

I made a total hash of the Common Entrance exam and scraped in to Eton in Lower Fourth, the lowest class but one. That did not really matter and I began six of the most enjoyable years of my life. Kerry wrote to my parents, 'Charles has taken to Eton like a duck to water.'

Kerry himself, 'm' tutor,' was a delightful man - short, round and bald, a good pianist and singer. Very keen on all sports, he had played football for the Corinthians (the leading amateur soccer club) and he taught higher mathematics in an intelligible way. He was at that time a bachelor, which (so it was said) accounted for the better than average food at his house. He was supported by 'M'dame,' Miss Hichens, whose brother had been a Chief Constable and lived at Sunninghill. She was short and round, too, with pink cheeks, and she looked like a robin. She came to watch all our matches at all sports and we adored her. She was most sensible about our health and, like an Army doctor, usually prescribed M&D - medicine and duty. We ragged her a lot but she loved us and to this day I can hear her cry out, 'You go too far. You know you do. You never know where to stop.' Both she and m'tutor visited every boy in his room every night between 8 and 9 pm where problems and successes were talked over in private, since every boy (except those 'in college') had his own bed-room/study.

On the top of the pack were Dr Monty James, the Provost, a great scholar and teller of ghost stories; Sir Henry Martin, the Vice Provost, a notable historian; Dr Cyril Alington, the headmaster, a stern disciplinarian and moralist - we were all scared of him; and Dr Ramsay, the 'Ram,' the Lower Master, a classical scholar. These four ran the school of about 1000 boys and over 100 masters, the 'beaks.' We admired these men and were proud of them; we wanted to please them and we did not want to offend them. We knew that if we did we would be punished by losing cherished privileges or having to write out 100 lines of Latin verse - or even, if our sins were mortal, by being beaten on the bottom with a cane by the Headmaster.

Discipline in the houses was maintained by the top half dozen boys, the 'Library.' In my last year at Eton I was captain of the House and Captain of Games. Kerry told me never to ask him whether I should beat a boy, but always to tell him when I had done so. The offenses were such as ragging in the passages, missing a call for carrying out errands, 'fagging' as it was called, cutting a games training session, being 'complained of' by senior boys or masters, or bad manners in the street. I always investigated each case with every boy and never gave more than 6 strokes, good hard ones, with a bamboo cane. There is no doubt we all had a healthy respect for authority at the receiving end and a sense of responsibility in administering it, which I guess has been life-long for most of us.

Games of all sorts dominated our lives. Eton was apt to play its own games in 'the Field,' at 'the wall' and in the fives courts, but we competed with other schools - at cricket with Winchester and Harrow, at Henley in the Ladies' Plate for rowing VIIIs, and in squash and rackets and boxing. If you were good at games it did make life much easier and more enjoyable; it was a passport to 'Pop,' the self-selected Mafia which ran the whole school, from the boys' point of view. My lack of co-ordination excluded me from all games except football, where I charged around to some effect, and rowing, where I sweated my guts out in the 2nd VIII, which was not very distinguished; years later I was delighted when my son

Nicholas got into the 1st VIII. I was a year (1931) in 'Pop,' which was heady stuff and I have no doubt I was both conceited and arrogant; it was a group which, despite war and fair wear and tear has shown remarkable survival capacity; a third are alive and working well as I write and a few have remained my good friends and led distinguished lives in different fields. There was no one really to cut members of 'Pop' down to size, but I scored an 'own goal.'

Eton had an Officer Cadet Corps and we wore an amazing pit uniform with puttees and a service dress cap. We took it all very seriously, so long as it in no way endangered our amateur status. The Commanding Officer was a housemaster called J.D. Hills. He had lots of Great War medals and we always called him 'the man who won the war.' The Adjutant was a regular soldier, either from the Brigade of Guards or from the Rifle Brigade. Then there were Cadet officers of whom, being quite large and with a loud voice, I eventually became the senior. Once a year we were inspected by the Major General, London District, and we had to march past him under command of the Cadet officers. We had 4 companies and I got mine into the right position on the parade ground. They were all spruced up and standing at ease and I turned round facing the saluting point and drew my sword with a flourish. Then, for reasons which now escape me, I roared out, 'Quick march.' As any soldier knows, such an order from a 'stand at ease' position is impossible to perform, but some tried while others did nothing; the remainder burst into uncontrollable laughter. I wished to die and be swallowed up in the grass of the parade area. Of course the regular Staff Sergeant sorted everything out in no time and the review went on under the totally crestfallen Senior Cadet officer. I have always tried to avoid doing something like that again!

Sometimes I did a bit better, as when singing sea shanties and songs from A.P. Herbert's 'Tantivy Towers' at the school concerts; this went down well. As secretary of the school Musical Society I arranged events with Dr Henry Ley, the most musical man I ever met. We acted, too, and I remember being the policeman in William Douglas Home's first skit, 'Murder in school yard.'

It is often said that there was a lot of homosexuality. Healthy, energetic young people do, of course, have longings and yearnings for others. At girls' schools it is called 'having a crush' on someone. At Eton it was 'crashing' on someone. No-one was in the least interested in me and I was too 'pi' ever to suggest such a relationship to anyone else. Of course, we did talk in the most vulgar way - stories, jokes and rhymes, some of which were witty but most of which were filthy. Tattered copies of La Vie Parisienne, all tits and legs, were highly valued and I guess that most boys as soon as they could get their hands on a girl, did so and forgot their schoolboy longings. But sexy we were.

We went to Chapel every day and twice on Sundays and we sang Hymns Ancient and Modern with great gusto. I was in the Lower Chapel choir, which was fun, and I learned a lot of music. My piano lessons were a disaster because, I suppose, of my wretched lack of co-ordination of hand and eye. In School Chapel the choir was found by the choir school and a few professionals. The services there were very impressive. Dr Alington gave relevant and entertaining sermons and he invited important clerics to preach on Sundays.

The pulpit was up a winding stair and very tall and high when you got there. An extremely short and small colonial bishop delighted us with a sermon whose text was 'Here am I! Send me!'

'But where is he?' was the muttered response from the aisles.

One evening, which lives in my mind, the preacher was the Reverend 'Tubby' Clayton of Toc H (being signallers' language for Talbot House where Tubby had set up a rest house just behind the lines at Poperinghe, during the battle of Passchendale in 1916, for officers and men.) This was so popular and successful that he had, after the Great War, set up a number of similar houses, mainly round London. He himself was Vicar of All Hallows by the Tower, next to the Tower of London. The text of his sermon that evening at Eton was 'Service is the rent we pay for our room on Earth.' I was very moved by this and went with several others to the Headmaster's house to have more talk with 'Tubby.'

No only did 'Tubby' strike religious chords in some of us, but also he spoke of Toc H as 'the university of life.' That appealed to me very strongly. I was about to leave Eton and I knew no-one who was not an Etonian, except some of the staff at Stanstead and Briggens, who were inevitably deferential. I had an uncomfortable feeling that at that time the Gibbs family had little time for anyone who had not been to Eton or Winchester or Harrow. The year was 1931 and I was persuaded that it was better to go into the City and earn, rather than go to Oxford and spend. I asked 'Tubby' if I could work for him in Toc H and he took me on as a sort of ADC 3 months after leaving Eton, at a wage of £2 per week.

Before recounting that formative experience I would say a last word about Eton. It was and is an extremely good school where you were and are encouraged and enabled to study any subject in the wide curriculum. If you did not want to study, too bad, but no-one chased you so long as you could keep up. If you could not keep up, goodbye. It was blatantly élitist, maintaining the Upper and Middle class culture. A former Provost once said to me that the destiny of Etonians is the British cabinet, or Government House, a Bishop's Palace, an Embassy, Head of the Civil Service, or a Field Marshal's baton. That was so for a long, long while, but not so these days under the meritocracy created by Margaret Thatcher. It was a 'macho,' 'top down' philosophy which was triumphant during the first 500 years of Eton's 550 years of existence. I can remember thinking in the late twenties, as other Empires declined, that the British Empire - occupying a third of the world's land surface - would never decline. But it did, and I watched it, thinking that we had been too confident, too complacent, too unquestioning and all for far too long. We had been caught unready for the world slump of the thirties, for World War II, for the secession of India, for Attlee's Government, for United Europe and for the collapse of the Russian Empire. We react to events, we are not pro-active.

Eton has changed as fast as, but not faster than, the rest of upper and middle class society, although it no longer opens all doors, as it did for us. Eton teaches leadership, above all, and there is never enough of that; but it is leadership of institutions which spend wealth, rather than of those which create wealth - and by wealth I mean not money but goods, 'things.' For 50 years now, Britain has needed more and better 'things.' Etonians' leadership in that field has been negligible and, to be honest, I am not sure that the impact of Eton on factory life would be helpful; that is where you need a 'shop floor' approach, which is not part of Eton's culture. The dynamic force pacing everything in today's world is techno-logically-advanced products for global markets - a far cry from the 'right little, tight little island.' Eton has, of course, moved far beyond Botany Bill's biology lectures of my day, but I do not find many Etonians (although I do find some, to be sure) who are willing to start life as industrial apprentices, to get their hands dirty, to become grafters, to live in the beautiful industrial counties of the North of England, and to defer rewards till their knowledge, experience and skills have made their efforts a success. I have lived with such people for many years and they are the salt of the earth - worth any number of City yuppies, whose behaviour and performance are nothing to be proud of.

Eton, as I have watched it over sixty years, lacks a dimension or two. First the tradition of service and duty, so strong in the past, has faded into an assumption, untested and usually unfulfilled. How can we lead without that? Secondly I can identify little 'real world' culture - the world of fear of failure, of profits or losses, of intense international competi-tion, of innovation, of high technology, of communication, involvement and participation, of working in professional teams and networking, of economic collaboration taking the place of traditional economic individualism. Of course 'Work Experience' is fine - never too much of it. However, 'Business Studies' are deemed better and I am sure that Business Week at Eton is an excellent innovation as is the Careers Convention for boys and parents. I read that technology at Eton has become 'important as a subject.' I think the school itself is doing a great deal to teach and stimulate young minds in 'Wealth Creation'.

What I fear is a drain of excellent human resources from Eton to the City. This drain robs the Britain in which we now live of leadership needed in other creative occupations. Eton used to train people to run the Empire; now we need people to run great industrial and commercial, technically-based, globally-operating empires of vital importance to the continued well-being of all those who live here. Running colonies needed generalists. Running businesses needs awareness and expertise in what the Germans call 'Technik.' Our brightest and best still do not have that culture, nor will they easily adopt it in competition with the 'me, more, now' culture of the eighties. Perhaps the nineties will be different. I do hope so, but I doubt it, unless we can find a sense of national purpose to take the place of selfish materialism.

All that is with hindsight. During the years I was at Eton, with 'Tubby' and at Oxford - the 10 years to 1935 - I had only a worm's eye view, although there was a whole range of opinion going on all round me. As I recall, the recession and slump of the early thirties was blamed first on Winston Churchill who, as Chancellor of the Exchequer, had put the £ sterling back on the gold standard at the pre-war parity, an over-valuation which called for a blockbuster by Maynard Keynes: 'The Economic Consequences of Mr Churchill.' Much blame also fell on Wall Street, which had indulged in a tremendous boom with a subsequent collapse in 1929. Lastly, the rather hopeless Labour government of Ramsay

MacDonald was thought to have dithered and missed opportunities. The economic recovery of Britain from the depths of 1931 was attributed to a housing boom, stimulated by cheap money (Bank Rate at 2%) and to the re-armament programme, triggered by alarm about Hitler's intentions.

In fact, of course, it now appears that these 10 years were full of innovations of lasting interest. The first of these, it seems to me, was the decision of the Tory party, under the leadership of Stanley Baldwin (and despite their victory in the election of 1931), to form a National Government, leaving Ramsay MacDonald as Prime Minster and making Stanley Baldwin Lord President. In this way the odium for the wage, salary and dole cuts was shared out between the parties. This arrangement lasted till the election of 1935 when the Tories took over the Government entirely, and so continued till 1945. Tories have been called 'the stupid party,' but keeping Labour and Liberals in the Government till the crisis was past was a political move of great sagacity. Indeed, Baldwin was a most sagacious man, a man of the middle way, like Disraeli before him and Macmillan after him. He believed in 'one nation,' and even die-hard Tories, like the Gibbs family, supported him.

The National Governments (1931 - 1935) did not pursue Socialist policies or seek a New Deal, as in America. They invented a policy which can best be described as 'managed capitalism,' which was market-driven on the laissez-faire principle, but which used government intervention to get the economy going again. There were 3 million unemployed in Britain in 1931-2. The price of commodities fell out of the sky and during this period the value and volume of British exports were halved. The burden fell mainly on the old, heavy industrial areas of Britain, but unemployed men and boys came south, usually on foot, and slept rough all along the Thames Embankment, in the crypts of churches and all around 'Tubby's' patch on Tower Hill. This visible misery and poverty put pressure on government in all its functions.

I have to say from my own observation that the 'upper ten' class was little affected, as I remember the 'coming out' dances of the 'debs,' including my sister's; when I asked Herbert Gibbs what he thought of the 1931 crisis, he commented with a chuckle, 'Well, the beaters will be cheaper on the grouse moors.'

The National Government did a lot for the coal, shipbuilding, steel and cotton industries, all of which started to do better. Much was done for agricultural marketing - milk, bacon, wheat and sugar. Transport, shipping and aircraft were modernised. There was even a policy for the 'special areas,' but this, it seems, was pretty ineffective; 5,880 firms were asked to help but the response was negligible. We were much more successful 50 years later, when we regenerated the steel and coal closure areas.

But perhaps the major innovation came, all unseen and unexpected, from a boom in consumer products and services. As the economy picked up, wages rose, but not extravagantly, though prices remained static or even fell. British production rose steadily in the period, while America, France and other countries stayed in the dumps. With more money about and hire-purchase beginning women, in particular, wanted labour-saving and other gadgets in the home; radios, gramophones and visits to the cinema became universal. The number of private cars doubled in the thirties. The consumer society was being born - and why not, provided the society can pay for its consumption out of current income, which at that time it did?

This was not of much help to the old, heavy-industrial areas, but it did wonders for towns in the South and Midlands, whose suburbs were ideally placed for the start up and growth of light industries, supplying consumer goods in demand at home. Indeed, Britain's trade started to move away from the 'staple' industries on which Britain's first industrial revolution had relied; these got inadequate investment and fell out of favour. In their place came the new consumer goods companies which needed to import many attractive components to meet the growing home demand.

These were the days of Birmingham, Slough and Watford, not of Manchester, Glasgow, South Wales or the towns of the North East. The 'two nation' tendency was greatly accentuated. The housing boom did, of course, reinforce the consumer boom, and by the end of the thirties there were more houses than families. The rearmament drive absorbed most of the unemployed people before World War II began.

Most of this was hidden from my ken when I went to work for 'Tubby' on Tower Hill in 1931. All I then knew was that Britain was going through a fearful economic crisis and that London was full of unemployed people, hungry and living rough. It was all a thousand miles away from Eton, Stanstead and all my inherited ideas and environment. But that was what I wanted and I was happy with 'Tubby' and his team of social workers. He used to introduce me like this: 'Charles came to us from Eton as proud as Lucifer and we made him scrub floors.' Walter, my stepfather, came to see 'Tubby' once, but not again; they disliked each other immensely. My mother wrung her hands but continued my allowance of £200 p.a.

I used to accompany 'Tubby' on his rounds and learned a new culture, direct and earthy. For instance, 'Tubby' visited a lady recently widowed who described her late husband to us: 'Yes, 'e was a loverly bugger.' 'Tubby's parishioners were like Eliza Doolittle and her dustman father in Shaw's 'Pygmalion.' I was to meet them again throughout my life.

The unemployed who drifted in and out had mainly northern accents, but some were Welsh and some were lowland Scot. They lived from day to day and I made the mistake in my first week of leaving my overcoat on a chair - it was gone by the time I turned round to pick it up. You could not blame them. 'Tubby' went round in a long black cassock with sixpences in the right hand pocket. Men were always coming up to him asking for a cup of tea or something to eat. He would always say 'Give me your hands.' If there were nicotine stains on the fingers he would say, 'If you can afford to smoke, I'll keep the money for those who can't.' He himself puffed away at a pipe from time to time.

I never quite made 'Tubby' out. He came from an old English family which had emigrated to Australia. He returned to go to St. Paul's School and Oxford, where he got a 'first' in Divinity. His accent was a clergyman's, accentuated by deep rumblings and pauses and stammers - quite unique, and well suited to his rumbustious, humorous, original but always Christian words. He was a very genuine Christian in faith, but he put the emphasis on 'works' - what you did, rather than what you were. He was tireless in working to relieve the needs, both spiritual and material, of other people. He worked mainly with and for men and was ill at ease with women. He was short, round and bespectacled, but he had magic. People of every class, from Queen Mary and King George on the one hand down to people who slept on the Embankment were drawn to him. He knew that and he used his magic to get money from rich people, service from motivated people (such as I) and devotion from the thousands who came to hear him preach or who visited Toc H functions.

He had been an army chaplain in the Great War and he realised that men coming out of the trenches needed rest, refreshment and spiritual comfort. 'The upper room' at Poperinghe was a chapel much frequented by tired and frightened soldiers, and all his work was based on the idea and practice of service to others: Christian duty. In 1931 we were still living in a Christian age, although Professor Joad and Bertrand Russell pooh-poohed the whole Christian ethic, but 'Tubby' gave Christianity a practical interpretation - you could 'do' something about it, helping others less fortunate than yourself.

'Tubby' gathered round himself a group of people who shared his enthusiasm and were attracted by his magic. A lot of them were Church of England clergymen of a rather high-church inclination. 'Skip' Moore was a Mirfield father; Tom Savage heard my first confession; Cuthbert Bardsley, an Etonian, became Bishop of Coventry. He was my guide, philosopher and friend - besides, he had a small car which most generously he used to lend me at weekends. The lay helpers were satisfying their need to do something about the misery and poverty which were so prevalent and obvious in Britain at that time. I was in that category, getting at the same time experience of what 'Tubby' had called 'the university of life.'

At first I lived in a dormitory with 20 others, mainly vagrants. There was no privacy and what you had you wore. We fed at a bare table in a mess where you ate what there was that day - and there was no alcohol. Then down to the skittle alley below the house, number 42 Trinity Square, on Tower Hill, where drivers and dockers and policemen came for tea and skittles, for which they paid. Then over to All Hallows with 'Tubby' for a service; the church was always full. 'Tubby' drew crowds: one day in the pulpit he said 'The text of my sermon this evening, many of you will find in your hats. It is 'Hope Brothers' (the menswear emporium).' Then off with him to a school or board room or some audience where he was needed to inspire people and in return he would collect some money for our endless work. I once got him to a train a quarter of an hour early. He was furious. 'How can I work sitting in this beastly train? Don't forget, I am about God's business.'

Toc H grew and grew in membership; branches and marks (as the managed houses were called) were set up in Britain and all over the Commonwealth where ex-soldiers carried on with the work of promoting an active and intelligent sense of brotherhood among men of all classes and standing for the fullest development of the individual. (Everyman should think and act with judgement and unselfishness). In addition we should all recognise the dominating claims of the spiritual factor in human life and of reconciliation between man and man in joy and service for the common good.

'Tubby' had written this on 'a crumpled piece of pink paper' in 1920. It was endlessly embroidered and encapsulated, but the themes continued. I think that all of us who worked in Toc H remember them and have done something about it. I find it sad that the idea of service to others has become less and less widely accepted as part of the British ethic.

'Tubby' was made a Companion of Honour in 1933; he became sick by exhaustion soon after. I used to go and see him and was saddened by his failing capacities. In December 1940 'Tubby's' church (All Hallows) was hit and burned out by incendiary bombs. Other shocks were to follow but 'Tubby' kept going till 1962, when he retired. He died in 1966, loved and admired by Kings, Queens, Princes, Field Marshals, Chairmen of great concerns, and all the rest of us whose lives had been touched by him. His memorial service in St Paul's Cathedral was attended by so many that overflow services were held on the pavements all around.

I cannot forget those days, which changed the direction of my life permanently. For a while I wanted to be a clergyman too, but Cuthbert Bardsley was insistent that I was too earthy for that job. I am sure he was right and it was not long before I got an invitation (organised by my parents) to go as a volunteer trainee in Glyn, Mills Bank in Lombard Street. Tom Savage asked me to be Warden of Toc H Mark VII House in Pembridge Gardens, so I went to live there and I worked with the other residents when I got back from the Bank in the evenings.

For a while I flirted with Frank Buchman's 'Oxford Group.' Frank was an outstanding American revivalist, of utter integrity and conviction. What I remember best was his insistence on 'a quiet time,' when one got up in the morning, with a note book and an open mind, writing down what one's conscience told one should be done during the day. I still like to 'sleep on it,' when I am not sure what to do and nearly always I know next morning where my duty lies. Frank's positive mental attitude began to take root in me.

For two years I did not go home or see my parents at Stanstead. They simply could not understand what had got into me. They dismissed me, saying, 'Charles has gone slumming.' When they were away from home I used to take a few Toc H people down and we slept in the barns and stables and went for country walks. BYOG (bring your own grub) was the order of the day. My sister 'came out' as a debutante at this time and I used to put on white tie and tails and go by the Underground to 'deb' dinners and dances. By the time the dance finished the Underground had stopped, and I used to take a taxi back to Toc H, saying, 'Stop when you have two bob on the meter.' I would then get out, give the driver half a crown, and walk the rest of the way to bed. The Toc H people I worked with thought this sort of thing was utterly unsocial and ridiculous and I doubt if they ever accepted me as 'one of us.' I have hovered between these two worlds ever since, trying to reconcile man to man, as 'Tubby' had taught me.

The people in the bank where I worked were equally suspicious. I was unpaid and was posted round the bank, attached to the senior clerks, who rather resentfully explained to me what they did. They seldom actually let me do it, for fear I would 'mess up their books,' as I probably would have done. Everything was hand written, exquisitely neat and tidy, much of it in copperplate. The Chairman, General Maxwell, used to walk round the bank, talking with the senior clerks, and I recall one old, but low-level clerk running along behind him saying 'Look, Chairman, this is the book I work in.' There was pride in the work and no-one could go home till all the accounts had been balanced, every letter answered and all telephone calls dealt with.

At the end of 1931, when I joined, the £ sterling had just been savagely, but rightly, devalued and all costs had to be cut. We could only go *up* in the lifts and had to walk *down*. All envelopes had to be re-used and we had to write on both

41

sides of all paper. One customer came up to the cashiers with a canvas bag of gold sovereigns; he surprised the counter clerk by saying, 'I suppose these are no good now.' I learned the basics of banking and said I would like to take the Institute of Bankers Examination. 'Better not,' said the Partners (it was then still a private bank). 'It would never do if you failed.' I was thought of as a 'do-gooder,' which I was, and I could see myself being shunted off out of mainline banking, so I did more and more in Toc H and Mark VII and with the Oxford Group, as Buchmanism was then called.

My parents and the partners in the bank, who were old friends, thought that enough was enough and that Charles should start again and go up to Oxford. They got me into New College (recently six hundred years old) without examination, because the Warden of New College, H A L Fisher was a friend and admirer of my grandfather, Herbert Paul. My father's marriage settlement just covered the cost and the bank said they would take me back after Oxford.

It was at this point that I was cornered by my mother and Walter one evening at Stanstead. 'When are you going to settle down, Charles, after all this chopping and changing?' I was 21 years of age, a bit cocky and had Oxford in prospect. It was perhaps the wrong question at the wrong time, but I remember answering without hesitation, 'I want to be independent.' That tore it!

My poor mother looked sadly down her nose and I knew she was thinking, 'Why is Charles always so difficult?'

Walter hugged his shoulders round his face and reached for a Martins Turkish cigarette, which he always smoked.

'Charles, your mother has always given up everything for Theresa and you. She could not possibly afford to make you independent.'

'I know that, Pa, and I am very grateful for all that you both have done for us.'

'You have been away from home a lot and we hope that you will now make your home with us.'

42

'Thank you, Pa.'

And that was the end of the conversation. They would have been embarrassed to go further; they found great difficulty in dealing with this sort of situation. Nevertheless they were kind and generous and I never forgot it. I regarded Stanstead and then Briggens as a 'safehouse,' where I and my family were always welcome.

The independence I was starting to seek was more in the world of ideas than physical or financial. I wanted to be free of the 'Jolly boating weather' culture of my peer group and I suspect that they felt the same. I felt stifled by the High Toryism of the Gibbs's. I was terrified of becoming a bank clerk, although I was devoted to them and enjoyed working with them. I was worried by the whole syndrome of 'class,' which pervaded everything. I wanted to be free to choose where to do my duty and how to serve, as Tubby had taught me. I thought of my namesake repealing the Corn laws and of Grandfather Paul writing and writing, till senility overtook him, so that later generations would understand the performance of the English in the 19th century. I remembered my mother telling me that my father's 'bête noire' was what he called 'Poverty of outlook.' I hated the thought of heading down a 'dead end.' I was searching even then for a newer world.

Of course, all this was pompous, high blown, adolescent stuff, which perhaps I would grow out of. But I didn't. I got deeper into it. I suppose that all young men feel from time to time that there are deeper springs of action within them than they use in everyday life and for me 'independence' summed it all up. I can imagine few young men going up to Oxford with greater anticipation than I felt in the autumn of 1933. Independence I had established - temporarily, at any rate. Now for philosophy, which I then thought was psychology, and politics and economics, which had already become major interests in my life.

CHAPTER 4

OXFORD AND THE GRENADIERS

Oxford in 1933 was bliss - not of course a real world, but after Toc H, Dr Buchman and the ground floor of a bank it was an amazing and utterly enchanting world of old friends, new bright people and of ideas. It was an intellectual paradise; from Plato to Descartes to Freddie Ayer, just made a fellow of New College and on his way to becoming the outstanding British philosopher of this century. There was Warden Fisher - Minister for Education in Lloyd George's last administration, pouring out Liberalism, and Richard Crossman, also just a fellow of New College, trying to create a new political philosophy for the Workers Educational Association. The economic scenario had just been laid out by Lionel Robbins, who had left for the London School of Economics, where his brilliant gifts came into powerful play. This was a panorama of overwhelming brightness and the problem for the undergraduate was how to participate. I determined not to take the relatively narrow path laid out for those going for first class honours, but to keep my independence by stretching the seamless web as far as I could, thus continuing Tubby's idea of the University of Life. For instance at my first tutorial with Crossman on the philosophy of Bishop Berkeley I dealt mainly with the culture of the man and of those days. 'You'll never get a first if you waste time on all that,' he said. But I got what I wanted out of it all.

I revelled in it and made many lifelong friends, mainly among Etonians, Wykehamists and Rhodes scholars. I ceased to hover between the classes because the half of the under-graduates who were scholars or paid their own college dues kept their distance from the half who were state supported - and 'never the twain shall meet.' A pity, of course, but there it was and I felt a need to mend my fences with my own class from whom I felt alienated, having left the herd. They thought I was pretty barmy, but were prepared to give me another chance. Brian Johnston was a friend at New College from Eton and later to be a friend in the Grenadiers: he was the best company, the funniest man and the truest friend anyone could have. After World War II he became the BBC's cricket correspondent and the 'presenter' of 'Down Your Way' on no less than 500 occasions. He was the centre of a group of young men including William Douglas Home, the playwright and brother of Alec, the Prime Minister. Tony Swann and Roger Wilkinson, became stars in the Colonial Service, serving in East Africa, Jimmy Lane Fox became a leading estate agent; Rupert Raw was later an adviser to the Governor of the Bank of England, Mike Robson was to be the power behind the throne in the Standard Bank. James Harmsworth was a future Chief Metropolitan magistrate; Simon Ramsay, later Gover-nor General of the Central African Federation, was at 'The House,' Christ Church, and a most wonderful sportsman with gun and rod. He succeeded his brother as Earl of Dalhousie and has been one of my dearest friends. Toby Low, a scholar of Winchester and New College, now Lord Aldington, whose illustrious career covers half a column of 'Who's Who,' has always been very close to me. (I was glad to give evidence for him in his libel action against Count Tolstoy, who had called him a war criminal. Toby was awarded £1.5 million damages by the jury).

The Rhodes Scholars fielded a very strong team and Fritz Caspari, a German (at St John's), Lewis van Dusen, an American, and Jan McShane, an Australian, (both at New College) were my constant companions. I used to spend vacations with Fritz and his family at Heidelberg on the

Neckar and go on long 'Wanderungen' in the forests and hills with his father and friends. Fritz got out of Germany just as the war began, and became a Professor at Chicago University and, after the war, German Ambassador to Portugal. With him I learned to be pretty well bilingual German-speaking and after the War we resumed our long friendship. Jan McShane was fly-half in our and the University rugby football team. I can see him now, using a hard scrubbing brush on his bleeding knees after a game, so that the blood washed the dirt out. But of them all Lewis van Dusen, an 11th generation American from Philadelphia, has remained my most constant companion and friend. His father and brother were both judges and he has been for many years senior partner in a leading law firm in Philadelphia. We shared rooms in the garden quad at New College and I remember walking his future mother-in-law round and round that garden while he was proposing to Mia, his beautiful, adoring and adored wife. There is scarcely any month in the subsequent 55 years when we have not been in touch by letter, phone or visit. Our first encounter was not very promising; I was lounging around the entrance lodge of New College, when a sturdy, rugged figure in a sweater and sneakers came at me straight across the hallowed turf, where no man walked except an old gardener with a long white beard who clipped it with shears after midnight and before dawn, or so the story went. The figure came nearer and nearer and thrust out a hand saying very positively, 'Van Dusen.' I was unused to this head-on introduction and, feeling rather a shrinking violet, I only smiled back. 'Well,' he said, 'what's your name?' I thought this was a bit much and just kept on smiling. 'Don't you remember it?' he said. Well, of course at that point my defences collapsed and I confided my surname and we went off to the steward's pantry in the Junior Common Room for some mulled claret, for which the steward was famous. The Rt Hon H A L Fisher, the Warden of New College, was very grand. His wife was very bubbly. They were both prodigious writers of books. His were very stately and classical, hers were also history books, but more fun, and I remember one sentence which typified them: 'Then all at once everything started to happen at the same time.' Brian Johnston always insisted that when, in their political career, a French person asked where her husband was, she replied, 'Il est dans le Cabinet avec beaucoup de papier.' We enjoyed, admired and felt in some awe of the Fishers.

I read for a popular degree, then as now, Philosophy, Politics and Economics. My philosophy tutor was Isaiah Berlin, a fabulous man who spoke so fast that one just hoped to catch one word in ten to give one a clue to what he was talking about. His rooms in All Souls, of which he was a Fellow, were exquisite, but entirely filled with books and a colossal gramophone horn, much bigger than the one which advertises HMV, from which Bach, Beethoven and Mozart blared out when pupils like me found Descartes, Locke, Hume and Kant too heavy to understand. I loved tutorials with him for the sheer fun of talking with this immensely erudite man; I came away bemused, but aware that I had been enjoying a great privilege. His Life of Karl Marx remains the standard work on that formidable but disastrous man.

For politics I was again lucky. Dick Crossman was my Tutor. He was a Fellow of New College and lived just outside the gate in a converted barn with his German wife. He married again later and more happily. He was a tempestuous man, highly intellectual, a committed socialist, brimming with enthusiasm and energy, continuously brushing away a forelock of hair which got in his eyes. He never stopped talking. I noted, however, that in commenting on my essays he would begin on one tack and, as he talked, slowly veer round to the opposite argument. It was fun, but confusing, to watch his mind working. I stayed with him at his home in North London, Buckhurst Hill, and met his father, a very conservative and highly respected Judge. Dick came to stay at Stanstead, where he roused Walter to one of the very few fits of fury I ever witnessed. Dick then complained that I was the laziest of all his pupils and would probably not get a degree. I thought this was a bit much, in one's own home; not a successful visit.

Nevertheless, Dick destroyed in my eager and impressionable mind the ethos of the British establishment, as I then perceived it. It was impossible for me to stand up against his immensely powerful mind and persuasion. All the evidence and anecdotes were 'agin the Government' - at that time run by Stanley Baldwin, as Lord President, and Ramsay MacDonald as Prime Minister. He ridiculed Ramsay, who was then gaga, for his speeches which began, 'We must go on and on and up and up.' 'Round and round would be truer' commented Dick. But his arguments in favour of Socialism never convinced me and I moved into the middle ground of politics, where I have stayed to this day.

My two years in the real world of working people made me doubt if the Socialist ideal could ever be made to work in practice. Oxford put me into the 'extreme centre' as Crowther, Editor of the *Economist* , once described it. Of course, as I write, I am a Tory 'wet,' in excellent company, but regretting that the Alliance of Liberals and Social Democrats has collapsed. Middle of the road people are likely to be run over. Dick Crossman is not to blame, but he certainly triggered impulses, which I had probably inherited. As I read the Crossman diaries it all comes back and I agree that Dick probably became an active politician in order to be able to write those diaries.

But politics is not only about theory, it is also about history, and in that domain my tutor was Richard Pares, also a Fellow of All Souls. This was a scholar, son of a scholar, to whom objectivity was all. A gentle, thoughtful, helpful man who, I suppose, saw in me a pupil to be coached into a degree. I responded to this treatment and worked harder for him than for any of my tutors. When the results of the examination were known he asked me to see him in the garden of All Souls and I remember his saying, 'You did much better than I expected and you were viva'ed for a 'first,' but you made a hash of economics.'

I could not get any excitement out of economics, 'the dismal science,' although I was expected to do so because I had worked in a bank! My tutor was Henry (later Sir Henry) Phelps Brown, appointed in 1959 to be one of the Three Wise Men advising Prime Minister Harold Macmillan on the relationship between prices, productivity and incomes, a problem which still dogs Prime Ministers. Our economic Bible at Oxford was then Alfred Marshall's 'Principles of Economics,' written in 1910 and a tough old read. I look, as I write, at my slips inserted in the book for reference back. Some of it has stuck, such as the principles of supply and demand, but 'supply of labour is governed by earnings' and 'rate of interest is anticipated earnings from new investment of free capital' seemed even then to be very remote from the real world. What seems strange to me is that the work of Maynard Keynes was never recommended to us in Oxford at that time. True, he was a Cambridge man, but his diatribes against the Peace Treaty in 1919 and against Mr Churchill in 1925 were already classics. So, also, I may add in passing, was his essay, 'The Great Villiers Connection,' about the Duke of Buckingham's tactics, to which I referred earlier.

When Keynes published his 'General Theory' in 1936 he was breaking new ground and was regarded as a radical thinker whose ideas needed to be digested before being fed into naive, undergraduate minds. Oxford was, and I believe remains, sceptical of radicals and prefers to chew over past and present thoughts to see if some more juice can be squeezed out of them. My own, recent visits there have been unrewarding. As a business man I had in the thirties already been trained and began to train myself to try to forecast economic data, such as rates, prices, volumes, wages and taxation in Britain, Germany and America (and now in Japan). I had already observed that, although this data was in the main market-driven, there were endless and weighty influences on the actual result, due to social, political, national and international factors, to say nothing of cock-ups. These upset the ideal, theoretical answer and often became dominant over market forces. Keynes was already writing at that time that in the end market forces would prevail, but 'by then,' he said, 'we shall all be dead'.

In the thirties the economic policies of Britain, based on a managed economy, were proving more successful than the classical 'Adam Smith' policies of America and France. We grew and they did not. In Germany preparation for war, and in Japan the Manchurian 'Incident,' produced quite different economic growth and development, from which we were all to suffer. In Britain 'coming off the Gold Standard' in 1931 was a major event. Ramsay MacDonald, whose Labour Government had collapsed, said ruefully, 'They never told us we could do that.' The National Government which followed had no hesitation in abandoning the Gold Standard, which meant a substantial devaluation of the £ sterling, and a good boost to our export trade. It was the beginning of Britain's recovery from the 1931 recession. In the viva voce examination which followed 'schools' in Oxford in 1936 I was detained much longer than I expected. After some, as I thought, rather easy skirmishing, one of the examiners, I think it was Roy Harrod, asked me, 'What should replace the Gold Standard?' I lost my head and started burbling about a steel or commodity standard, which I had seen mentioned in the newspapers. I knew it was rather a ridiculous idea and soon got lost. I should have said 'nothing,' which would have got me by. As Richard Pares said, I made a hash of it and the viva came to an abrupt end. It is reported that at the same session William Douglas Home when asked 'What is the future for coal?' replied, 'Smoke'.

Perhaps we took Oxford too light-heartedly. For me after Toc H and all that, it was rather necessary to regain my sense of humour, without which there is no success in Britain. But I learned to learn and have continued to learn throughout the subsequent 55 years. I learned good French and German, much history, the ground work of politics, and enough economics to make political economy an abiding interest. Specialists divide this great subject into its two component parts. I have always looked on it as a single, integrated complex. It is a talisman with which to find one's way and to see what should happen and what is most likely to happen... quite different perspectives.

I got a tremendous amount out of Oxford. Mind-stretching lectures, tutorials, conversations, books, essays and the cinema were going on all the time.

There was sport, even for duffers like me; there was good cheap wine in the college and we mopped it up; there were clubs like the Bullingdon, Boojums and Vincents, hearty, traditional, ruling-class clubs, where one met contemporaries, whom one was to meet again in war and peace, usually in charge of their local situation. We had no doubts about our future function in life which was to be in charge of a piece of our Empire, command in the Army, a political constituency or a Government Department, a profession or even a bank! (No-one talked about industry). Architects, artists, writers and entertainers were all there. As I look back I see the entertainers having done best. William Douglas Home still fills theatres (including the Theatre Royal, Windsor, where I have been chairman for 20 years), Brian Johnston at the BBC and with his books has entertained millions, as has Freddie Shaughnessy, with his nostalgic 'Upstairs, downstairs' epic. As Ouida wrote of the Oxford and Cambridge boat race, 'All rowed fast, but none so fast as stroke;' who then was stroke at New College in the thirties? Freddie Ayer, who made a singular contribution to philosophy. Joe Grimond who saved the Liberal Party, Lionel Brett who set a style of architecture of which the Prince of Wales would approve... Lionel Robbins the economist... Dick Crossman the socialist teacher and politician... H.A.L. Fisher, the downy old bird. Hard to say, and does it matter?

New College was brimming with brains and leadership, but I was not sad to 'go down.' I longed to get back to what I saw as the real world, away from the dreaming spires, back to where people did things, won and lost, got on or got out. As I went down (too broke to take up my degree), my father's first cousin, Lord Clarendon, asked me to join his son Nicholas as volunteer ADCs in South Africa, where he was Governor General. Not much real world about that! No number plate, but a crown on your car, and no stopping at traffic lights ... Wonderful sports and terrific girls ... Then up to Humphrey Gibbs at Bulawayo, fishing for tiger fish in the Zambesi and so home to find that Walter's father had died and that the family had moved from Stanstead to the big house at Briggens; and that was not the real world either.

I know I paused for breath and thought at that moment, mid-1936. I was very conscious of the advantages and responsibilities which the genes and the environment had conferred on me. I knew that my education had been specifically designed to prepare me for work as part of the ruling class in Britain, which was then very much in control. It enjoyed watching the success in most fields of its own culture; a state of affairs which seemed broadly acceptable to most people. The move towards a meritocracy had certainly begun, but Labour and the Trade Unions were still overwhelmed by the recent recession and a General Election, in which Conservatives had great victories. There was certainly an undercurrent of leftward-moving culture, mainly stimulated by public school boys and those who had been at Oxford or Cambridge. There was literature showing distrust of the fundamental soundness of society, anti-British and pro-Russian - the world of Burgess, MacLean and Blunt. My old school mate George Orwell spoke of 'England ruled largely by the old and the silly.' There was dislike of an industrial society and so of technical progress. The idea grew that technology represented constant change, so things were not so genuine because they were not what they had been!

It was the last time the ruling class could display wealth without concern. One quarter of working women were domestic servants. But visitors to Britain commented, 'even the poorest are loyal.' Others identified the two nations as the difference between rich and poor in 'income and capital, nutrition, the death rate, infant mortality and shelter'.

All this was to surface later but meanwhile, economically, Britain's recovery from the great slump of the early thirties had been remarkable and the concept of a managed economy and the middle way was widely approved. Baldwin, Prime Minister till 1937, and Neville Chamberlain, who succeeded him were generally respected and trusted. I knew I was isolated, still searching for a newer world without class distinctions.

The nigger in the woodpile was Germany, and that 'demented Adolf Hitler,' as Churchill called him. Churchill, out of office, was thundering away in Parliament about Britain's lack of preparation for a war which he by then saw as inevitable. He was supplied with inside information about, particularly, Britain's poor position in aircraft production, but, as I was soon to see, our military poverty was not confined to that.

I came to the conclusion that I must go and see for myself what was happening in Germany and I traipsed round to my friends in East Prussia, in Berlin, Bonn and Heidelberg. Finally I attended, as an observer, the Reich's Parteitag in Nuremberg - the Nazi party rally, marching in uniform, flags waving, bands playing and addressed by Hitler. Much beer drinking in the Keller in the evening, where boastful talk was the order of the Nazi evenings. I felt sick and frightened. I saw clearly for the first time that Germany meant to go to war and that included Britain - 'Wir marschieren gegen England.' My rather naive, complacent, goody-goody world was blown apart. Whatever my idea of the real world had been, it was now something very different. I kept thinking of my father dying in 'a war to end wars' and here I was going into it all over again, just as Lloyd George had said.

Back home I was astounded at the complacency on all sides, but I should not have been surprised, because not many had seen what I had seen in Nuremberg. My Oxford friends, the young Astors, asked me to their home, Cliveden, built by another Duke of Buckingham, where a group of politicians and authors, including the Editor of *The Times,* met to plan 'appeasement.' I did not dare to speak up; perhaps these great and good people were right and I was wrong, frightened by one bad experience. Once again I found myself hovering between two stools. The Cliveden stool was comfortable, weighty, 'establishment,' as we would say now. The other, the Churchill school, was pooh poohed as alarmist, exaggerated - and anyway what did Churchill, out of office, know that Chamberlain, by then Prime Minister, did not know?

I made up my mind and asked a family friend, Arthur Penn, an old Grenadier, if he could get me into that wonderful regiment as soon as possible. He did, and before long, together with Joe Buxton, whose father's property was next door to Briggens, I was marching up and down the parade ground at Wellington Barracks in the young corporals' squad. We had been admitted to the supplementary reserve of officers and appointed 2nd lieutenants in the Grenadier Guards on 2nd September 1936.

Later in that year Walter was shooting with Lord Desborough at Panshanger. Chamberlain was one of the guns and he walked with Walter from one drive to another and said, 'I have to buy time till our fighter aircraft are ready. I hope I can buy enough.' Chamberlain, of course, knew the truth, as did Baldwin before him, but he could not tell it in public or British determination, not strong at that time, might well have wilted and gone down the path to appeasement with the Cliveden group.

I was glad I had joined the Grenadiers, but it was terrifying. As senior Cadet Officer in the Eton OTC I thought I knew about peacetime soldiering, or something, anyway.

That is not what the Grenadiers thought. Joe Buxton and

I went back to Square One. We had been very impressed at our interview with the Lieutenant Colonel, Colonel Guy Rasch, DSO, and the Regimental Adjutant. I had been scared about my short sight and having 'bogged it' at Eton by marching the corps off on the wrong foot. Joe said he could not take his eyes off the mirror-like polish on the Adjutant's shoe. But we were admitted and taken to be measured for our uniforms at Johns and Pegg, the regimental tailors, who knew the officers well, because we were very dressy. When an officer went in to have his tunic let out, Mr Johns said to Mr Pegg 'I never mind letting 'em out; it's when they want 'em taken in that I fear we shall be losing a customer.' But before the uniforms arrived we had to get out on the square at Wellington Barracks in dark civilian suits and bowler hats with the young corporals, who were of course in guardsmen's uniforms. Saluting, which we had to do very often, was a regular drill. We had to stand to attention, lift the bowler off the head with the right hand and bring it smartly down the right side of the body... pause and then replace the bowler with a sharp, smart movement. We got very hot and sweaty during drill and one day Joe, who had borrowed his father's bowler, smartly removed the rim of the bowler, leaving the crown still on his head. Had he saluted or not? I found this deliriously funny, Joe was abashed, but the Sergeant Major was not amused.

We were alarmed at going into the Officers' Mess at Wellington Barracks. We had been warned that the senior Major would probably greet us with, 'Well, Mr Bloody, what's your name?' But that never happened and we were ignored during our first attachment of 3 months, but we were welcomed when we went back for a month's training each year. Then we had to attend the Adjutant's 'Memoranda,' or Orderly Room, each day to learn how to deal with offenders.

One day the Sergeant Major marched in a Guardsman who had missed parade on the previous day. 'What action did you take Sergeant Major?' asked the Adjutant, 'Sir, I went to the canteen and the barrack room and then to the latrines. One door was shut and I banged thereon and said, "oos there?" A voice replied, "Jesus Christ." Not believing this to be the case I opened the door and confined this guardsman to barracks.'

Life was not very strenuous doing London Duties. There might be a parade after lunch, but usually one was free. Lunch was preceded by drinks in the Mess, usually port wine, which was said to be good for a parade ground voice. Often the Prince of Wales, then the uncrowned Edward VIII, would look in to the Mess before lunch, especially if the Welsh Guards were at Wellington Barracks. He would always talk with the young officers and we became fond of him. Later we were sorry when he was forced to abdicate.

The training programme was another matter and the long marches and then advances 'by bounds' over Chobham Common and Salisbury Plain were hard, but we were young and fit. The older officers wanted to get back to London Duties, what they called 'real soldiering,' going on guard at Buckingham Palace, St James's Palace and at the Bank of England. The young officers enjoyed the life immensely. It was strict, precise, smart, according to the book, deferential in public to seniors (including the Regimental Sergeant Major) and if you erred for any reason you did extra pickets. I have tried, but cannot get this way of life out of my system, although it sometimes clashes with 'independence.'

We learned to use the .303 rifle, the Bren Gun, hand grenades, and the bayonet. Tactics were a bit elementary, but I practice to this day 'time spent in reconnaissance is seldom wasted.' We learned to drive and maintain our vehicles. Above all we learned to give orders in a clear, logical sequence and to ensure that everyone under our command understood what we were trying to do, why and how. After the initial training I was sent to command a platoon of 3 or 4 sections of 7 or 8 men, each under a Corporal. My platoon sergeant was the key man. I learned then how to use middle management (foremen, supervisors and shift managers in industry). These non-commissioned officers were the backbone of the whole system. They were well trained and educated over many years. They had their own mess, traditions and even language. They were an elite class, who understood their men and were understood by them. They knew their profession and what to do next. They relied for support on their officers and King's Regulations, and their officers could, with confidence, turn round and say, 'Carry on, Sergeant.' This was the old world at its best.

When we were serving with the Regiment we had to live in Barracks. Otherwise I shared a flat in Davies Street, Mayfair, with my Oxford friend Simon Ramsay, who was with a firm of stockbrokers. My main occupation was back with Glyn Mills bank in Lombard Street, who had taken me back without penalty and put me in the 'Advance' Department. Later I was moved to 'Personnel.' At Glyn Mills I learned in a very professional way the two business disciplines which I have used all my life; first, how to measure a credit risk and second, how to choose a successful manager. It so happens that these two arts, they are not sciences, are basic to all business. I have not by any means always been right, but near enough not to come a cropper. Even in the Army one had to make endless judgements about people's capacities, and in business you have to combine that with estimates of credit risk and forecasts of results. That early training in a fine bank has stood me in good stead over the years.

I was then 24 years old and girls played a large part in my life. I had a decent job, but very little private money. I was, however, considered rather 'unsound' for going off to work for Toc H and following Frank Buchman. But I was strong and healthy and had some success fishing around, falling in and out of love many times. And then I got bowled over by a wonderful girl, Pamela Constance Flower, and we married in 1938. Our son Nicholas was born the next year and she died when our second son was stillborn in 1942.

Such tragedies, in one form or another, seemed to be part of life in war time. It all happened so soon and so quickly that one 'scarce could take it in.' Pam loved the country, horses and dogs and she drew and painted beautifully. A lovely, soft, bright, quick girl, with friends everywhere. Her father, Major John Flower of the 60th Rifles, had been killed, like mine, in the Great War. Her mother was a scatter-brained lady, who could not really cope with Pam and her sister, Rosie, so she was brought up by two aunts; both were kind, warm hearted, generous, delightful ladies. Aunt Daisy was the mother of Anthony Head MP (later Viscount Head) who was Eden's Minister of Defence at the time of the disastrous invasion of Suez. The other aunt, Phyllis Buxton, was the wife of Major Toby Buxton, and the mother-in-law of General Monkey Blacker, a famous horseman and soldier. Phyllis Buxton and family came to live at Stanstead when we went to live at Briggens. So in a way I married the girl next door. We lived in Chelsea till war came. We could afford a Nanny for Nicholas, a cook and a butler - all on £1,200 p.a. as I see from the accounts I then kept. We hated being away from each other, but I was called back to the Grenadiers early in 1939 and Pam went with sister Rosie to live in a house we rented in the country. I got there when I could. In 1942 Granny Paul died and we went to live in her house in the village near Briggens. Pam was having a difficult pregnancy and one morning I took her to Hertford hospital, where they instantly performed Caesarian section. When she came out of the theatre I took her hand and her pulse was very faint. I tried to talk her back to consciousness, but, after a while the surgeon tapped me on the shoulder and said gently, 'She's gone!' There is no moment so sad and so final as that. No hope, nothing to want or enjoy, nothing to look forward to.

I thought I would never get over Pam's death, but time and the support of family and friends work wonders. My mother was marvellous and took care of Nicholas till he went over to Rosie and her family. Friends like Simon Ramsay, after he escaped from an Italian prison camp, and Arthur Grant, my best friend in the Grenadiers till he was killed in Normandy, made all the difference. When one door closes another opens, and life offered me another chance in a totally unexpected way.

CHAPTER 5

WAR

Part of the Supplementary Reserve of Officers was called up in April 1939; I was mobilised into the 2nd Grenadiers at Pirbright Camp. I lost Joe Buxton who went to another battalion and then to North Africa, where tragically he was killed in action - a super guy. His son is now in line to be chairman of Barclays Bank. I had been attached to the 2nd Battalion for training and I knew the young officers, but SROs were mostly older men, such as Peter Fleming, brother of the inventor of 007, and Lord Burghley (later Marquess of Exeter), the Olympic hurdler. After we had been at Pirbright for a couple of weeks the officer commanding our brigade (7th Guards Brigade), Brigadier Jack Whittaker, a Great War character, summoned us to meet him in the mess and asked, 'Well, you've all had time to see how we are, and what do you make of it?'

There was deadly silence till Fleming said 'Sir, it reminds me of the theatrical profession.'

'Good God, Fleming. The theatrical profession, what do you mean?'

'Well, Sir,' said Fleming, 'we all seem to hope it will be all right on the night.'

Collapse of stout party, as Mr Punch used to say, and exit Fleming to join Military Intelligence 'R,' a forerunner of the Special Operations Executive. One of us brought his dog, which made a fearful mess on the floor. The Mess Sergeant, called up from the Savoy Hotel, said in a loud undertone, 'I never thought I was called up to shovel up shit in the Officers' Mess.'

We trained and marched and got to know our NCOs and men. We practised rifle shooting on the ranges but we always had to economise with ammunition because there was never enough. Everything else was in short supply; not enough trucks nor Bren guns or anti-tank guns, which we had been promised, nor Bren gun carriers - lightly armoured tracked vehicles - and we wondered how we would get on when facing the Germans who, it was said, were armed to the teeth.

A strange event remains in my mind of those days at Pirbright when the men were coming back from their civilian jobs, many of them pretty sophisticated, to the Regiment they had left many years ago. In one company of the Grenadiers there was what amounted to a mutiny; the men locked themselves into their barrack rooms and refused to report for duty. Brigadier Whittaker set up a court of enquiry under Major Venables Llewellyn, of which I was named as the junior member. We called witnesses: first the company commander, who was a very zealous, strict disciplinarian Grenadier, who complained to the Court of the slack behaviour of the men returning to the colours and how he had to bawl them out. We then saw the 'old soldier' among the men who were being disobedient. There always is a senior soldier, being the man who served longest. In this case it was a quiet, grizzled, handsome, sensible man and I have never forgotten what he said. 'The men were willing and happy to return to the Regiment, but the Captain treated them like recruits from the depot and gave ridiculous and foolish orders. The men became incensed and locked themselves in the barrack rooms.' Those were, as well as I can remember, the exact words used. Llewellyn turned to me as the junior officer on the court and asked my verdict. I had no hesitation in replying, 'Case explained.' The other officers imposed a formal penalty and life went back to normal; Llewellyn had a quiet word with the Company commander, who continued to be, as he had been,

61

a first class officer, but no doubt better for this incident.

What stuck in my mind is that even the best of the British will not stand for what they consider to be unfair treatment. If you treat them right they will die for you, and later many did so, but get them wrong and it is you who are in trouble. When later I had responsibility for over 200,000 steel workers, who are like Grenadiers, I remembered these things and tried to act accordingly.

The war we were preparing for was declared on 3rd September 1939. Chamberlain said, 'We are now at war with Germany. We are ready.' That seemed to us just as fatuous as his remark on returning from Munich a year earlier, 'I believe it is peace for our time.' We moved down to Sherborne in Dorset and on 29th September left Southampton and landed at Cherbourg, and thence went to an area between Lille and Roubaix in Northern France, where we found a rather decayed anti-tank ditch, full of water, and some very smelly pill boxes. This was the end of the Maginot Line, said to be impregnable, and we were stretched out over 2 miles of it. There was only one thing to do and that was to strengthen what came to be called the Gort Line, after our Commander in Chief, General Gort VC, a famous Grenadier.

The winter of 1939/40 was cold and wet, and the water table in the Gort Line rose steadily and we were always digging, revetting, sandbagging and working in rotten conditions. But the men's billets in the French villages were good and the locals were friendly and hospitable. The officers' mess was excellent and, because I spoke French, I was made Mess President of our two company mess - some 10 officers when we were all present, which we seldom were. To help me I chummed up with a sprightly French 'commerçant' whom we always called 'Cliquot.' He produced large quantities of 'The Widow' at very low prices (the bottles must have fallen off the back of a lorry) and we had a good cook and lived quite well. Cliquot also arranged a number of personal services, which were much appreciated by officers far from home. My Company Commander was an American, 'Hoover' Harrison. His 2 I/C was Sir Arthur Grant of Monymusk, and there was another subaltern, Chandos Pole - like myself, commanding a platoon. The third platoon was commanded by Platoon Sergeant Major Hackett, who was really the best soldier of us all. He rose to high rank in the Regiment.

Our battalion Commanding Officer was Lt Col 'Billikin' Cornish, who had won a Military Cross in the Great War. The conditions that winter did not suit him at all and in 1940 he was replaced by Jackie Lloyd, considered to be one of the outstanding officers in the Guards regiments.

Major Dick Colvin was 2 I/C the battalion. Dick was a fine officer and when the German offensive began on 10th May 1940 I marched alongside him into Belgium and to the university town of Louvain. At one moment in that long march he did confide to me that he thought the Germans would get the shock of their lives when they met trained troops for the first time. That proved to be the case on the very few occasions when we had a fair fight with the Germans in the campaign, but for the most part we had to fall back, to remain in touch with the French on our right flank and the Belgians on the left. No sooner were we at Louvain than I saw from my position on the extreme left of the British line the Belgian Chasseurs moving unexpectedly. We were totally exposed and fell back to the River Dendre where all 3 Grenadier battalions were next to each other on the 'thin red line,' a very rare occasion. Then to the River Escaut and into what Lord Gort called 'a besieged fortress.' There the ammunition began to run out. Then to the slums of Roubaix where we were heavily shelled for the first time. Our guns were down to 5 rounds per gun per day. We just had to sit and take it.

Most people, fortunately, have never been directly and continuously shelled. I hated it, but 40 years later, when we were shelling Port Stanley in the Falklands War, I felt sure the 'Argies' would not stand it. At Roubaix we dumped everything we could not carry and on 27th May we made for

Dunkirk on foot, in a very orderly manner. On the following day King Leopold of Belgium asked for an armistice, which began at 4.00 pm. Again my platoon was on the extreme left and I must say the Belgians did seem relieved that their war was over. The 7th Guards brigade, including 2nd Grenadiers and my little platoon had, with others, to plug a huge gap. We had marched and fought for nearly 3 weeks non stop. I never remember being so tired and the Guardsmen were moving like Daleks, quite automatically. However we got down the road to Furnes, a small town near the coast, with a canal through the middle, in the afternoon of May 28th.

In my mind's eye I can see what I suppose was the 'Grande Place' in Furnes and in a side street I can see half a dozen British officers huddled over their maps. I can hear a rattle of rifle fire and there on the ground was the Commanding Officer, Jackie Lloyd, and two company commanders, Dermot Packenham and Christopher Jeffreys, all dead or dying. My Company Commander and the Adjutant were not hit. Tony Jones, with his Bren gun carrier, dashed in and brought out the bodies. There was absolutely no sign of panic. Dick Colvin took command of the battalion. 'Hoover' took over from either Dermot or Christopher and Arthur Grant took over our company. It was done in a twinkling by very tired men in a desperate situation. The Guardsmen knew all about it at once, but just kept going. It was a superb example of Grenadier morale and training - when in doubt KBO, which to the uninitiated means 'keep buggering on.'

That night we crouched section by section in the houses facing the canal in Furnes. The Germans had infiltrated the town and were shooting all night long at and from the burning houses, but they never crossed the canal in any strength. We sank their boats as they tried to cross and got them as they reached our bank. We hung on there for 3 days, living on the food we found locally while the evacuation from the beaches was going on behind us. At around midnight on 31st May we tied sandbags over our boots to avoid noise, broken glass was everywhere, and we stole away in single file back out of Furnes, towards the beach at La Panne.

Arthur rallied all our Company. He and I were the only remaining officers and we made our way to the beach, just as the sun was rising on the 'glorious' first of June 1940. There was no organised force between us and the Germans and our orders were set to get into any ship or boat and get home, carrying only our small arms. Had the Germans used their remaining strength and energy they would have followed us on to the beach and mopped us all up. Indeed, had the 2nd Battalion not held on at Furnes the story might have finished very differently.

The scene on the beach was as we expected: thousands of British and Allied soldiers were wandering about without officer control. A quarter of a mile out at sea were boats of every description waiting for the tide to turn so that they could come in over the sand.

Our Company was still intact and Platoon Sergeant-Major Hackett said, to Arthur, 'What about those boats up on the dunes?' There were indeed three long, black, fisherman's boats, without oars, up above the waterline. Hackett's platoon went to one, and my platoon to another. We tried them both, then just one, but they would not move. At that precise moment two things happened: Arthur made the only Dunkirk joke when he said 'I am finding it harder and harder to convince myself that this operation is going according to plan;' and then two Messerschmitts roared low over the beach with all guns firing. A lot of men seemed to go down, but none of us was hit and the first then the second long fisherman's boat slipped over the dunes into the sea, as though on a greased slipway! Immediately, we were surrounded by men from other regiments, desperate to get away. Arthur stood up in one boat and yelled to me, 'Charles, get into the other and shoot any man who gets in without your orders. Hackett, you do the same.' The voice of confident authority always calms a situation and the loading went steadily ahead - wounded first, Grenadiers next, and there was not much room for any more. Fortunately, it was a fine day and the sea was dead calm so we could load to the gunwales. We rowed with our rifle butts and many swam alongside, holding on. I held a Guardsman's hand for as long as possible, but after a while he gave up and went down with a peaceful look on his face. Poor chap! I think with sorrow of those who died in that retreat and on the beaches; they really were the best of British.

As our boats approached the 'Margate Belle,' a paddle steamer brought over by its ex-Naval owner, an excited officer on the bridge shouted at us, waving his revolver, saying, 'Go away, get out, we're full up.' This was too much and one of my corporals who had been swimming alongside, naked, said 'I'll get 'im.' Seconds later, or so it seemed, Corporal Woodrow, still stark naked, appeared on the bridge of the 'Margate Belle' and jumped on the back of the unsuspecting officer, who was still shouting at us. We were up and into that paddle steamer in no time.

There were lots of Grenadiers already on board, and we organised squads to collect ammo and shoot at enemy aircraft if they attacked us. They came for us all the time and we blazed away with rifles and Bren guns. It was quite ineffective, but it kept our spirits up. But we were dead-beat and I cannot even recall at which port we landed.

I know the Guardsmen were very annoyed at having to give up their rifles to a port official and Corporal Woodrow, now reclothed, managed to conceal a Bren gun down his trouser leg. We telephoned home, free for once, and got into a train bound for nowhere. There were Grenadiers everywhere.

In my carriage was one man who continuously played with a hand grenade, practising removing the pin and the throwing action. Fortunately, he dozed off before he did any damage. Another had a nasty wound on the hand and he suddenly sat up and said 'God in heaven, this is my home station, but I don't have a movement order.' The train slowed down and we pushed him onto the platform. Later he was Captain of the British Ryder Cup golf team.

All along the line were people offering drinks and buns and cakes and fruit. You would have thought we were conquering heroes, instead of an army which had retreated for 3 weeks and escaped capture by the skin of our teeth.

Eventually we got to London and stopped at a railway station which I have never subsequently discovered. On the platform were all the senior officers of the Grenadiers to greet us before we set off again in the train for an unknown destination. Not even the driver knew - it really was a ghost train.

That evening we stopped at Oswestry in Shropshire. At a military camp we found ready for us new battledress and baths and beds and blankets. I remembered that my uncle Eric, 'Brandy' Villiers, lived nearby and he had Pam and Nicholas and me to stay in great style for a few days. Then Lord Howard de Walden invited our whole company to Chirk Castle, where the Guardsmen had a riotous day with the maids and the officers demolished Lord Howard's port.

But this respite was short and we were soon back again with the rest of the battalion in the Sherborne area of Dorset, from which we had set out for France 9 months earlier. New equipment poured in and our divisional General, Bernard Montgomery, the famous 'Monty,' came to address us. He boasted that he had persuaded the War Office to send our division back to France immediately and that this was a great honour! The King came to inspect us and we moved down to the coast for immediate embarkation.

On 18th June reinforcements arrived for our brigade, including my half-brother Vicary Gibbs, who went to the 1st Grenadiers. As we were greeting them in the bar of a hotel Churchill began to speak on the radio, 'The news from France is very bad, but whatever happens....' The rest of his 'finest hour' speech was lost in the cheers of Grenadiers, who knew they would not have to go back to France. France sued for peace and Marshal Pétain set up his government in Vichy. We therefore attacked the French fleet at Mers-el-Kebir in North Africa. The Germans opened the Battle of Britain with day-light bombing raids, and were expected to launch the invasion with the next full moon. The 2nd battalion moved to Poole Harbour to defend a long coastline.

Sections of 7 or 8 men were placed at least 100 yards apart, protected only by coils of barbed wire at the waterline, though these were soon clogged up with seaweed. Our only consolation was Churchill saying, 'We are waiting for them. So are the fishes.' The Battle of Britain began in earnest and I remember lying on the cliff tops watching the dog fights and the vanquished spiralling down into the sea. Our propaganda greatly over-estimated the number of enemy planes shot down, but it was one of the decisive battles of history, 'Never in the field of human conflict was so much owed by so many to so few,' said Churchill on 20th August. There was an invasion scare on 7th September, but it was a false alarm and the 2nd battalion settled down, out of the blitz on London and in some comfort, to wait and see.

And now, as they say on commercial television, we take a break. We can look back and forwards. First, how on earth was it possible that nearly 350,000 Allied soldiers escaped over the Channel from Dunkirk? It was to be the last time that the British could move a few miles over the sea out of extreme danger into complete safety. Churchill himself thought that only some 20,000 would be evacuated. It must be said that the discipline of the soldiers, and the courage of the owners of the fleet of small boats which rescued us, made the incredible operation possible. But why did the Germans allow it? As I saw with my own eyes, they needed only a minimal extra effort to put us all in the bag. Why did they not make it? We can only guess at the workings of Hitler's crazed mind. My guess is that he reckoned the British were defeated and done for and would be ready to make peace when he had defeated the French, who were on the run and did, indeed, sign the armistice terms on 22nd June. The picture of Hitler dancing for joy on that day at Compiègne indicates that he did not believe that we could carry on the war single-handed. He had a non-aggression pact with Russia, and America was still slumbering in isolation. Perhaps he even thought that in negotiating peace terms with Britain he would be able to claim some credit for not annihilating the British Expeditionary Force. Whatever he thought, he made one of his classic mistakes, which were the cause of his defeat.

Secondly, what was the mood in Britain in June 1940? There is no doubt that the majority was filled with euphoria. We had gone into the war unprepared, but united under Churchill, who by his bearing, his speeches, his political and military actions convinced most people that somehow, some-time, we would win this war, as we had won all other wars throughout history. We were proud and confident and ready for anything.

Our reaction to Dunkirk, the Battle of Britain and to the blitz was undoubtedly 'Britain can take it.' There were cer-tainly some faint hearts and a few, very few, who were suspected of treachery but they were isolated. Everyone was on the look out for spies; the sign posts were removed or turned round to point the wrong way. One old gentleman, leaning out of his window at night, was arrested for puffing a cigar in a suspicious manner! Several German spies were caught in Britain during World War II and some were exe-cuted.

Lastly, what about my active interest in political economy? Churchill's national government contained both Tory, Lib-eral and Labour ministers, and they agreed that every British resource should be dedicated to the single purpose of winning the war. It soon became clear that Churchill himself, as Prime Minister, was devoting his prodigious energy to strategy, diplomacy and military, naval and air force issues. He left the home front to Attlee, Bevin, Cripps and later to Butler and Beveridge. Thus it began to be clear that in order to defeat the Fascist countries Britain was adopting socialist, or anyway, collectivist policies. Every man and woman was drafted into something that would help the war effort. Agriculture, shipping, transport, industry, finance, commerce and the whole administration were centrally directed and controlled. The Emergency Powers Act of 1940 gave government absolute powers. Churchill is reported to have said, 'People say I am a dictator. I am not. All I ask is that they do what I say, when I say.' We felt we were fighting for liberty, but could not at that time enjoy it, for reasons we understood. We, therefore, accepted a managed economy, planning of resources, a sort of Welfare State and a considerable degree of nationalisation. I do not recall that we objected strongly, although we complained. We expected to unravel it all when the war was over. After all, much of it had been introduced by the national governments of Baldwin and Chamberlain. Tories went along with Churchill. Labour and the unions and workforce were disarmed by Russia's non-aggression pact with Hitler. Liberals, led by Sinclair who was Minister for Air, felt they were playing their part. The House of Commons had been bombed and MPs met in the House of Lords. The country was solid, industry performed production records, everyone was at work, we all had the same, rationed food; there was enough, but not too much, money about. The blitz levelled the classes. As so often the British people, in time of crisis, excelled themselves. We were squeezing every available ounce out of ourselves and out of the economy; we felt we had no other option, and, like most others, I went along with it.

Back to the Grenadiers. Our sojourn at Poole went on too long, but, unknown to the young officers, great changes were being planned. In 1941 the formation of a Guards Armoured Division was made known to us and we made our way to Warminster, on the edge of Salisbury Plain, where we started to learn how to drive and maintain and to use the guns and the wireless communication sets of Crusader tanks. I was amazed at the speed with which Officers and Guardsmen mastered these new techniques. I was made gunnery officer of a squadron of the 2nd armoured battalion. Major Sir John Little Gilmour ('Jock') was the Squadron Commander and Lt. Col. Venables Llewellyn ('Mike') was the battalion Commanding Officer. Both were superb soldiers and wonderful human beings. Mike's brother had been a close friend of mine at Eton and Jock's son, Ian, was to become a Tory Minister, considered by Margaret Thatcher to be a 'wet,' but considered by me to be a true One Nation Conservative. We were a closely-lit group. Old friends like Arthur Grant were there; Brian Johnston turned up in charge of tank recovery; Peter Carrington was there; Robert Cecil was in my Squadron, and all around were brother officers, totally committed to professionalism in tank warfare.

We were carefully and intensively trained. I went to the tank gunner ranges at Linney Head in South Wales, but there was so little ammo available for actual use that the course was more theoretical than practical. Pam and Nicholas came to stay in a farm house near Warminster, but it did not work out very well and they went back to a house near Hertford, where Rosie was living and where I could get for a weekend's leave and see them before Pam died in 1942.

There was a great stir in April 1942 then because we heard that Winston Churchill was coming to Salisbury Plain to see how the new division was getting on. By then our training was well advanced. We did not know the date, but on Monday 13th April the young officers were told to go up to Imber Down and watch a rehearsal of Hurricanes shooting up dummy tanks and troops before the visit of the Prime Minister, who would be accompanied by General Marshall, Chief of Staff of the American Army. Three of us went up together in a pick-up truck, Jock Askew, Robert Cecil (later Marquess of Salisbury) and myself. My account of what happened next is taken from a piece in the Grenadier Gazette of 1987, which the Lieutenant Colonel asked me to write, following a lunch he gave to mark the 50 years which had passed since I first joined the Regiment.

'We settled down to watch the show with several hundred other officers, mainly from 7th Guards Brigade. Over they came from behind a hill, Hurricanes flying very low, firing live ammunition at the mock-up targets, tanks and troops. With field glasses we could see the bullets spattering round them. Then suddenly came a different sound - a Hurricane was coming directly at us from our right. I turned my head to see and, at that moment, the pilot, mistaking spectators for targets, opened fire and a bullet went through my right cheek, jaw and collar bone, and came out over my left tit! The scars are still there. Robert, next to me got a bullet through his arm and into his lung. Others down the line were hit and, I believe, some were killed.

I sat down with a bump and as blood was spurting from my facial artery I prepared to meet my Maker. Robert was making a fearful noise, breathing through the hole in his lung. We might have gone, if a brother officer, Miles Howard (later Major General the Duke of Norfolk) had not grabbed the Divisional Medical Officer and brought him immediately to us. He gave us an injection of morphia, slapped a first aid pack on to my bleeding face and said 'Buck up, it's only a flesh wound.' This was absolutely untrue, but I abandoned my previous project and started to struggle for life. Jock Askew bagged the first ambulance to arrive and, Robert still making that frightful din, we were taken to Warminster Cottage hospital which had no spare blood! By some miracle Robert's father then arrived with the blood, as though he had had it in his fridge all the time at nearby Cranborne, and we began the long fight back to active service.'

Fifteen months and sixteen plastic surgery operations later I was pronounced fit, with a new jaw made with bone from the crest of my hips, and the regiment posted me to the Training Battalion at Windsor, with the suggestion that I had 'done about enough.' I really did not agree. I had gone to France with the 2nd Bn. in September 1939, come back off the beaches on 1 June 1940, was a competent tank gunner and, perhaps conclusively, I was a widower.

As luck would have it a regular officer in the Royal Fusiliers, Peter Wilkinson, who later married my sister, and has had a splendid career, was looking for one or two volunteers for a rather harebrained scheme to drop into Jugoslavia and cross the Alps into Austria, to stir into action the Austrian Resistance Movement, which was said to exist, as part of the Prime Minister's 'set Europe ablaze' campaign. I spoke a bit of German and jumped at the opportunity. The Regimental Orderly Room thought I was quite mad, but let me go. So began life in the Special Operations Executive and the training and practice of banditry.

As I sit at home, forty-seven years later, and read my report dated November 1944, written in the 98th General Hospital in Bari, Italy, I realise that SOE was more a political than a military operation. Of course we wanted to stir up trouble for the Germans in occupied Europe, which would deflect their war effort and destabilise their confidence. However this produced problems for us in the occupied countries because the political parties there wanted to make capital out of the Resistance Movements for use post-war. The Communists everywhere were extremely active from the moment Russia was invaded. In France the Gaullist and non-Gaullist movements were rivals. In Jugoslavia we supported both the Royalist Mihailovich and the Communist Tito and they harassed each other whenever they got the chance. Further, the Jugoslavs wanted to get territory from both Italy and Austria after the war and their support of our efforts varied with their perception of how we could be used to further their ambitions. It was not possible to disentangle the political from the military and we had to be constantly alert to the possibility of being dumped in extremely dangerous situations.

Preparation for SOE was largely based on Lawrence's 'Seven Pillars of Wisdom,' written after his amazing experiences in Arabia in the last years of World War I. 'Hit and Run' was the clue to it all, requiring extreme physical fitness, strength and endurance, broad experience with explosives, quick reaction with hand and tommy guns, competent use of 'one time pads' for communication, knowledge of the local language and political complications and, of course, being a reliable parachutist and swimmer and able to live off the country. I loved all that, learned at SOE's schools on the West Coast of Scotland and in Southern Italy.

In Italy the month of May 1944 was good for the Grenadiers. The 3rd Battalion had won their battles at Cassino and were about to take part in the dash for Rome with the 5th Battalion which had played a crucial role at Anzio, where Bill Sidney (the late Viscount De L'Isle) won a Victoria Cross. The 6th Battalion, sadly, after terrible casualties, was withdrawn from active operations at Salerno. The Allied invasion of Western Europe was evidently about to take place. The German armies were not yet defeated but in the occupied countries there was a strong belief that they soon would be. The Allied Balkan Airforce dominated the skies of the Adriatic. Tito's star was rising. The 'propustnica' permit and authority to get help from Partisan forces, arrived from Marshal Tito, through the good offices of Brigadier Fitzroy Maclean, Churchill's personal representative with Tito, and I felt confident that we could get from Slovenia in northern Jugoslavia, into Austria and stimulate internal mayhem there, which would help the Allied war effort in Western Europe.

Two wireless operators, Corporal Roberts and Corporal Warman and myself, were standing by to drop into the Tito Partisan IX Corps 12 miles north east of Gorizia, not far from Trieste. Twice we took off, but were unable to identify the target area, as the agreed ground flares were not to be seen. We came back to a small house near the airfield where we 'Joes' were held until we dropped. To my amazement there was a close friend from school and university, then a major in a Brigade regiment. Even more amazing was the discovery that he was due to drop to the Royalist Mihailovic. We were supposed to know nothing about each other, but by next morning we could both have picked up the other's brief!

On 15 May we tried a third time. Our pilot, a New Zealander, said over the intercom that we were over his best guess at the target area. I said 'OK, we'll jump.' Out we bundled at about 10,000 feet, much too high, but it was a still, clear moonlit night, and it seemed an age before the trees on the top of some low but rocky mountains came rushing up at us. We scrambled together and collected our kit, including a charging engine for the wireless batteries. Soon a sound I was to get to know only too well, came ringing through the trees 'stoi' - stop, halt! Two young men in Italian army uniform came towards us and we were very tempted to shoot, but they said in German that they were Partisan Generals. We lay low, but they come on and there was no one with them. We felt we were in the right place and we made friends; one of them was aged twenty-one, the other nineteen - we called them 'Arso' and 'Arsitch.'

The HQ of the Partisan IX Corps was in a relatively safe area, a 'republic' into which German soldiers seldom ventured, but we had to get up north over the Alps, aiming for Klagenfurt in Southern Austria. We got to the foothills of the Alps by the end of June, travelling along well-established Partisan courier stages, some 20 miles each night, cursing the weight of that battery charger and living off the local porridge, boiled rough grain with animal fat and, if you were very lucky, an egg. The Partisan couriers never left us as they were personally responsible for our safety and we were valuable property because we could bring in 'drops' of rifles, tommy guns, mortars, ammunition and explosives. We followed the principle of Lawrence of Arabia and never stayed to fight, but hiked up to the top of the tree line if a German patrol appeared. The Germans stuck to the roads and tracks, leaving the forest paths to us, but they would interrupt the courier stages daily and cause us huge detours. On the day we crossed R. Save we moved continuously for 21 hours.

We crossed the main road at the Loibl pass, one at a time,

very quietly at night. I looked pretty odd up there in battle-dress with 'Grenadier Guards' on the shoulders. The Partisans mainly wore the uniforms they had taken from the Italians who had capitulated. We reached what I always call Logarthal, just out of sight of Solcava which was a German HQ. Logar was a big, brave Slovene who hated the Germans. He had a wood and stone house and a small farm on the road to Solcava. He always befriended Partisans and, when I left, I gave him my field-glasses to watch for German patrols coming out of Solcava. Twenty-five years later, at Tito's invitation, I went back there with my own family, and Logar's son gave me back the field glasses saying 'My father always said you would come back and that I was to give you your glasses with many thanks.'

On 27 June 1944 I came down out of the woods into Logar's 'hotel' and up to the first floor, where I found my friend, Major Hesketh Pritchard, on reconnaissance mission. He was thin, worn and tired, but he was driven by a fanatic determination on what he himself described as a 'one way journey,' from which he failed to return.

Together we planned the crossing of the Karawanken Alps and the R. Drava and the occupation of an area round Volkermark in southern Austria, which was said to be the home of Slovene farmers sympathetic to the Partisans. Hesketh Pritchard eventually did that in the winter of 1944/45; we never knew exactly when because he went off the air. There he died, probably killed by the Partisans in the wild dementia of exhaustion, hunger, cold, danger and conflicting interests. We never found his body.

The conflict of interests bedevilled us. We wanted to find the Austrian Resistance, if any, and the Partisans wanted us to supply them with arms and keep out of southern Austria, to which they laid claim post-war. We did, however, find a Slovene Kommissar, Ahac, a red-haired, wild, clever devil who travelled far into Austria for us, seeking news of Austrian resistance. He returned empty-handed. We could find nothing on which to build. I remember sitting with him in the Northern foothills of the Alps on 10 August looking down into rich, peaceful Austria as he told us of the 'gemütlich' and comfortable Austrians, who said 'Hitler has already lost the war. Why should we risk life and family for the Allies? All we ask is that the Allies get here before the Russians.' This was a terrible disappointment for us. We were on a wild goose chase. There was no such thing as the Austrian Resistance Movement. We had come all that way for nothing... or had we? Perhaps Ahac was lying, put up to it by the Partisan HQ - perhaps he was working for the Germans, or had just invented it all.

Hesketh Pritchard never gave up. I felt we had more immediate problems at hand.

We were by now virtually the prisoners of the Partisans, about 450 men and women organised in 2 'odreds' whose Kommandant, Gaspa, was a fearless, shrewd Slovene peasant, who liked to dress in SS uniform. The Nacelnik (adjutant) Marko was a regular Jugoslav army officer, efficient, ravaged by scurvy and difficult to deal with. The Kommisar, Ciril, had the dominant voice in that part of the world; he was clever and able, but a great dealer in half truths. The Vice Kommissar, Bogo, aged 20, was trustworthy and devoted to us. Without the support of these men we could go neither forward nor back. They were themselves under heavy pressure from the Germans, who were maddened by their guerilla tactics which were, of course, as everywhere else in Europe, sifting unwelcome grains of sand into the well-oiled German war machine. There is little doubt that these Partisan odreds were in a key position to tie up German reserves and slow down troop movements through Slovenia into Italy for what was to be a crucial battle on the Gothic line, which stretched across Italy from Pisa to Rimini. The 3rd and 5th Battalions of Grenadiers were fighting hard there through the month of September 1944. So, while Hesketh Pritchard concentrated on building up a team to cross the Drava into Austria, hoping thus to attract Austrian resisters to join him, I concentrated on the build-up of the Partisan odreds in their interference with German troop movements into Italy. During July and August 1944 we delivered from DC3s 17 loads of arms, ammunition and explosives, and the strength of the odreds rose to 700, although not everyone was armed. Two things were essential: first the wireless communication with our base at Bari had to be perfect and the second was pilot skill and daring in coming in low to small clearings high in the Alps, and dropping supplies in two or three runs over our flares, lit up in an agreed pattern.

My two wireless operators never failed. They had to keep on the move with the rest of us most of the time, they had to keep their batteries charged, they had to keep their 'skeds' precisely, they had to send without a single mistake the messages we wrote on one-time pads. They were badly fed and in continuous danger because the Germans were able to pin-point their exact location with their own directional wireless. Those two lads performed in the most professional way and in the best traditions of the Royal Corps of Signals.

We could only do our 'drops' in the moonlight, for about one week in the month. Without moonlight and clear skies the pilots would never have found our minute dropping zones and we would never have found all the precious equipment and been able to clear away all trace by dawn. To this day I can tell a DC3 engine from any other and remember the excitement as it came nearer. Then 'Feuer machen,' light the fires, I shouted, and the 'planina,' forest clearing, came ablaze. The dark shape of the DC3 was lit up by the firelight, so low did the pilots dare to come, and we saw the canisters and bundles float down on their parachutes. Round again they came for another drop and then away while we collected everything. 'Pushka, pushka' (rifles) Gaspa would shout with delight, and he loved to have a grenade always swinging from its ring, attached to his belt. He was killed in one of the endless, small, demolition engagements with the Germans and we never had another Kommandant as good as him.

Inevitably this sort of action infuriated the Germans, who always called us 'Banditen;' they reinforced their local security forces, put a price on my head (greater than any salary I have ever been paid!) and mounted a major drive, a Hajka as the Slovenes called it, to round us up once and for all. While I was there four Hajkas took place, all of which, except one, were foreseen and forestalled by the Partisans. The one exception came as a complete surprise. We were in an empty house, which backed on to the forest and I happened to look out of a first floor window and see a German patrol on the road 500 yards away. We were out of the house with all our kit, except for one important item, within a minute, but the Germans had spotted our movement into the forest and they were after us.

The next four days were miserable. The Partisans, just like us, were on the run without food and uncertain of the German encirclement plans. I was nagged by the thought that we had left behind the directional wireless sender which enabled the aircraft crews to pinpoint our dropping zone. It was a wretched, heavy contraption which had been wished on us, but I feared the Germans would use it to trap a DC3 before I could send a signal to ignore it. We were quicker on the hill than the Germans and Hesketh Pritchard and I thought we were safe on the top of a low mountain, but another German patrol came up on the other side and we crawled into a deep thicket. The Germans had dogs and the risk of being caught was very great. I held my revolver at Hesketh Pritchard's head and he held his at mine; we would both have pressed the trigger, simultaneously, if the Germans had found us. We believed we would be tortured for all the information we carried in our heads and then shot, so better to end it all before that happened.

The Germans moved round and round our thicket and then moved off. It had been a very close call, from which our wireless operators and Partisan liaison group all escaped. We moved fast every night and hid by day. On the fourth day the Germans returned to their barracks and we went to a farm and killed, skinned and boiled a bullock. Twelve us demolished the whole animal in an hour, with fearful stomach pains to follow. Both sides were really exhausted by this Hajka and peace reigned for a while.

In October I began to feel dreadfully ill and could only move with difficulty. Peter Wilkinson recalled me from the field and I made my way painfully in 20 days down towards Ljubliana, where another 'Republic' had been established by the Partisans. A DC3 could land there and, together with other sick and wounded (including Tito's son, who had lost an arm), I was evacuated to the General Hospital at Bari. I was emaciated, covered with lice and in the grip of typhoid fever. The doctors said it was impossible to march for 20 days with typhoid; they evidently did not know what humans can do when they are really frightened! I then heard that my half brother, Vicary Gibbs, to whom I was devoted, had been killed commanding Kings Company in the attack on the Nijmegen bridge over the Rhine. It was a bad time for us.

I recovered quickly and reported in January 1945 to Mr Harold Macmillan (later Prime Minister) who was HMG's Minister in the Mediterranean, at his enormous headquarter building at Caserta near Naples. I was all kitted up to go back to Slovenia. The wireless operators had been evacuated, but Hesketh Pritchard was, I supposed, still alive and out there, and I felt had to get back to him. Macmillan was adamant:

'You can't go, you know.'

'Sir, you don't understand, I HAVE to get back there.'

'I do understand, but the skies of the Mediterranean are dark with the crows of your organisation returning to roost, and I won't have any more of it!'

Well, politics again, but I suppose Macmillan saved my life because if I had got back in the fearful winter weather, I should no doubt have suffered the same treatment as Hesketh Pritchard. Instead I had to become a staff officer in the 8th

Army. Our leader, Peter Wilkinson (now Lt Col Sir Peter Wilkinson, KCMG, DSO, OBE) was to be recruited into the Foreign Office, in which he held many distinguished posts, including British Ambassador in Saigon and later in Vienna. I took command of No 6 Special Force staff section which organised other attempts like ours along Austria's frontier with Italy. We finished up in Klagenfurt, Austria, where the unit was disbanded in October 1945. They were a wonderful lot of men and women; I think of them with affection.

I was no good as a staff officer and I was embarrassed when the German General commanding the Cossack Corps (General von Panwitz) insisted on disarming himself and his Corps in front of me personally. They rode past Von Panwitz and myself, throwing away their arms and I passed them on to the regular British Army regiments. (There has been a fearful row about the consequences of this, which still rumbles on). I longed for the freedom of the field and a small group of buddies dedicated to immediate action. 'Once a Grenadier always a Grenadier.' But 'once a bandit...?' Perhaps twice or even three times, that should be about enough for anyone!

Southern Austria at the end of World War II was in utter confusion. Refugees flooded in from all sides. Prisoners of war were everywhere - the Cossacks, of course, and the Yugoslav Chetniks, White Guards and Ustashi. Many had their women and children with them. The only authority was the British 5 Corps, part of the famous 8th Army, commanded at the end of the war by the Canadian General Crerar. 5 Corps consisted of only 15,000 men under General Keightley, whose Chief of Staff was Brigadier Toby Low, my great friend from New College days. The prisoners and refugees totalled about a quarter of a million all told and the lines of communication back into Italy were long and vulnerable.

What made the task of the British Army infinitely more complicated was that the Yugoslav leader, Tito, had laid claim to a slice of Southern Austria and had, indeed, invaded the area up to and including Klagenfurt and had got there before

5 Corps arrived. There were probably no more than 2,000 of Tito's partisans in Austria (the numbers grew substantially in the next ten days with the arrival of Tito's army divisions) but the last thing 5 Corps wanted was to get into a fight with them - our allies. I had persuaded the Partisans to stop fighting the Cossack Corps and I did my best to persuade them to leave Austria but they reminded me that, when I was with them, they had always told me of their claims on Austria and Italy, and that they were now forcibly presenting these claims. They went on to claim that all Yugoslav nationals should be returned to Jugoslavia where the 'Kriminali' would be legally tried and punished and the remainder 're-educated' - from monarchists to communists.

There is no doubt that this was Tito's intention, and 5 Corps acted upon it. The Cossacks were returned to Russia under an agreement made at Yalta between Churchill and Stalin. All Jugoslavs were withdrawn to their own country, between 20th May and 30th May 1945, thus greatly easing the difficult and dangerous situation of 5 Corps.

I assumed at the time, and still suspect, that Tito agreed to withdraw his Partisans provided the Chetniks and other Jugoslavs were repatriated at the same time. Documents show that the repatriations took place because of an order given by Field-Marshal Alexander on 14th May. The Titoists withdrew on 21st May because of an order given by Tito on 19th May as the result of Stalin telling him that he would not support him against the USA and Britain.

Leaping forward 45 years, I gave evidence in the libel action brought by Toby Low (now Lord Aldington) against Count Tolstoy, who undoubtedly (as the jury in the case agreed) libelled Toby by calling him in a widely circulated pamphlet, 'a war criminal.' This allegation was based on a pamphlet accusing him of many things but may best be summed up in the sentence: 'The man who issued every order and arranged every detail of the lying and brutality which resulted in these massacres (i.e. the alleged massacres of repatriated Cossacks and dissident Jugoslavs) was Brigadier Toby Low, Chief of Staff to General Keightley's 5 Corps, subsequently ennobled by Harold Macmillan as the 1st Baron Aldington.' He was accused of giving these orders knowing they were contrary to the orders from above, and hiding from his superiors what was being done. The trial showed all these allegations to be false and wrong. In the same document I was accused of 'doing his dirty work' and watching Chetniks commit suicide, all of which was pure Tolstoy invention. I know from the evidence of my own eyes and ears that Toby acted under orders emanating from the British Government and confirmed at all lower levels. It is sadly and dreadfully true that some dissident Jugoslavs were massacred on repatriation with or without Tito's complicity. Toby, however, at the moment of repatriation had no reason to feel so sure that Tito's known intentions would be disregarded that he should take the unprecedented action of flatly disobeying the orders he had received through 8th Army from Field-Marshal Alexander, originating with the British Government in the case of the Cossacks. The jury in the libel action awarded Toby £1.5 m damages, subsequently greatly reduced on Toby's initiative.

There remains, however, a widespread feeling that the British action in repatriating the Cossacks and Chetniks in May 1945 was somehow 'wrong.' Toby clearly could not be held responsible, but, so it is felt, we should have acted differently. No-one has, however, suggested what other action the British could reasonably have taken in all the circumstances pressing upon us at the time.

In October 1945 my 'release group' came up and I returned to London to Wellington Barracks to collect my 'civvies' and demobilisation papers. There was a final happy moment, when I went to Buckingham Palace with my mother and Nicholas, to receive a Military Cross from King George VI, who asked in the most friendly and informal way about the Regiment and my part in it. It wasn't much, but I am glad to have done it!

83

CHAPTER 6

THE CITY

The way back from the Grenadiers and Jugoslavia to the City of London was not nearly as difficult as I had imagined: every person and institution in Britain was anxious to help returning service men and women. Briggens was at that time returning to civilian life after being Station XIV, used by the Polish underground for training and printing false identity documents during the war. Rosie angelically continued to look after Nicholas with her own sons, with whom he was very happy. Glyn Mills took me back into the Bank and I started to pick up with old friends such as Simon Ramsay and Brian Johnston. I missed Joe Buxton and Arthur Grant and as I looked at the old photographs of Eton and Oxford clubs I was sad to see that so many had not survived. As in the Great War, it was the young officers who had suffered most. But the young survivors were working for a newer world - most did not want to go back to Square One.

I settled into a small flat in Manchester Square, London, and the Bank sent me on a number of trips round Europe to re-establish their connections with other European banks. I enjoyed that, especially visiting a Norwegian bank where the manager looked at my card and said 'Ah, yes, Glyn Mills. Tell me, are you cotton mills or timber mills?' But the best moment came in Brussels, where I got jaundice, all yellow; I tripped on the way to the loo and hit my head on the bidet, giving myself a gash and a black eye! A Belgian-born friend, Toinon de Bellaigue (now Toinon Ladd), who was teaching French

to Princess Elizabeth and Princess Margaret, asked two wonderful Belgian ladies to visit me. They were both delightful
and I could have married them both! I did, in fact, marry one
of them - José de la Barre. Later, I asked her why she accepted
me and she said, because I looked like the Belgian flag -
yellow, red and black. Subsequent experience has produced
longer-lasting attractions and now, more than forty years
later, we live happily together in the house we built on the
edge of the Great Park at Windsor where our children and
grand-children are regular visitors.

José, 'the underground girl,' was a heroine of the resistance
movement. She has told her story in a successful book
'Granny was a Spy,' published by Quartet in 1988. Her father,
Count Henri de la Barre d'Erquelinnes, was a distinguished
and popular minister and senator in the Belgian parliament;
her mother, a beautiful, but rather shy lady, was the daughter
of le Marquis du Parc, head of a very old family which
originated in Brittany. Her son was for many years Belgian
Ambassador in London. José's family was exceptionally kind
and welcoming to me and I have made many firm friendships
among them.

We married in the family chapel at Jurbise near Mons. Toby
Low was best man, and the wedding breakfast was a superb
example of Belgian cuisine, so soon after the privations of
World War II. For our honeymoon we drove an old Chevrolet
van from Cairo to the Cape and back through the Congo; we
had every sort of adventure. Our eldest daughter, Diana, was
born soon after we got home, none the worse for being
bumped over the worst roads in the world. An old friend from
Eton days, Sir John Gilmour of Montrave, whose father had
been Secretary of State for Scotland, had inherited a huge
house in Cadogan Square, Chelsea. He, out of the kindness
of his heart, lent us two floors, which we occupied in great
state and comfort for some years. Our two daughters were
born while we were there, and we have very happy recollec-
tions of that splendid house and of the generosity of the

Gilmours.

When we got back from our honeymoon I returned to the Bank, which had treated me so well, and confessed that I did not really want to continue life as a commercial banker. I had come to see that dealing with capital and investments was much more interesting than looking after income and current account, and much more influential when pursuing my social objectives.

The Chairman of the Bank asked me to be a local director, but I refused; the only person I believe ever to do so. But, lovely man that he was, he said 'If you ever want money, be sure to let me know.' I was always short of cash thereafter, but I never went back to him. I suppose I looked on him, while he lived, as the ultimate long stop.

But how was I to get into the capital and investment business? I knew some of the bosses of the merchant banks, friends of my step-father, Walter, but I did not think he would be a strong supporter as he had got me into Glyn Mills in the first place. But luck came to my rescue: my kinsman, Lord Clarendon, at that time Lord Chamberlain, gave a huge party for the Diplomatic Corps and all the 'good and the great' at St James's Palace. José and I were invited and I was told to 'look after' anyone who looked lonely. I think that I myself was probably the most lonely man in the room, but I beavered round and suddenly found myself in front of Lord Harcourt of Morgan Grenfell, a leading merchant bank in the City. Bill had been a boss of SOE in Italy and I had worked closely with him.

'Charles, what are you doing now?' he asked.

'Funny you should ask, Bill,' I answered. 'Actually, nothing.'

'What do you want?' said Bill.

'To get into a merchant bank. How about Morgans?'

'No room, but Helbert Wagg are looking for people. They are good: you would suit each other. I'm seeing them tomorrow and I'll have a word.'

Did I imagine it, or did naughty Barbara Villiers, whose portrait hangs in the gallery of St James's Palace, wink at Buckingham on the opposite wall? The 'connection' was still working! A week later Bill took me round to see Alfred Wagg and Lionel Fraser, and within a few days I was in Helbert Wagg and soon became the junior partner. Whew!

Now, it might be thought that this was 'the old boy net' working at its worst, but the story of Helbert Wagg shows that it was quite logical. Heilbert and Waage were Jewish people living in the Frankfurt Ghetto at the end of the eighteenth century and they both married relatives of Nathan Meyer Rothschild. When that amazing man came to London in 1808, to extend the family banking network, they came along too and set up, separately, as stockbrokers in the City. Every day, so Alfred Wagg told me, they called on NMR seeking orders and business. NMR eventually knocked their heads together and set them up in a stockbroking firm with the anglicised name of Helbert Wagg. Alfred was rather scathing about Helbert, whom he always called 'the murderer,' and he dropped out early on. The Waggs all lived to a tremendous age and Alfred eventually inherited the firm. Between the wars, he took it out of the Stock Exchange and set up shop as an issuing house and investment manager, in a beautiful house in a courtyard just off Threadneedle Street. This housed his staff, which never exceeded 100 people, but they were special people and on that the success of the firm depended.

Alfred was a bachelor, a philanthropist - a 'dreamer,' some called him. He loved and sponsored the Eton Manor Club in the East End of London. His co-sponsor was Arthur Child Villiers (a distant Jersey relation) who slept on a truckle bed at the Club, always had a bottle of champagne for dinner and, in the morning, rode up on his bicycle to the offices of Baring Brothers, perhaps the best of all the merchant banks in the City, where he was immensely influential.

I did not know the earlier generation of Alfred's partners,

but he took two of his nephews into his firm. They eventually went their own separate ways. I remember Sir Nigel Campbell, an industrialist, and Bernie Barrington who was Chairman of Legal and General Assurance. Later Alfred promoted one of his staff, Lionel Fraser, who was the son of Gordon Selfridge's butler and an ardent Christian Scientist. He roped in Albert Palache, a Jewish man from Holland, originally from 'mittel Europa.' Albert was the first man I ever knew who could 'see round corners.' Then he promoted more of his staff; James O'Brien, who managed the investment trusts, and Gordon Gunson, a chartered accountant, who managed new issues and mergers. Later came Alan Russell, son of an earlier generation of partners, and Michael Verey, son of Alfred's great friend at Eton. 'Verey and Wagg rowed pluckily and well' was an oft-quoted comment from the Eton College Chronicle.

This was a very mixed bag; half had been to public schools and half had not. I had accumulated some medals for years of 'undetected crime,' as they say in the Army, and seemed likely to fit into this small partnership. It was all new to me and I have no doubt that I was a bit arrogant, but they disciplined me in their various ways and I learned to get new capital business from industrialists and to fit into the financial network of the city. For the next twelve years I was junior partner, keeping the minutes of the weekly partners' meetings, and learning the practice and personalities of the people at the centre of City life. Each firm had its own speciality and strength and you had to select the one most suitable for each share deal.

It was all very personal, informal and trusting, as between friends. The Governor of the Bank of England was the leader, arbitrator and disciplinarian of the City. He was, in those years, Kim (later Lord) Cobbold. He seldom gave orders: a wink or a nod was enough, and his professional officials worked in the same way. The Governor had a tremendous position in the country and, indeed, internationally. Most international deals were carried out in £ sterling or US $. The Governor was responsible for the sterling area, the integrity of the national currency, the level of the Bank Rate, the rate of exchange and the volume of money supply. He also had to attend to the raising of money by Government, both central and local. This is a huge job and it was very well performed. I do not believe the performance was improved when the Bank of England was nationalised in 1946 and it became known as the 'East End Branch of the Treasury.'

It is strange that the British privatisation programme of the eighties did not include making the Bank of England independent. I am convinced we would do better to make the Bank independent in its judgements of how to maintain price stability as in America, Switzerland and Germany where the Central Banks have their independence supported by law.

In the City of London in the fifties the various markets were kept separate. Stock jobbers made the market in the Stock Exchange, fed by orders from stockbrokers. Similarly Lloyds was divided into insurance underwriters and brokers. The money market was made by the discount houses, moving money from where it was in surplus to where it was wanted. The big banks ran the foreign exchange market, and the merchant banks and issuing houses ran the capital market. The 'institutions,' such as life assurance funds, pension funds and investment trusts, stood back and waited for attractive investment propositions to be put to them. The commodity markets, the Baltic shipping exchange and the gold market were active, but smaller. The Bank of England kept a watchful eye over them all, relying on self-regulation and the 'old boy net.' The foreign banks were small players at that time.

By and large, in the years immediately following World War II, you could say that the City of London was perhaps the best of Britain's industries. It was self-absorbed to a great extent, but if you wanted to expand abroad you got a lot of help, especially into America and into the old Empire. There was little interest in Europe. Most of us were still under the spell of the victorious, but centrally-managed and directed, Britain we had known since 1940. The strong sense of national purpose - 'Victory' - was still in our minds, although it had become 'Recovery' - but back to 1939, or on to what?

After the General Election of 1945 we had to accept that Labour had an overwhelming parliamentary majority: their Government was carrying out a radical, extensive and populist programme of nationalisation accompanied by the foundation of a National Health Service and of a social security system 'from the womb to the tomb,' as the saying had it. They were constructing a complete Welfare State, based on the vision of Maynard Keynes, conceived during World War II by Liberals, such as Beveridge, and Labour politicians such as Attlee, Morrison, Bevin, Cripps and Bevan. The new Education Act had been designed by the Tory, R A Butler. Churchill had tried, and failed, to stand against these ideas during the war but after he lost the General Election he put up only an ineffective opposition to them.

In the City, always a Tory stronghold, we moaned about the nationalisation of the Bank of England and of the steel industry, which had provided many firms, including Helbert Wagg, with good revenue, serving their capital needs. We were particularly irked by the imposition of a Capital Issues Committee, which greatly added to our work, slowed down deals and did not seem to be doing anything useful for the economy, which had been devastated by total war but was returning to health and some prosperity. The Americans were all-powerful and amazingly generous, and Britain got the largest share of Marshall Aid. Slowly, our exports rose above pre-war levels and Britain enjoyed a 25% share of world trade - only 8% in 1990! But everything was rationed and controlled, including wages. Exports were pretty free, but three quarters of our imports were controlled or rationed.

In 1951 the Tories won an overall majority in Parliament following a General Election fought on their slogan 'Britain strong and free,' and started their historic thirteen years of government. It cannot be said that the Tories dismantled the Welfare State they inherited. Rationing did not end till 1954. Economic policy was called 'Butskellism,' being a broad consensus between Rab Butler, the Tory Chancellor and Hugh Gaitskell, the new leader of the labour party. Walter Monkton as Minister of Labour, sought cooperation with the Trade Unions. Nationalisation, except of the steel industry, which was sold back to the public, was more or less accepted all round. Beeching at British Rail and Robens at the Coal Board produced vigorous plans for rationalisation and were provided with Government funds for massive investment. Full employment continued to be the main social policy. Expenditure on education was doubled during the period, and benefits under the Welfare State were increased no less than five times in thirteen years. Of these, the first four were under Churchill, as Prime Minister. Although 1940 was his 'finest hour,' these last years were an Augustan age when things generally went well for Britain. They were, however, as under Augustus in Rome, years when complacency started to return as a main national characteristic in British life, encouraged by Britain's high standing in the world and the long period of economic progress of the fifties.

Short-termism was not nearly as pronounced then as it is now. Markets will, of course, always look at what the price will be in the next few hours, or even minutes - that is their purpose and way of life. But in the capital market I recall many conversations which dwelt on what would be best for a company's fortunes in the long run. Major shareholders and managers would discuss and agree the best capital format with their merchant bank or issuing house in the City. I shall not list our successes and occasional failures, as they are all recorded in the Issuing Houses Year Book, carefully studied to see who was doing most and best. It was all competitive but often we agreed to 'go joint' with another house, to avoid bad blood between us. Perhaps it was too cosy to stand up to intense international competition, but there was not much of that. The customers thought we charged too much for what we did - 1% on the capital amount raised - but we never tried to undercut each other and thus break the rate.

Relations with industrial companies were quite close and were usually based on individual friendships, kept alive by regular visits to each other's territory. I know that my interest in British industry began at that time and I took every opportunity to visit factories and plants of our clients, and in that way I got their confidence. Lionel Fraser was, at that time, the chief Executive of our firm; he was very well regarded by industrialists as well as in the City. He was an immense man, topped with a shock of white hair. He cultivated his public relations and tried to get a better image for the City in the press. He was quite successful at this, but his devotion to Christian Science became well known and he was a bit stumped when one day in Whites Club an old friend addressed him, 'Good morning, Lionel, how's God?' He was a good, brave man, a 'natural.' His own story, 'All to the Good,' was published by Heinemann in 1963. Lionel was absolutely insistent that although his partners could have a free hand in negotiation none of them could commit the firm without the approval of a partners' meeting. Any infringement of that rule would lead to dismissal. Our business was on quite a large scale, but our firm was so small that we all knew what other partners were doing. That resulted from the skill of Alfred Wagg and Lionel in choosing compatible partners.

The partners of Helbert Wagg, as of other 'houses,' were much in demand in the City and in industry as non-executive chairmen and directors of public companies. Lionel was Chairman of Babcock and Wilcox, the power station builders, and of Thomas Tilling, an industrial conglomerate. He was deputy Chairman of Tube Investments and a trustee of the Tate Gallery. We thought we would not see much of him but he was in our office almost every day. The other partners of Helbert Wagg had many varied 'outside' directorships; we had to get consent of a partner's meeting before accepting these invitations and to turn the fees into the profits of HW.

There was a sharp division in the City between Gentlemen and Players. When I joined the boards of the Sun Life and Sun Fire Insurance companies I asked for information about various obscure matters at a board meeting. The ancient Chairman asked me to see him after the meeting and begged me not to ask questions.

I responded 'Why, for God's sake?'

The Chairman said, 'Well, it upsets the General Manager.'

The Players did not want the Gentlemen prying into their professional domain. I talked to other directors and we had a mini-revolution, which changed things a bit but not entirely. I have usually found it impossible to resist the temptation to play the 'enfant terrible' when I found stuffy resistance to change, which you could say was the root cause of the British disease. Of course, it had its comical side. When Sun Life amalgamated with the Alliance Assurance everything went very smoothly and there was a first meeting of the two boards to approve everything.

'But, what about the port?' asked an Alliance director.

'What port?' asked the Sun Directors.

'Well, the Alliance board has accumulated a magnificent cellar of port wine and we would not want to share it with the Sun board.'

This produced a deadly silence till the General Manager of Sun Life proposed: 'Perhaps we could put a special label on the decanter of Alliance port, in which Sun directors could only participate by invitation!'

The Players to the rescue!

I often found myself sitting next to Lord Chandos (previously Oliver Lyttelton), Chairman of Amalgamated Electrical Industries, and generally considered to be in the very top flight of British industrialists. With my growing interest in industrial management I asked him once, 'How do you mange AEI, what is your style?'

He paused and said: 'Honestly, Charles, I just tell the

buggers to do it.'

That was, indeed, the macho style of industrial management in Britain for many years after World War II. It didn't
work very well as I found fifteen years later when, in a very
different context, I witnessed the near-collapse of AEI and its
absorption into the General Electrical Company, managed by
Arnold Weinstock.

We had to choose whether to stay with Sun Life and the
Alliance or with the Sun Fire, on our own. I chose Sun Life,
but we all wondered what Sir Miles Thomas would do. He
had been Lord Nuffield's sales director at Morris Motors and
he was known as Tugboat Thomas, because he 'chugs from
peer to peer!' Fortunately, he was made Lord Thomas and
could chug quietly at home.

One of the first 'outside' boards I joined was the United
Premier Oil and Cake Mills in Hull, a mini-Unilever, crushing
vegetable oil seeds and animal fats and selling the treated oils
and fats as highly refined products. That company taught me
most of what I know about British industry. I started with the
financial controls and moved on to marketing, commodity
purchasing, production, innovation, quite high technology
and, of course, industrial relations with both managers and
men in the North East of Britain. I gave it quite a lot of time
and thought and the company gave me a Bentley. Many years
later the firm was bought up by Croda, a larger competitor. I
was delighted that most of the Hull people, who had become
my real friends, got good jobs in the amalgamation.

From that time on, I studied the problems of British
industry more and more closely. I did not, however, lose
interest in Africa, and Sir Frederick Leith-Ross, the Chairman
of the Standard Bank of South Africa, and a board room
colleague of Lionel Fraser's, asked me to join the board of the
Standard Bank. I made several trips round Africa, one of
which followed the granting of independence to India. As José
and I moved through East and Central Africa we heard
everywhere the cry, 'We do not want good government, we

want self-government.' We became convinced that the days of Empire were coming to an end and that we had better make the necessary adjustments to our business, our economy and indeed to our place in the world. It was then that my interest in 'Beyond the sunset' began to grow.

This shift in attitude was greatly reinforced in 1954 when the partners of Helbert Wagg felt I should become more involved in their American business. They sent me, plus José on an extended trip, first to New York, Philadelphia and Washington, then to Toronto, across Canada by train to Vancouver and home via San Francisco. This was a mind-stretching exercise, from which I have not yet recovered. Britain seemed small, timid, old-fashioned and slow in comparison with America in the fifties, when they were at the peak of their success. Everything was 'can do,' the opportunities were boundless, no-one seemed to be short of money, everything was available, everyone talked with everyone else, you had a really 'classless' feeling about society in America at that time. Wages were high and rising, but productivity by investment rose faster still. People were unbelievably kind and friendly to us. We were invited everywhere, from the floor of the Stock Exchange to the gardens of Du Pont at Winterthur in Delaware. All the time I kept thinking that America was a new but mature country, and that Britain has to buck up. As Tennyson has Ulysses say, 'Tis not too late to seek a newer world.'

All this has stayed and grown in me, and has encouraged my cult of a positive mental attitude. I have been able to go to America almost every year since that first visit; my lifelong friendship with Van Dusen has been a major factor. Our eldest daughter married an American who in 1990 is the US Ambassador to Mexico. We have been able to stimulate a series of dynamic, Anglo-American conferences of what we call the 'Successor Generation.' I am still a director of the Norris Institute in Minneapolis. I love the country and the people.

A City battle, waged in 1958, reinforced all these sentiments. British Aluminium, very much an 'establishment' company, was advised by Lazards, a top class merchant bank, to do a deal with the Aluminium Company of America (Alcoa) whereby Alcoa would acquire a large slice of British Aluminium's capital at a relatively low price. This was considered by Tube Investments (of which Lionel was Deputy Chairman) to be a 'steal' and he found support in this at Warburgs, who had an interested American client in Reynolds Metal of Virginia. TI and Reynolds put in a bid for British Aluminium, which kyboshed BA's intended deal with Alcoa.

This produced a tremendous furore in the City; the details are to be found in Lionel's autobiography. In the end TI/Reynolds won control of British Aluminium, and little good did it subsequently do them. The point I have to make is that the new young 'houses' in the City, Warburgs and Helbert Wagg, supported by Schroders, had defeated the 'old Guard' led by Lazards, Morgan Grenfell and what Lionel calls 'an alliance of bankers and friends.' He goes on, 'old citadels tumbled, traditional strongholds were invaded, new thought was devoted to the city problems, there was a freshness and alertness, unknown before, dramatic to watch.'

Only the British Aluminium shareholders directly benefitted, but Warburgs and Helbert Wagg were 'made' and Schroders came closer to us, as we shall shortly see. 'Siggy' (later Sir Siegmund) Warburg had come to the City in, I believe, 1930 from Germany, where Hitler was threatening the Jews. His first company called the New Trading Company, banked with Glyn Mills where I was one of the clerks who looked after it. He had three close and brilliant colleagues, Kroner, Grunfeld and Thalman, trading, as I recall, with South America. Soon they were into the traditional City money and share markets and they were able to acquire a small accepting house, Seligman, which had run out of management. They were still not generally credible in the City and they always brought their ideas round to Lionel at Helbert Wagg, and I cannot remember that we ever turned one down.

The deals were all complicated, involved, clever and original, but they worked and we all made money. I remember Carlo Bombieri of the Banco di Roma bursting into my room one day saying: 'I have just been at Warburgs. They create a huge cloud of confusion in which they do their monkey business.' I was able to pacify Carlo, who went back to Warburgs and completed the deal. But after the British Aluminium affair Lord Kindersley, Chairman of Lazards, said of Siggy, 'I shall never speak to that little so and so again.' But he did, as everyone else did. When I finished my job at the Industrial Reorganisation Corporation in 1970, Siggy said to me at lunch 'There's always room for you at the top of Warburgs.' I did not take him up, finding that the total dedication of that firm to profit and financial advancement would not allow me room for what were increasingly becoming my wider interests.

They were exciting years and there was always some new development awaiting the partners of Helbert Wagg. Through my directorship of the Standard Bank I was in regular contact with its Chairman, Sir Frederick Leith-Ross ('Leithers' to one and all), who had been a very highly regarded Treasury official. He was especially well thought of by the leading European bankers with whom he had done business in the closing years of World War II.

These bankers, led by the formidable Dr Alfred Schaeffer of the Union des Banques Suisse, had put together a group to form the International Institute for European Banking Studies (I.I.E.B.). This was an unappetising title, shortened to 'Institut Bancaire,' but Schaeffer had persuaded many European banks to support his idea and three or four bankers from each of the European capitalist countries had started meeting twice a year for a weekend to discuss a prepared paper, to have a free-for-all discussion on Saturday morning, a grand dinner on Saturday night and a visit to local beauty spots and historical buildings on the Sunday. The Banks represented had, of course, to foot the bill. The Bank of England at first considered the whole thing a waste of time, but Leithers persuaded Cobbold that it was a good listening post and he formed a British group to join the Institute. I became a member in 1959 and stayed till 1976, when I gave up all external appointments to become Chairman of the British Steel Corporation.

The Institut Bancaire was another eye opener for me. I knew enough French and German to get by and I had visited much of Germany between the wars. Through José I knew quite a lot about Belgium, but otherwise I was very ignorant about Europe. At first the meetings were mainly technical, either about commercial banking or about the banques d'affaires, as the merchant banks are known in Europe. But the free-for-all meetings were tremendously interesting. Anyone could speak and the subjects were mainly about politics and economics, from a banker's point of view, country by country. One could not help absorbing an immense and panoramic view of the European political economics. Although the European Common Market had been launched and endlessly debated, few of the thirty or so bankers at these meetings really expected that anything much would come of this 'grande idée' during their working life time. How wrong we were! But bankers follow rather than lead and although there were many bank mergers within national boundaries, there were very, very few international bank mergers. The day for that was still to come.

We had a good British contingent in the Institute and I think we pulled our weight in debate. Leithers was very carefully listened to, as was Lord Cromer when he had finished being Governor of the Bank of England, but the star was always Herman Abs of the Deutsche Bank. He always spoke in perfect English, quoting statistics of both macro and micro economics, and he gave us a strong impression of Germany's astounding recovery, not only in financial and industrial terms, but also in relation to political and social development. He had been adviser to Adenauer who had outwitted all the interest groups to fashion the democratic, capitalist, liberal, ordered state that we now see. Abs was in such demand to be Chairman of companies that the German Parliament passed the 'Lex Abs,' limiting to twelve the number of companies any one man could be chairman of. Abs was the 'Pope' of the Institute and he dressed me down once, when I got 'hot under the collar' with Karsten of the Rotterdamsche.

The social life of the Institute was very important. Everyone brought his wife and in many cases social as well as business friendships were established. It has to be said that some of the wives were not up to the intellectual standard of their husbands. At dinner in Luxembourg I found myself sitting next to the wife of a local dignitary.

It was hard work and I commented on the homard thermidor, 'It is a long time since this lobster was in the sea.' 'But I,' said my neighbour, 'have never been in the sea.'

One night I threatened to refuse to attend the grand dinner for fear of unexciting neighbours, so José dashed down and altered the 'placement' to provide me with more amusing neighbours. That night the wife of the President found herself 'au bout du table.' She was furious and we took pot luck from there on. I involved Toby Low (by then Lord Aldington), chairman of Grindlays Bank, in the Institute; his beloved wife, Araminta, created a tremendous stir when she declined a sumptuous invitation by Dior in Paris, saying she was going to buy guinea pigs on the Left Bank - just what the Europeans wanted as an example of the eccentric English milady.

The Institute was totally beneficial to its members and their banks. It was my first experience of international networking. Of course, there were more 'functionaries' than entrepreneurs. Baron Guy de Rothschild came once, and as he left he said: 'Just a lot of bloody bank clerks.' But this brilliant arrogant, unlucky man was wrong, and he made up for it by opening his magnificent Château de Ferrières for an Institute party. I believe we all retained quite a sharp mental image of the culture, capacity and credit-worthiness of all the European countries: this has made it easier to understand the will behind the Single Market and Monetary Union. Then, as now, the British tended to be the odd man out, except on single, isolated, deals and issues. My guess is that the others looked on us as people to be respected, even admired, but as living in another, different world.

1960 was an 'annus mirabilis,' a wonder year. Jack Kennedy won the election to President of the USA and the West rose up to welcome this young, bright, brave man who promised to make all things new. Macmillan, our Prime Minister, pulled us out of the mess of the Suez invasion and promised the 'wind of change' in South Africa. Kruschev banged his desk with his shoe at the United Nations, saying, 'We will bury you.' Gaitskell, now Labour leader, said, 'We will fight, fight and fight again to reverse Labour's unilateral, nuclear disarmament policy,' and National Service in Britain called its last recruits, my son Nicholas among them.

The film 'I'm all right Jack' set the pace for the swinging permissive sixties, but all the time complacency was at work and it would not be long before the old criticism, 'Britain is out of date,' was heard in the media and in the international competition. The affluent society produced inflationary wage claims. Bank Rate was raised and a pay pause was introduced. We had to have a loan from the IMF. The 'night of the long knives' (13th July 1962), when seven Cabinet ministers were sacked by Macmillan, was still to come.

Despite this economic and social turmoil, the City of London felt good and confident in 1960. We all talked of expansion and steady organic growth. Lord Cromer of Barings was hotly tipped to be the next Governor of the Bank of England. What should Helbert Wagg be doing, under the strong leadership of Lionel Fraser? We had no position in Australia, which was very much in the news as the up and coming country, having largely shaken off the dominance of the Trade Unions. I asked my partners if I could go with José and spy out the land for an issuing house and investment advisory firm such as ours. They were all intensely busy with the businesses they advised, and so off we went with only three contacts, but a lot of hope that 'there was gold in them thar hills.'

The contacts were given me by Geoffrey Gibbs, my favourite Gibbs uncle. Two were to banks, which came in handy; the third was a trump card. It was to Vincent Fairfax, then owner (and I believe editor) of the leading daily newspaper in Sydney, who was a personal friend of Geoffrey's. He at once rang up and asked us to lunch with him and some friends at his office in a few days.

Vincent Fairfax's office was at the top of a building from which one could see the whole of Sydney harbour and the famous bridge. Below us was bustling, ramshackle downtown Sydney - no opera house then. The guests were Vincent's friends and business associates, all interesting people. But one man, especially, I had noticed as he came in, broad, indeed rotund, smiling, confident - the sort of man of whom you say 'he's here.' His name was John Darling, son of a former Chairman of Broken Hill Proprietary, Australia's largest mining and steel making company.

Vincent asked me to 'say a few words' after lunch and I did my best. As we filed out, John Darling came up to me and asked, 'What are you doing this afternoon?' That was the moment of conception of Darling and Company, now one of Australia's leading investment banks. We talked all afternoon and it was clear that John, who was well heeled, would like to start some sort of money business, rather like Helbert Wagg. I thought, 'This is just what we are looking for' and I signalled Lionel who promised support. As I recall we put up a third of the capital, as did John Darling himself and also the Bank of New South Wales ('the Wales'). We found a manager, Rupert Burge, and set out our stall at 51 Young Street, Sydney.

Of course, like true love, all did not run smoothly all the time, but we were always able to find superb managers. Rupert got it going, but moved away from us. He was followed by Gleeson White, a very clever expatriate, and then by John Broinowski, who proved the ideal man. We were the right people at the right time in Australia. The stockbrokers had done our sort of business before. They naturally resented our arrival, but in their open-hearted Australian way they came to accept us as part of the Sydney scene. We always made some money and, as the saying goes, we went from strength to strength.

John Darling was too entrepreneurial to stay with the company for ever, and he has done many different things since then. I was a director till 1970, when I went to Guinness Mahon, but I often visited Darling and Company in Australia. They wanted me there at Christmas time 1965 and I said I would only come if I brought my family. 'Sure,' they said. Nicholas was just into a new job, but José and I and our two daughters flew out and what they remember was Christmas pudding ice-cream on Bondi beach. We came back via Saigon where my brother-in-law, Peter Wilkinson, was British Ambassador. Peter, as an old soldier, fitted perfectly into Saigon and the Vietnam War, but my poor sister, Theresa, was unhappy there in the heat and with the incomprehensible language, having to organise an embassy. They arranged for us to meet a number of Americans, including a young secretary at the American Embassy, who fell in love with our elder daughter, Diana; John Negroponte had to wait another ten years before he married her.

The first visit to Australia was for José and myself a climacteric experience. We had proved, (to ourselves at any rate), that we could start up and handle new business in a new situation. We gave ourselves a few days holiday in the Haleukenani (Breath of Heaven) Hotel in Honolulu, which at that time really did live up to its name. We visited the other islands and I took out an American driving licence. The grizzled old native policeman who tested my driving (I never went over 30 mph) said 'You drive well, but you drive too fast.' We got back to the hotel to find a signal from Lionel:

'Return at once for urgent talks about important developments.' That sounded like a merger. We wondered who with, as we bustled home.

When I got back to Threadneedle Street no-one wanted to hear about Australia: they were all agog with the negotiations started between Lionel and Gordon Richardson, who had just been appointed Deputy Chairman of J. Henry Schroder, a merchant bank established by Baron Schroder out of the 'maison mère' in Hamburg, at the end of the last century. We had been friendly with them for many years and they were on our side in the British Aluminium battle. We also knew Gordon Richardson who, when he left the Bar, became, among other things, a director of the Legal and General Assurance under the chairmanship of our partner, Bernie Barrington. In, I think, 1958, Bernie brought Gordon round to see Lionel with the idea that Gordon would make a good partner for us. Lionel was very impressed with Gordon but told him that his age-group was pretty well full up at Helbert Wagg. Lionel offered to take him round to see Helmut Schroder who we knew was looking for more good partners. Helmut, whose firm was perhaps over-gentrified, jumped at the idea of such a brilliant and attractive man as Gordon, who had been educated at Nottingham High School before Cambridge and Grays Inn.

Two years later Gordon had established himself at Schroders and was made deputy to Helmut. It was at that point that Gordon and Lionel started talking about an amalgamation of the two firms. It was quickly done and has proved one of the most successful mergers in the whole post-war City experience.

The shares of Schroders were quoted on the Stock Exchange so they offered their shares for ours and also bought out our managerial participation in the profits of Helbert Wagg. There was no real problem till we came to the future Chairman of the new group. Helmut was due to retire shortly because of trouble with his thyroid gland. He would embarrass us at lunch in the firm's dining room with visitors present by rising to his feet and saying loudly, 'They've come for me. Good night!' His driver would then take him to his car.

Lionel longed to succeed Helmut, if only for a short while, but the Schroder partners would not have it. They had chosen Gordon and they wanted him to succeed. As always in the City, if a firm is not bankrupt, it is the man with the majority of shares who wins. Helmut, who had a majority, settled on Gordon. At the next board meeting Lionel rose and said: 'I wish to make a personal statement. I feel I have been passed over, after all I have done for the firm and the City, and I now sever all connections with it. Please arrange for the Prudential to pay my pension.' And he walked out of the room; it was a sad moment. Every inducement short of the Chair had been offered him, but his strong pride, his strength, was wounded. He went on being Chairman of Tillings at Crewe House in Mayfair and he tried to get the Banque de Paris et des Pays Bas going in London. He died of Hodgkins' disease a few years later. Had he not been a Christian Scientist his life might have been prolonged, but his peak had passed and he was never the same again.

But the rest of us had to get down to it and make the new firm, Schroder Wagg, work well and smoothly. The Schroders did the banking and the Waggs did the investment and the new issues - the 'corporate finance.' We moved out of the labyrinthine offices of Schroders into a spanking new building in Cheapside. Business poured in and we were much in demand. Gordon became Chairman in 1962 and surrounded himself with other 'pros,' accountants and lawyers like himself. The firm became a meritocracy and we had to move with it. Gordon was cold and steely but no-nonsense, and intense care was the order of the day. He was aiming high personally, as we could see. He was up against Warburg and he knew it. Any slip by any of us was 'one down' and Gordon did not forgive. These qualities stood him in good stead when later he became Governor of the Bank of England.

104

I had a fine room overlooking St Paul's, divided only by our secretaries from Gordon, whom I saw constantly, but I never felt close to him. I expect he thought I 'flew by the seat of my pants' which I sometimes did. In 1965 I was doing a deal in New York with Ian MacGregor (later my successor at British Steel) and two other bankers, when Gordon pulled the rug out from under me; the others went ahead without us. That evening in New York I wrote to Gordon saying I would like to give up all my external appointments and concentrate on getting our group deeply established in Europe, which I felt I could do with all my Institute contacts. I read it over next morning, as usual, and posted it off. That gave Gordon the opportunity I think he was looking for, to shunt me elsewhere. When I was back in London he said, 'We can't afford to lose all those big fees you earn,' but I always suspected that he had suggested to Leslie O'Brien, then Governor of the Bank of England, that I might be a candidate for a 'quango' - quasi-autonomous national government organisation. I can't be sure, but very soon afterwards Sir Frank Kearton (later Lord Kearton) recruited me as managing Director of the recently created Industrial Reorganisation Corporation, of which more later.

I had been thirty five years in the City, broken by three years at Oxford and six years of war, and I had seen its life and work from several angles. I had been very happy and had accumulated a small pile - enough to contemplate 'independence,' which I seemed to be losing in Schroder Wagg, and I looked forward to a 'national interest' job. I had been for two years on the Ministry of Labour's Resettlement Committee, aimed to resettle Servicemen made redundant by the heavy cuts in the armed forces, which began in 1958. This was a fascinating job and I acted as consultant to hundreds of men who were really 'lost' on leaving the services. They all wanted to commute up to London or get some sort of clerical job. I tried to persuade them to stay and get a job in their local environment, where their service skills would be invaluable in running local businesses, such was builders, garages, stores and even shops. Some thought this was 'infra dig,' but lots took my advice and wrote to say how they had prospered. It was a good lesson for what I had to do in British Steel later on.

The City is a living, throbbing, changing part of British life. It has moved far since the meritocracy of the sixties and it has far to go. I am anxious about the 'me, more, now' culture of the later Yuppies; it needs a little more than that. This culture, I believe, sprung from the lack of national purpose which led many people to disregard service and duty in their lives. Short-termism is part of that culture. A business development board, of which more later, would correct much of that.

I have already commented on the need for an accountable Bank of England, independent in its market judgements of how to keep prices stable and eliminate inflation. I do also believe that only a Stock Exchange Commission, as in new York, will be able to deal with the shenanigans which break out so often in relation to share deals.

London is benevolently placed, time wise, between New York and Tokyo. If we were to lose that great advantage to Frankfurt, Paris or Zurich, it would only be because of gross errors and negligence on our part. There is however, I do believe, too much aggressive self-interest in the City to allow that to happen.

CHAPTER 7

INDUSTRIAL REORGANISATION
1968-1970

So, out of City life into what was to be a most exciting period of my life. The thirteen years of Tory rule fizzled out in 1964 when Sir Alec Douglas Home, a splendid Foreign Secretary and a non-economic Prime Minister, just lost the general election to Harold Wilson, the new Labour leader, and Ted Heath became the new leader of the Tories. Wilson went again to the polls and got a majority of 97, enabling him to 'act confidently,' but not for long. Wilson claimed to have 'ended the slide to social inequality and public neglect.' Unfortunately, this was done by increasing taxation and pumping up the money supply, which soon produced a series of worsening economic crises, leading to devaluation of £ sterling in 1967.

Against this unpromising background Wilson spoke of 'white hot technological revolution' in British industry and of a National Plan to be produced by the newly created Department of Economic Affairs under the mercurial George Brown. The Plan collapsed because it was based on wage increases of 3.5%, when the actual increases were 9%. The 'white hot' concept did, however, produce the Industrial Reorganisation Corporation (IRC) although it was not specifically technological.

The origins of the IRC can be quite clearly traced to the intelligent, inquisitive mind of Ben Cant, the head of an old-established family business, Hamworthy Engineering, part of the Powell Duffryn Group. In a long paper, 'Notes on Britain's Industrial Future,' Ben, who became an IRC board member at the same time as I did, argued closely to reach five propositions:

1. In the UK we must distinguish between the need for competition at home and the need to compete effectively in world markets.
2. We have to accept that international competition is the real spur to efficiency, rather than the Monopolies Commission etc.
3. We need, therefore, in Britain, bigger and better production units, capable of meeting the international competition.
4. The UK needs a catalyst to achieve this, which must be state-owned, to overcome the many sectional interests involved.
5. The catalyst should be a highly independent 'quango' with access to public money, with which to achieve identifiable re-structuring results.

The paper found its way to Sir Eric Roll (now Lord Roll) and to Sir Maurice Dean, Permanent Secretaries to the Department of Economic Affairs and to the Ministry of Technology respectively, and it finally saw the light of day in a White Paper in January 1966.

The White Paper emphasised the need for more concentration and rationalisation, to promote the greater efficiency and international competitiveness of British industry. Changes to date did not match the economic requirements. IRC would meet a national need not satisfied by existing institutions in the public or private sectors.

The appointment of Sir Frank Kearton (Chairman of Courtaulds and later Lord Kearton) as Chairman met with universal support, as did the board of directors, which was heavily weighted in favour of successful industrialists.

IRC's first Managing Director was Ronald Grierson (now Sir Ronald), a man of many parts. He came from Warburg's stable, brilliant, flexible, tri-lingual, ambitious, born Griesman in Nuremberg in 1922. They assembled the first and outstanding IRC team of executives, about eight in all, young men from the City and industry, of no particular political inclination but keen to do something for British Industry, which was by then seen to be the area thwarting the desired continuous growth of the British economy.

Grierson did a good start-up job, but when it came to the General Electric Company's bid for Amalgamated Electrical Industries in 1967 he felt that 'IRC should not publicly take one side against the other, or seek to influence shareholders in the choice before them.' This quote is from the official IRC History by Professor Hague and Geoffrey Wilkinson, published in 1983. The board of IRC felt that they should publicly back GEC and Grierson resigned. As the official history says, 'Without Grierson the IRC would not have been what it was; until he left it, the Corporation was not likely to become what it did.' Kearton ran the IRC from then till I was posted Managing Director on 1st February 1968, and he stayed very close to its decision-making centre till he returned full-time to Courtaulds at the end of that year.

Why, my friends asked, did I give up a safe job in Schroder Wagg and accept an appointment in a dicey little quango, working for Wilson, who was by then anathema to the City and the High Tories? My Villiers relations with their long tradition of public service were more understanding. My wife had no doubts: she said 'Have a go, Joe.'

I knew I had got to the end of my creative role in Schroder Wagg and that I had better get out of the way of younger professional men who were straining at the leash under Richardson. How well they have done! The business, still Schroder family controlled and chaired by Helmut's son-in-law Gowi von Mallinckrodt, is top of the league for corporate finance; having avoided the mistakes made by other merchant banks at the time of the so-called 'Big Bang' reshuffle in 1987, it is a clear leader in its own specialised field of operations. I have never sold the shares allotted to me at the time of the merger with Herbert Wagg.

The terms Kearton offered me to go to IRC were good and Labour leaders had a hard time swallowing them. Kearton described the job to me as 'prestigious;' certainly it was always in the public eye. I really did not know what I was in for, except for the fine words in the White Paper, but I knew that governments loved words such as those. But how on earth was the job to be done? Grierson had packed it in. Why should I hope to do any better?

I suppose that at the back of my mind there were two considerations which I had constantly thought about as I studied political economy in Britain. The first was that the generally accepted policy of full employment was OK politically, but disastrous economically, when combined with the other main economic policies - economic growth and a surplus in the balance of payments. Like amateur jugglers, successive British governments were always letting one ball or another fall to the ground and having to start again. Usually the employment ball stayed up and that policy worked (to the benefit of Members of Parliament). But when growth went up the balance of payments went down, as it did when employment rose too fast or too far.

I had studied the economic fortunes of Britain from 1951, when the Tories returned to power, to 1967, when Harold Wilson devalued the £ sterling, using the incredible phrase, 'This does not mean that the pound here in Britain in your pocket, purse or bank has been devalued.' It is almost unbelievable, but the Bank rate had been raised or credit otherwise squeezed in no less than nine out of the sixteen years. The relaxed periods, on the other hand, covered only seven out of those sixteen years. The remedies for economic crises had mainly been through demand management; bank rate, special deposits, reduced hire-purchase and 'the regulator.' Peripheral experiments such as the formation of the National Economic Development Organisation (NEDO), the 'pay pauses,' the 'guiding light,' the Prices and Incomes Board and George Brown's National Plan never had sufficient teeth to function effectively. There was an inexorable pressure for higher wages, supported and sometimes stimulated by the Trade Unions. When I was talking with Kearton about IRC it was crystal clear that Britain was getting nowhere dangerously fast, under what we called the 'Stop-Go' regime.

The second main consideration in my mind at that time was that the 'supply side,' manufacturing industry, had never been directly involved in government measures to remedy the production gap. As Professor Bernard Smailes, the economic historian, has said, Britain's problems were 'mainly due to the failure of Britain's visible export trade to grow at a sufficiently rapid rate to match the ever increasing quantities of imports, combined with the decline in the ability of invisible exports to support trade deficits.' The clincher for me was that my friends and business associates in America, Europe and Australia unanimously warned that Britain's exports were delivered too late, of poor quality, of old-fashioned design, carelessly sold and anyway too expensive - a litany that we have heard over and over again. The case for industrial intervention was clearly made - for me anyway.

Still, I hesitated. The IRC was, I could now clearly see, a red-hot potato. My carefully assembled business 'connection' would not forgive my intrusion into their sacred domains: 'fools rush in where angels fear to tread.' Strangely, conviction came through industry itself. I was sitting at my desk at Schroders when the telephone rang - 'This is George Harriman of British Motors. Can you pop down to Piccadilly to meet my directors?'

'Sure, Sir George, what's the problem?'

'Well, I'll keep that till we meet.'

'OK. I'll be with you within the hour.'

'Don't be late!'

As I walked into that board-room I could literally feel crisis. I knew many of the members, who greeted me in a rather hopeless sort of way, and the Chairman, Harriman, said 'Charles, British Motor Corporation has run out of money, models and management and that little so and so Stokes is just itching to put in a bid for us at a ridiculously low price. Do we accept his offer or liquidate? What is our duty to our shareholders?'

I knew, of course, of Sir Donald Stokes' intentions (Chairman of Leyland Motors and later Lord Stokes) because one of the Schroder partners was advising him, and my first thought was, 'Here is the conflict of interest situation.'

Harriman said, 'We've heard the rumour that you are going to the IRC, so you should be free to advise us.'

Well, Stokes was also a director of IRC, so that would have to be carefully handled to prevent Stokes from getting inside information about British Motors. Nevertheless, it was at that moment I decided to accept Kearton's proposition and go to the IRC - if this was the sort of thing the IRC would be asked to do, it would be vastly exciting and, hopefully, beneficial to British industry and to the political economy.

I delved into the British Motor problem and explored every avenue, as the diplomats say. In the end Harold Wilson, Prime Minister, Tony Benn, Minister for Technology, and the leading members of the accountancy profession, plus Frank Kearton for the IRC and Siggy Warburg for good measure, fixed and imposed merger terms on British Motor and Leyland Motors. Stokes became all-powerful Chairman and some of the best British Motor people departed in both sorrow and anger. I was by then at IRC and had offered the newly merged Company, British Leyland Motor Corporation, a large loan to sweeten the marriage. At the press conference to announce the deal Stokes and Harriman said they did not need the IRC money. This was only the first of a series of accidents to which the new Corporation was prone, and from which many lessons were to be drawn: above all the difficulty of getting good, new practices down through the layers of management to the shop floor. Meanwhile, I had to get down to understanding the IRC and what we could expect to make of it.

I had barely walked into the new, but spartan, offices of the IRC at 46 Pall Mall, in the centre of London's Clubland, when I was surrounded by the executives demanding attention to the mergers and deals they were preparing. They were an exciting group of men aged between 30 and 36, picked up by Kearton and Grierson mainly from the financial sector, none yet quite at director level, but all itching to show their paces, full of confidence in their own abilities - 'brash' was the description sometimes applied to them. They were all convinced that the IRC was of some national importance and that they could make a visible contribution to the regeneration of British Industry.

The first call was to bring about the merger of Broom and Wade with Holman Bros, both in the compressed air industry. They had been flirting with each other for ages and the merger made sense: 'industrial logic' was the phrase IRC invented for that. I got the senior directors of both companies in the same room in the IRC offices and, after hours of further flirting and dithering, I got up with my back to the door and said, 'Gentlemen, we have heard it all and I am not going to let you leave this room till you all have initialled the terms for merger which you have before you.'

This was highwayman stuff and they looked very surprised, but they accepted the terms, calling it a shotgun wedding. In fact, they were making honest women of each other. The result, International Compressed Air Corporation operated successfully for many years till it met further problems, but by then IRC had been disbanded, so we could help them no more.

So far so good, but there was sterner stuff to come. I might have been appointed Managing Director of the IRC, but Frank Kearton had been in at the beginning, had been executive Chairman after Grierson left, till I arrived, and had established a firm hold on the board of directors and on the executive team. Kearton is blessed with a tremendous personality. As he said to me once, 'Wherever I go things happen.' He is a year older than me but his track record by 1968 was very different. From Hanley High School he went to St John's College, Oxford and thence to ICI, Billingham. He spent the war on project 'Manhattan,' developing the atomic bomb in America. After the war he joined Courtaulds, in charge of chemical engineering. He soon became a main board director, then deputy Chairman, when almost single handed he fought off ICI's take-over bid for Courtaulds and thus became the obvious man for Chairman in 1964. He felt passionately about the post war failures of British industry, about which he knew an enormous amount, both from technical and business points of view. The IRC was his baby.

In the IRC days Kearton spoke with the speed of a woodpecker drilling a tree. He was a lion of man, as determined as a mule, with the vision of an eagle and a tendency to occasional buffalo charges.

Once he got going he was unstoppable. He poured out energy and experience and enthusiasm as from a tap. Alastair Morton, one of the IRC executives (in 1990 Co-Chairman of Eurotunnel), said to me, 'Frank will blow a fuse one day,' but he never did. His fear was that, like Grierson, I would prove too 'bankerly' and not confront the business establishment of Britain as he had done with Courtaulds over ICI and as he was determined to do with the IRC. The test came in the spring of 1968 and I nearly failed it.

The issue was, would IRC not only choose between contestants in a take-over battle, but also use its cash (£150m voted by Parliament under the IRC Act) to support its choice? This had never been done before in such circumstances. The situation arose because two IRC executives, Chris Hogg (now Sir Christopher, Chairman of Courtaulds and of Reuters) and Mike Knight (in 1990 a leading business consultant) had made a penetrating study of the scientific instruments and process control industry, in which Britain's position had been undermined by German, Swiss and American companies. The IRC board was determined to build up this essential, but ailing, sector of British Industry.

For some while the Rank Organisation had been trying to persuade Cambridge Instruments to accept a take-over bid. Rank was diversifying out of cinemas and had made an astonishing success out of its purchase of the Xerox copier, from which many other companies had turned aside. Rank's chairman, John Davis, was ebullient at this result of his entrepreneurial vision. Cambridge was very much smaller, highly specialised, technical and inventive. Its Chairman, Dr Erasmus Barlow, belonged to the founding family, was an excellent technician and wanted only to be left alone to develop his company in his own inventive way. The third player was George Kent Limited, chaired by Rodney Kent, who wished to keep his efficient, successful family business moving steadily forward in the instruments and process control business. He wanted to bring Cambridge into his group, but lacked the financial resources to do that in competition with Rank.

We had a number of very straight-talking meetings with the three chairmen and their executives and came firmly to the conclusion that Rank was too impatient, instant-profit conscious and lacking in the technical expertise needed to make a good foster parent for Cambridge. Kent, on the other hand, seemed much more suitable for that purpose, but they were not strong financially and in an open fight against Rank for Cambridge, they would certainly lose. Cambridge had become resigned to being taken over by one or other, but they greatly disliked the Rank Organisation and felt that they would be compatible with Kent. The Royal Society owned 583,000 ordinary shares in Cambridge - a key shareholding, watched over by Lord Fleck, former Chairman of ICI.

Kearton had made up his mind that this was a test case for

IRC and that if he failed to use our muscle to the full in this case our credibility would be gone. Many board members and executives agreed with him. All my previous experience told me that to support Kent in taking over Cambridge was a dicey deal financially and that it would arouse deep hostility in the City and in industry, which would make life more difficult for us in the future. Was it worth it?

Kearton was in his unstoppable mood. I was due to leave for an meeting of the Institut Bancaire in Venice on a Friday evening. That evening was chosen by him for an IRC dinner at Courtaulds' magnificent chairman's residence at Sunning-dale. I decided to postpone my flight to Venice to the follow-ing day. It was just as well I did so.

At Friday night's dinner I found myself in a minority over the action IRC should take to support Kent in its take-over bid for Cambridge... My arguments cut no ice and I was thrown by the news that the Ministry of Technology and the Department of Economic Affairs (to which IRC was account-able) were neutral on the use of IRC cash for this purpose - it was up to us. I played for time and left for Venice.

I can remember nothing of that meeting of the Institute, except leaving one of the sessions and going to Saint Mark's Basilica in the Piazza San Marco, under the Winged Horses, into the gloomy dark church, smelling of candles and incense. I had been brought up as a Protestant and became a Catholic soon after marrying José. The teachings of Tubby Clayton and Frank Buchman never left me - now they must all help to resolve my dilemma. And they did.

I found the interior of St Mark's intolerably stuffy and the continuous shuffle of priests and worshippers all round me made it hard to concentrate, so my mind was open. What should I do? Quite suddenly, I knew. There was no vision, no blinding flash, but, ridiculously, I thought of the Whig's battle cry for the Reform Bill of 1832 - 'The Bill, the whole Bill and nothing but the Bill,' which unlocked the Age of Reform in England. So, I thought, would the IRC unlock the regeneration of British industry by cocking a snook at the British Establishment, by using Government money to get the preferred solution to an industrial problem. It did not quite work out like that, but never mind, my conscience was clear and we would be doing the right thing. I bought some dreadful gold embossed long glasses (which José would never use) and hurried home.

The whole deal was lined up by our executive colleague, David Ewart (in 1989 the Financial Director of Morgan Grenfell) and announced on 5th June 1968. We underwrote Kent's offer for Cambridge, we bought Cambridge shares in the market and we bought Royal Society's holding direct. We finished up with 24.9% of Kent's equity; we undertook to make more money available to Kent, if necessary, and our colleague Roger Brooke (later founder and Chief Executive of Candover) joined the board of Kent. John Davis of Rank said, 'I can only leave it at that' (*Times* 6th June 1968). He had more to say later.

As I turn the pages of my scrap book I find a great variety of press reactions: 'sharp claws for the paper tiger;' 'taxpayers takeover;' 'IRC stumps Rank;' 'Rank blasts the IRC;' 'Rights and wrongs of the IRC Rank battle;' 'IRC: off with the velvet glove.' Even the former Archbishop of Canterbury, Dr Fisher, joined in with a letter to *The Times* saying, 'I am ready to trust IRC's judgement. The Chairman of IRC says he preferred to risk incurring criticism than to miss opportunities of promoting industrial reorganisation which will bring wider benefits to the economy. That seemed to be a most laudable preference.' The CBI said 'IRC interfered with normal market forces involved in a take-over. Worse, it had done so with public money.' Harold Wincott, the greatest financial commentator of the time, said, 'I happen to believe that the IRC is run by honourable, efficient people, but recent events have endangered the revival of confidence which the IRC was beginning to enjoy.' *The Times* on 21st June commented, 'To succeed, a body like the IRC needs to be able to convince the business community that it is absolutely fair.' Antony Bambridge in *The Observer* remarked, 'It's no damn good knowing what is the right thing to do, if you've no way of doing it.' William Davis, then at the *Guardian,* wrote a piece headlined, 'Why I think Villiers was right.'

Politically there is no doubt the IRC damaged itself with the Tory party. Keith Joseph pressed Peter Shore (Secretary of Sate for the Department Economic Affairs) hard to say that the IRC would never do such a thing again. Peter Shore flatly refused. Tories saw IRC as 'a kind of talking shop.' Joseph then said, 'When we are in Government we shall reconsider the width of its powers very carefully.' I listened to the debate from the Gallery of the House and later had lunch with Keith Joseph and Iain Macleod. The latter said, 'The Tories would change your riding instructions.' 'Surely,' I said, 'you would still wish us to ride to win?'

The subsequent history of Kent plus Cambridge was not happy. Profits fell away to an actual loss in 1974. Kent tried to get rid of Cambridge and the Swiss engineering group Brown Boveri made a bid for the process control activity. The stake acquired by IRC was sold to Brown Boveri by the then Labour government, and Rank with 18% followed suit. The truth was that IRC had over-estimated the strength of Kent's rather middle-aged management and under-estimated the magnitude of Cambridge's problems. IRC never again used its clout to the full. We did not need to; the sword was more effective in the scabbard.

The consequences of this small, but in some ways historic, contest were twofold: in the short term IRC's influence was greatly increased in the British economy and our deals went through more easily; in the longer term the Tories and CBI became IRC's implacable enemies.

Life became very hectic at the IRC after the Kent/Cambridge affair. We were sought out by Chairmen, large shareholders and indeed Ministers to investigate possible improvements in British industry and to suggest remedies.

The Author *(photo: Sunday Telegraph).*

We were poor, very 'pi,' but everything had to be 'done proper.' We lived in a house called 'Cherry Orchard.'

My earliest and strongest influence was my father, killed in France at Cambrai in 1917.

I was left much in the care of Grandmoth Herbert Paul's wife, who was a most splen lady, both in appearance and intellect.

As far as my sister an were concerned Brigge our new home, was a be tiful place. My stepfath Walter Gibbs, s sequently became L Hunsdon, and later L Aldenham. My mot sometimes got a bit m dled!

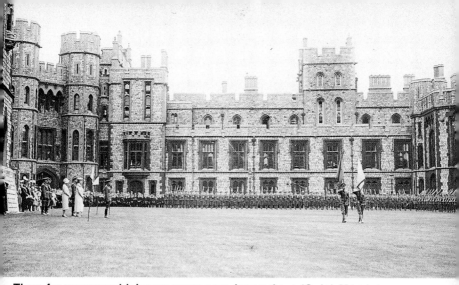

Then, for reasons which now escape me, I roared out, 'Quick March.' As any soldier knows, such an order from a 'stand at ease' position is impossible to perform, but some tried while others did nothing; the remainder burst into uncontrollable laughter. The Eton Officer Cadet Corps.

The figure (an 11th generation American from Philadelphia (front row right) thrust out a hand, saying very positively, 'Van Dusen.' The New College, Oxford, Rugby Fifteen. I am in the back row with spectacles.

Part of the Supplementary Reserve of officers was called up in April 1939. I was mobilised into the 2nd Grenadiers at Pirbright Camp.

Tito

Standing by to drop into the Tito Partisan IX Corps 12 miles north-east of Gorizia.

I concentrated on the build-up of Partisan odreds in their interference with German troop movements into Italy.

The Partisan couriers never left us as they were personally responsible for our safety and we were valuable property because we could bring 'drops' of rifles, tommy guns, mortars, ammunition and explosives.

We were in an empty house and I happened to look out of a first floor window and see a German patrol on the road 500 yards away. They had spotted our movement into the forest and were after us. (Jugoslavia July/August 1944).

I was no good as a staff officer and I was embarrassed when the German General commanding the Cossack Corps (General von Panwitz) insisted on disarming himself in front of me personally.

(Inset opposite): We crawled into a deep thicket. The Germans had dogs and the risk of being caught was very great. I held my revolver at Hesketh Pritchard's head and he held his at mine. We would both have pulled the trigger simultaneously if the Germans had found us.

I asked her (José de la Barre d'Erquelinnes) why she accepted me and she said (after my fall) I looked like the Belgian flag: yellow red and black. *(Inset*, Jurbise, her family home near Mons).

Helmut Schroder was looking for more good partners, and conscious that the firm was perhaps overgentrified, jumped at the idea of such a brilliant and attractive man as Gordon Richardson, who had been educated at Nottingham High School before Cambridge and Grays Inn.

I think of the dozen or so IRC executives I cannot choose between them in their energy, inventiveness and loyalty. Thank goodness they all found other outlets for their talents when IRC was wound up. *Photo: Michael Ward.*

The Bank of England at first considered the Institut Bancaire a waste of time, but Sir Frederick Leith-Ross persuaded Cobbold otherwise. One could certainly not help absorbing an immense and panoramic view of European political economics. Saturdays' business was followed by grand dinners afterwards.

HEDEGAARD GREEN VERHOUSEL COLLIN SCHOELER VILLIERS

Bob Scholey and José at the opening of the Rod Mill at Scunthorpe in September 1976.

José at Shotton. My work was not all to do with closures.

Her Majesty Queen Elizabeth The Queen Mother about to open the Hunterston Ore Terminal on 5 June 1979. I was able to brief Her Majesty about meeting the leader of the ISTC. *Photo: F & J Adam.*

Mother The is 'an ord person and extraordina human be said José visit after 1979 Inte tional Iron Steel Inst Conference Sydney, Au lia.

Unless there is more money on the table there is nothing to talk about. *Photo: Morris Benjamin.*

There was a big crowd shouting and throwing things. I got hard pears on the face and a woman poured a bucket of bad fish over the policemen who were trying to get me through the crowd. *Photo: Evening Gazette, Middlesbrough.*

José launched the BSC ore carrier *Ravenscraig* in Belfast.

Prince Philip, a supporter of our work at British Steel (Industry).

Paddy Naylor had sniffed out that there was a market (for small business) for space with a roof, a water tap and an electric light point at a very low rent. *(Photo: Mac Rhind)*

Everyone concerned wanted the Prince of Wales to open the proceedings. Here he is at Blaenau Gwent Workshops, 1981.

When MacGregor succeeded me at BSC he kept the financial support and property transfer to BSI going strong.

One, above all the others, stays in the mind. Kearton and I invited Arnold Weinstock (later Lord Weinstock), managing director of General Electric Company (GEC), and Lord Nelson, Chairman of the English Electric Company (EE), to meet us at IRC on 22nd July 1968 to discuss the rationalisation of their turbo-generator businesses. We made some progress and Weinstock said to us, 'I would like a word with you.' We said goodbye to Nelson and moved next door with Weinstock, who at once said, 'We are playing around with this. GEC is now ready to take over the whole of EE and with their assets and facilities on the chess board we can play a much bigger and more successful game.' Kearton and I knew how well Weinstock had remade AEI after GEC's successful take-over bid in September 1967 and we looked at each other and simultaneously said, 'OK.'

Then the fun began. Out of the blue came a £260 million bid for EE by the Plessey Company. Plessey was smaller, but was earning almost the same amount of profit and had less debt than EE. Nelson at once said 'English Electric doesn't want Plessey's help.'

Tony Benn, then Minister of Technology and IRC's new sponsor, said, 'This is one the market should not decide.' Intensive talks then began between Nelson and Weinstock; Plessey backed down after a tactful statement by Warburg, their merchant bankers. GEC did well by this deal, increasing its capital by 140%, but its sales by 373%. Toby Low, by then Lord Aldington and an ever-present good fairy in my life, stood down as Chairman of GEC in favour of Nelson, which greatly greased the merger wheels. Nelson asked me to be present at the EE board meeting which approved the merger. Lord Poole, Chairman of Lazards, EE's merchant bankers, strongly recommended it, and at the vote only one hand was raised against it. There was a last-minute kerfuffle when Anthony Crosland, President of the Board of Trade, thought he should refer the merger to the Monopolies Commission. We at IRC made a strong pitch for no referral.

The civil servants took the opposite view and it was a great relief when Crosland ended the matter: 'I settle for the IRC.'

The GEC/EE merger, on top of the take-over of AEI the year before, proved a great success. For many years GEC was Britain's largest industrial company and has been able to stand up to international competition from the world's biggest companies. Looking back over the 23 years since those exciting events I feel that this was the best work done by IRC. Recently I have felt that GEC was getting a bit constipated and I noted that Weinstock in a *Financial Times* interview said, 'The object of our policy is to increase earnings. It is perfectly simple.' The *FT* published my comment that 'This is not the object of our Japanese competitors. Their object is to increase market share, supported by their banks and at times by MITI (a Japanese Government department with some resemblance to IRC).' This view was supported by Professor Jonathan Brown. I met Weinstock shortly afterwards and he held my hand for ages, not in sorrow or anger, but in need, I felt, of comfort in facing the new dilemma with which the Japanese have confronted the whole of industry in the West, including America.

Some idea of the pressure of those days appears in my diary for Thursday 5th September 1968:

9.00 To Mr Ryland, GPO
10.15 Sir Leslie Rowan - Vickers
11.00 Mr Baring - Bishopsgate
11.45 Fortune Magazine
12.00 Lord Nelson. EE.
1.00 Mr John Clarke - Plessey
2.30 Lord Nelson
3.10 Sir Harold Mullens
4.00 President of Board of Trade
4.45 Mr Lord - Chairman Whessoe
5.30 Sir Douglas Allen - Treasury
6.30 Lord McFadzean

7.30 Lord Nelson and Lord Poole

This schedule was busy enough, but it does not happen to include the study of the ball bearing industry which IRC started in the summer of 1968. Almost everything that turns around in industry does so on a ball bearing, a series of steel balls in a cage through which a bar can turn without overheating or undue wear and tear. No car, aircraft machine tool, tank or ship could move without ball bearings. I recalled how my uncle Gerry Villiers was sent to buy ball bearings from Sweden during the war and how the Royal Navy smuggled them back to Britain, so important were they.

IRC had been alerted to the likelihood that Skefco, the Swedish ball bearing giant (whose British subsidiary already supplied 27% of the British market), would shortly seek to dominate our market by bidding for control of Ransome and Marles, one of three British ball bearing makers, the others being Hoffman Manufacturing and Pollard Bearings. These three together supplied 35% of the British market.

As IRC said at the time, 'For industrial reasons and from the point of view of the national interest this would be wrong, a view which the Government shares. IRC therefore invited the three British owned companies to enter discussions with a view to merging their interests, but leaving room for participation by foreign based companies.' To get a firm base for this difficult operation IRC made a bid for Brown Bayley, a Sheffield based special steel maker, which owned 60% of Hoffman. The board of Brown Bayley supported the IRC bid, which was successful.

It was during this negotiation that I had the unenviable task of ringing the Chairman of Skefco, Jacob Wallenberg, and telling him of our intention to merge the three British companies, leaving room for Skefco participation if desired. I told him that we had enough cash for this and that the British Government supported the plan. I knew Wallenberg's brother Markus, who was an Institut Bancaire member, but that was

121

no help. Jacob was almost speechless with fury and said he would make a bid regardless. I said we might then outbid him, but hoped he would take a participation in the resultant group. He yelled 'NO' down the phone and rang off.

Skefco continued to feel very flouted and Wallenberg, flanked by his advisers, Lord Goodman (later an IRC director) and a very senior Hambros partner, strode over to the Ministry of Technology, to confront the formidable Sir Otto Clarke (then Permanent Secretary), David Ewart and myself. After some pleasantries, which included Lord Goodman calling me a monster, Otto repeated my offer of participation in the British Ball Bearing Company we were creating. Wallenberg said 'Where I invest, I control.' Otto rose and said, 'Then you won't be investing - good afternoon.' Lord Goodman said, 'Negotiating with Villiers is like playing Mah Jong with a mule.'

Having secured 60% of Hoffman through Brown Bayley, of which I became chairman for a while, we lent Brown Bayley the money to buy out the other 40% of Hoffman. The next step was for Ransome to acquire Pollard, which at that time was chaired and largely owned by John King (later Lord King and Chairman of British Airways and of Babcock and Wilcox). I negotiated the terms, which was done on a friendly basis at lunch in Brook's Club. IRC underwrote for cash a convertible loan stock offered by Ransome. Sir Edward Senior became the chairman of the new group named RHP. It sounds simple and easy, but it did in fact require great originality and care exercised by our IRC executive colleague, David Ewart, who later became RHP's chairman.

The reorganisation made possible by this new grouping was very far reaching. The number of different bearings made was reduced drastically from 15,000; stocks of finished but unsold bearings were enormously reduced; and the *Financial Times* reported on 27th May 1970 that 'the UK's position in bearings is one which has seldom seemed healthier.' Sales, which used to be mainly to Commonwealth countries, were expanded into the American and European markets. A heavy investment programme got under way.

A serious set-back came with the deep recession of 1981/2 and factories were closed. RHP was weakened by this storm and in 1990 the shareholders accepted an offer from a Japanese ball bearing maker which had set up a factory in the North East of England. As Lord King then wrote to me, 'These Japanese are very thorough little people.' But it was a sad day for many of us.

It was not till some months later that I had time to digest all that IRC activity and write in the annual report what I thought IRC had become: 'IRC is not a banker, though on occasions the ability to deploy funds is crucial. It is not a holding company, though the capacity to own shares for a limited period is essential. IRC's main job is to improve the international performance of our manufacturing industries by promoting structural reorganisation. It would be difficult for merchant bankers or other private sector agencies to do this, owing to the limitations imposed by their relationship with their individual clients. IRC's client is the national interest, where this is identifiable. IRC's priorities for action are the scope for improved productivity and the scope for improving the balance of payments... Where fragmentation is impeding performance the IRC approach is to support those managements of proven success in taking practical steps to concentrate effort and resources. The critical element in IRC work is the capacity of industrial management to do the job and it is above all on this that the IRC board must be satisfied before lending its support to industrial reorganisation...

It soon became apparent to the IRC board that to discharge its statutory job effectively it would have to intervene directly on occasions, or to act as an accelerator, or in a steering capacity, or to use the market mechanism directly... the use of public funds for such purposes is a novelty in Britain and is queried, not only in the sense that 'the bottomless purse' is unfair, but also because of the need to reduce public expenditure. The real test of IRC's judgement is the capacity of the companies which it assists to prosper in world markets and satisfy their public shareholders... The IRC is a prod and not a prop and will stand convicted if these investments do not through time come good. In all cases its independence was scrupulously respected by Government, who have neither insisted on, nor prevented, any course of action.'

After the publication of this statement in April 1969 the IRC continued very actively till it was wound up by the incoming Tory government. Altogether we did in three years some 70 deals of which a half can be said to have stood the test of time. We were, of course, dealing all the time with industrial problems rather than with the successes. We had disbursed £107m out of the £150m available to us. IRC had seen that inadequate investment by British industry was one of the main reasons for British failures and, at the end of 1968, Kearton (before he returned full time to Courtaulds) and I went to see the Prime Minister, Harold Wilson, and Roy Jenkins (then Chancellor of the Exchequer), to ask about the possibilities of increasing the IRC's borrowing powers. We sat opposite the Prime Minister across the table in the Cabinet room, but he did not seem to be listening and just sucked away at his pipe. Roy Jenkins was very alert and enquiring but he shook his head and we got the message.

The economy was improving after the devaluation and the balance of payments was actually in credit, but the Government was holding down expenditure as tightly as possible and industrial investment did not have a high priority - sadly and wrongly. IRC's other resource, people, was also sparingly used. We never employed more than 30 people, of whom at any one time only a dozen were executive. The total running costs were £300,000 a year, so it was a cost-effective operation.

The death of IRC at Tory hands had been forecast and well leaked. By 12th October 1970 John Davies, former Director General of the CBI and the new Tory Minister of Technology, had said, 'No place for the IRC in the reorganisation of Government,' but the official notice did not come till the budget statement on 27th October. Press comment was varied:

'IRC to be killed in costs purge;' 'IRC dies without dishonour;' 'Intervention to go;' 'Tories to axe IRC and six little Neddies;' 'Lamented death for IRC'; 'Please don't kill the IRC;' 'IRC leaves a gap to be filled;' 'The IRC, sheer wanton murder;' 'Davies was wrong on IRC'; 'Institutions will need an IRC of their own.'

Thirteen years later José and I were staying with Walter Annenberg (formerly American Ambassador in London) near Denver, Colorado, and Ted Heath was a fellow guest. Ted drew me aside and said, 'Charles, about the IRC. I made a mistake.'

'God in heaven, and it's taken you all this time to tell me that.' Ted shrugged his shoulders and smiled. We have been friends since then.

Perhaps the IRC would have 'grown whiskers' and started looking round for things to do if we had continued. Perhaps we thought 'one crowded hour of glorious life is worth an age without a name.' Certainly we became much more careful in choosing strong managements to which to give support. We were definitely moving away from mergers towards being the Government's non-political merchant bank, using public funds quickly and effectively in a way which avoided the controversy aroused by Kent/Cambridge. We had come to see that continuing industrial investment, not interrupted by 'stop-go,' was the essential element in Britain's industrial recovery, combined with greatly improved industrial management.

A verdict by Professor Grigor McLelland, an IRC board member, is very well informed. He picked up my phrase 'IRC is a prod not a prop' and commented on IRC's role: 'active, initiatory, discretionary or discriminatory, non-bureaucratic, commercially orientated, change-promoting almost free wheeling wheeler-dealing and buccaneering. The best of British merchant venturing was for once harnessed to the public interest above all else... It will be surprising if, in one form or another, the erstwhile experimental prod does not return.'

The official history by Professor Hague and Geoffrey Wilkinson comments, 'It is not possible to be so enthusiastic about the initial concept that the promotion of mergers was a general solution to the UK's industrial problems... The IRC tried to help to improve management standards in British industry, to remove some of the obstacles to good management and to increase understanding between government, the City and industry.'

Later still, in May 1983, Christopher Lorenz, commenting in the *Financial Times* on the official history of IRC, remarked, 'The lack of consensus about industrial policy among the political parties, industry and the Civil Service makes it virtually impossible to formulate, let alone act, upon the long-term vision of the future, which characterises the Japanese approach to these matters. There is a lack of continuity, of follow-through, in the British system, which reduces the value of even the most sensible ad hoc interventions.'

My own summary of an important period of my life is that those of us who worked in IRC did see a 'vision of the future,' which grew as we worked and thought and talked, not only to each other but in public as well. We could imagine a regenerated British industry, competing world wide. We could see the huge gap between the best managers and the rest. We could feel the love of 'as is,' preventing the break-out to 'as could be.' We realised that the problem is a management and investment problem, not a Trade Union or workforce or macro economic problem, although all these do have an effect. We saw the downhill slope staring Britain in the face, together with the probability that Britain would go on rolling down it, unless we and others did something about it.

I incurred large debts to people: to Kearton and to Sir Joseph Lockwood, who succeeded him as Chairman of the

IRC - they stretched my mind till I nearly screamed for mercy; to Sir Les Cannon, General Secretary of the Electrical Trades Union, who introduced me to trade union leaders, at that time Vic Feather, Len Murray, Jack Jones and Hugh Scanlon, whose motivation I got to understand; to Sir Michael Clapham, Sir Maurice Bridgeman and Lord Stokes who inducted me into big industrial business; to Frank Schon (later Lord Schon) who taught me about the Labour party; to Lord Goodman from whom I learned the secrets of negotiation; to Geoffrey Robinson an IRC executive, successful industrialist and Labour Member of Parliament, with whom I first went to Japan to visit MITI (Ministry of International Trade and Industry) and began my twenty-year study of the culture and practice of Japanese industry - so threatening and yet so much admired. We also went to Paris where the French government copied IRC exactly.

I think of the dozen or so IRC executives. I cannot choose between them in their energy, inventiveness and loyalty. Thank goodness they all found other outlets for their talents when IRC was wound up. Today they are pacemakers in industry and finance and I have watched their careers with delight. They have not 'run out of puff' and they do continue with the very necessary industrial revolution which the IRC began. We have all continued as prods, not props.

CHAPTER 8

IRELAND AND EUROPE 1970-1976

The Tory victory in the General Election of 1970 was a considerable surprise and nearly all the pollsters had 'egg on their faces.' Edward Heath promised 'strong and honest government' and that was what the people wanted. Harold Wilson's government, with Roy Jenkins as Chancellor of the Exchequer, had got the balance of payments back into surplus but this was at the expense of growth and investment. What upset the electorate was constant change within the Cabinet and the obvious split over Wilson's and Barbara Castle's proposals to limit Trade Union power, as set out in 'In Place of Strife,' which was a moderate social-democratic proposal. This infuriated the left wing members of the Cabinet, who voted against it. Wilson had to be content with the TUC's promise of good behaviour by the unions, but wages and prices went on rising unchecked; as Wilson said, 'Strikes did not diminish in number, scale or duration.' The Tories, following their Selsdon Park conference, promised more law and order, less government spending, no incomes policy and a 'new style of Government.' This made an instant appeal. What particularly interested me was that Heath's description of Labour as 'men of straw,' trampled upon by greedy, strike-prone unions, proved more effective than Wilson's description of the Tories as 'yesterday's men.' The Tories obtained a working majority in Parliament, pledged to the slogan, 'There has been too much Government; there will be less.'

My contract with IRC expired at the end of 1970, but I agreed to continue as a non-executive director for another year, to help in what would now be called the 'unbundling.' Fortunately for me, I got offered a number of jobs, including 'overseas marketing director' of Courtaulds, by Kearton, which I would have enjoyed, but it meant being away from my family, which I had neglected while at the IRC; but Kearton offered me a non-executive seat on the main board of Courtaulds, which I gladly accepted. The other offers were mainly from the City and I had a visit from James Guinness, the Chairman of Guinness Mahon (Holdings), which controlled the small merchant bank and accepting house of Guinness Mahon (GM) in the City, and Guinness and Mahon in Dublin. James would not take 'no' for an answer and he offered me generous terms. I became Chairman of the bank on 1st March 1971 but I promised myself a return to the public/private interface if an opportunity arose.

The original Mr Guinness and Mr Mahon were Irish agents collecting rents and looking after the estates of absentee English landlords. They had the use of the money for a while and started a local banking business. Their cousins set up a brewery on the banks of the River Liffey, which runs through Dublin. Between them they had family businesses of great success and value. Mr Sam Guinness, who moved the bank from Dublin to London, became Senior Partner on his father's death in 1936. The partnership was dissolved in 1964 when the bank became a limited company and his nephew James succeeded him as Chairman of the Holding Company. Sir George Mahon, my contemporary at Eton, stayed in Ireland, devoting himself to Christian charitable work. The City rhymesters were soon at it again:

The Kleinworts came from Cuba,
The Morgans from New York,
The Guinnesses came from County Down,
And not from County Cork.

129

As may be imagined, the Guinness family dominated this small bank. 'Mr James' in London and 'Mr John' in Dublin were looked up to as sources of favour and promotion. They were both excellent men but anxious above all to preserve their bank and their good name, which they wanted to do by organic growth rather than by merger or acquisition. Fair enough! But I had seen what was happening to Anthony Gibbs and Sons as a result of just that attitude. GM was really a family money box which took in money from the family and from the money market and lent it out again at a favourable rate on short term. At this they were very good. They were also good at investment trusts; one was, as James put it to me, 'top of the pops.' The long term loans were really 'lock ups,' many to Norwegian ship owner, Leif Hoegh, a friend of Mr. Sam, whose wife was Norwegian. They had virtually no corporate finance business, but they had an assortment of shareholdings in small companies which may have been hopeful situations at one time but looked sick by the time I got there. GM was considerably overstaffed, as family businesses often are, and their main asset was a brand new, but rather inconvenient, freehold office building in Gracechurch Street, not far from the Bank of England, which they occupied in rather gloomy state.

I had seen all this before accepting James' offer and had invited three IRC colleagues to join me in trying to revive GM's fortunes. David Ewart was a success and very nearly got the corporate finance business going. Mike Knight soon sorted out the small company shareholdings and then made his way back to George Kent. Stefan Steiner got mixed up in some unfortunate business in Nigeria and sought other employment. I came to rely at GM heavily on Harry Everitt in everything to do with the money market, on Hugh Sassoon for managing the investment trusts, on Derek Matthews for a sound view of our shipping interests and on Joan Roberts for keeping and presenting the accounts clearly and reliably. Alan Rushton computerised the whole business. This was a professional team and I thought we would be able to do a 'turn around' - that most difficult operation - from a family money-box to a credible, publicly-accepted merchant bank.

We had a chance and we nearly did it - but not quite. On 18th June 1971 my good friend Michael Webster, recently appointed Chairman of the famous brewing company, Watney Mann, asked me round for a talk about the future. I took with me David Ewart and began a negotiation which lasted for the next twelve months. Michael Webster had got himself a new Chief Executive, George Duncan, not previously in the brewing business, and between them they wanted to expand Watney's traditional brewery into the wines and spirits trade. They started well and got control of International Distillers and Vintners, but their plans were interrupted by Maxwell Joseph, whose Grand Metropolitan Hotels had recently acquired Trumans brewery in East London. Joseph was keen to move out of property development, where he had started, and become Britain's biggest brewer - into the 'beerage' as it was called. Grand Met made a bid for Watneys.

We assembled a strong defence team with Cazenoves as our stockbrokers and Philip Shelbourne, of the Drayton Corporation as our co-defendant. Grand Met was advised by Warburg. We slugged it out for four months in the Stock Exchange, with the financial institutions and in the press. At the close of the final offer by Grand Met they claimed to have 50.06% of Watneys shares and we had to accept defeat. It was the largest hostile take-over bid ever to succeed in Britain up to that time. The small shareholders stayed loyal to Watneys, but the financial institutions and the Hennessy brandy family, who were substantial shareholders, were fascinated by the brilliance of Maxwell Joseph and came to the conclusion that they would do better with him than with the more traditional Watney management. It was a sad blow for Michael Webster, who was 'stunned by disappointment,' and for David Ewart and me. One gets no marks for losing, however hard one may have fought.

131

While the struggle for Watneys was going on I found myself getting involved in the affairs of Northern Ireland, where matters had gone from bad to worse. In August 1969 Wilson sent in troops and from then on there was in fact civil war in the Province: the worst 'troubles' since 1920. Heath had promised no change in Ulster without the support of the Stormont Parliament, but in 1971 Faulkner became Prime Minister of Ulster and began talks, not only with Heath, but also with the Irish Prime Minister. This infuriated the Protestants in Northern Ireland. Heath imposed 'direct rule' in 1972 and appointed Willie Whitelaw to be, in effect, Governor of Northern Ireland.

In the spring of 1971 I was approached by Civil Servants in the Treasury and Home Office (at that time responsible for Northern Ireland) to join Sir Alec Cairncross in making a review of economic development in Ulster. Alec had been Economic Adviser to the British Government till 1964, when he became Master of St Peters College, Oxford. We recruited Darwin Templeton, a chartered accountant in Belfast, to help us. We reported to Willie Whitelaw in December 1971 that 'the tragedy of the present situation is that before the civil unrest, measures taken to improve the economy were beginning to operate quite strongly... it will not be easy now to get back to the previous rate of expansion, much less to improve on it. The overriding problem now is to preserve the industrial and commercial fabric and to provide reassurance that there will be adequate support for this purpose.' We proposed:
1. That a Northern Ireland Finance Corporation should be set up to offer financial assistance to undertakings threatened with closure, provided there were reasonable prospects of solvency, long term.
2. NIFC should have a life of three years - renewable.
3. £50m should be earmarked for its use.

This was announced in Northern Ireland and in the House of Commons on 15th December 1971. On 4th January, after one or two rather waffly meetings with Reggie Maudling, then

Home Secretary, he wrote me a letter asking me to be Chairman of the new NIFC, which I agreed to take on for two years only. On 13th February Heath invited my wife and me to lunch at Chequers, which we greatly enjoyed, even watching Ted conducting a gramophone record of an orchestra playing music conducted by himself. I expected he would refer to Northern Ireland, but no, he said there was a job he wanted me to do in Europe. Did the right hand of the conductor know what the left hand was up to?

It was a tough job and I did not enjoy it much, although it was more fun when Whitelaw became Supremo, and I reported to him. He asked if £50m was enough money, because the start is the time to get more, before the difficulties appeared! I really could not say how much more might be needed, but it looked like a bottomless pit. I had to get some good people to do the work on the ground. I was lucky to find John Watt, a man of huge energy, enthusiasm and integrity. He came over with two colleagues from PE Consultants (who have never forgiven me for hijacking them) and they performed magnificently all the time I was there. I could only get to Belfast on one day a week but it worked out quite well. With the help of Darwin Templeton we put together a useful board of directors, all of whom 'knew where the bodies were buried;' Ulster was, and remains, a graveyard.

By August 1972 we were in business in a small office in the centre of Belfast which, sadly but unsurprisingly, was twice burned out by IRA action, either on purpose or by mistake. In the first period we investigated 119 companies, of which we directly helped 13; 26 were helped by other, more appropriate, means and 49 were refused.

This little tally tells its own story. Too many companies in Northern Ireland simply did not have the management, the product, or the prospects to justify support. Our £50m looked as if it would last a long time!

As can be imagined, we used IRC criteria and techniques, which proved easily transferable. We had quite simply to assist

133

the economy of Northern Ireland by preserving the fabric of business and improving the industrial structure, which consisted of a few big British companies such as GEC and Courtaulds and a mass of small companies, for which there was not enough management or investment funds but this was no good without the management. Most of the best managers had gone to England for bigger jobs and fatter salaries. We were mainly concerned with survival, then with growth and only occasionally with new industry.

I served out my stint and came to understand the root of the Ulster problem: 'the Ascendancy.' The 'implantations' of Southern Scots into Ireland during the 17th and 18th centuries by the Stewart kings, Cromwell and 'King Billy' were intended to bring order and wealth to the impoverished Irish. The implanted Scots were given land, jobs and the vote, to which they have clung with intense ferocity. It so happens that most of them were Protestants, implanted among the Irish Catholics, but that has never been the vital issue: it has been the cover story. The heart of the problem is the whole idea and practice of the Ascendancy, which is less and less relevant as the vote and other divisive issues are generalised. Perhaps the essence came out when a number of company chairmen were giving me a farewell dinner in Belfast at the same time as Whitelaw was running his optimistic 'Sunningdale Conference,' which looked like reaching a wide settlement of political problems. At the dinner I asked,

'Are you optimistic or pessimistic?'

The growled reply was, 'We're very, very pessimistic.'

'But', I asked, 'don't you think Willie is going to get a settlement?'

'That's why we're so pessimistic,' they replied.

Struggle is a way of life in Ulster. Small boys are brought up as little terrorists. Death is never far away. One side, Protestant Ascendancy, wants to drive the 'Candlesticks' back into their bog. The Catholics want to drive the Protestants into the sea to achieve the great dream of a united

Ireland. The IRA want an anarchist, nihilist state, motivated by an insatiable hatred of Britain.

My friend, Sir Kenneth Cork, of Cork Gully (the liquidation experts), and later Lord Mayor of London, took over from me, and did a fine job of work. He is a hero. But whether he or I did much good is open to doubt. The Northern Ireland Economic Research Centre reported in 1990, 'Unemployment in Northern Ireland at 14% is two and a half times the rest of the UK. It is unresponsive to government policies such as years of wooing inward investment, subsidising private industry on a massive scale and maintaining a high level of public expenditure. All this has had only a minimal effect. There is an over-supply of labour in an area with the highest birth rate in Europe. As in all else, management is the key element and if that is missing, there is little result!'

I had been invited in May 1971 to give the Lubbock Memorial Lecture in Oxford and I reminded the audience of Ted Heath's saying in 1965, 'We need fresh policies to speed up the reform of management at all levels.' My recipe was, 'Find tomorrow's management - men and women: they exist. Train them formally and informally, and it is no tragedy if they move around. Test them early and, if they can stand it, promote them fast. Look at their capacity for leadership and above all at their vigour. To reinforce this, the Companies Act should define the duties of non-executive directors, who should report annually to shareholders whether they are satisfied with the performance of their company. A two-tier board structure should follow. In addition there should be an ombudsman to hear complaints of shareholders, which would speed the process of renewal. This has begun but it has a long way to go and the longer we leave it, the poorer we shall all become.'

I have been developing these themes ever since.

Meanwhile, the other ingredients of my Irish Stew had not been neglected. Following the lost battle of Watneys, I had come to the conclusion that Guinness Mahon in London would be able to fend off predators and that we would do better to seek out a compatible partner than to sit still waiting to be gobbled up. I therefore put out a number of feelers, with the knowledge of the Bank of England, to see where I could detect a warm response. I did in fact meet a series of cold shoulders for a variety of reasons, but mainly because other similar businesses in the City could not see that we had a really viable business worth buying for anything other than our name, our cash and our new building. Nevertheless, Lord Goodman had introduced me to Harry Kissin (later Lord Kissin) who was Chairman and chief shareholder in Lewis and Peat, a commodity merchant, food distributor and insurance broker, which had done very well and wanted to increase the range of financial services which it offered.

Harry Kissin was born in Danzig in 1912. His father was a grain merchant there, an impressive man with a white spade-shaped beard and a twinkling eye. Harry was largely educated in Switzerland and studied law and several languages. He came to London in the thirties and became Managing Director of Paul Winn and Co. In the fifties he moved to Lewis and Peat and was its Chairman in 1958. He bought control of Fenchurch Insurance and Thomas Linnell and a shareholding in Esperanza Trade and Transport. He became a great expert in Britain's commodity markets and exchanges, which are renowned for reliability, validity of contracts, international coverage and sophistication. We soon got on well together.

Now it so happened that in October 1972 Harry and I were both invited to speak at a seminar in Copenhagen on the City's financial services. Harry was very nervous and I think he ducked out of his speech, but we had plenty of time to talk about our companies and whether they would make a successful merger. I have before me the notes I made day by day from then till the merger was announced on 8th December 1972, as the Guinness Peat Group. The honeymoon was short but intensive.

The Bank of England, through its Deputy Governor, was very helpful - 'come and talk to me at any time.' The insurance companies had to be briefed as large shareholders. The Commercial Union was most encouraging and wanted to take a large stake in Guinness Peat, but found too many merchant bankers already on its board of directors. Weinstock was tremendously congratulatory and wanted to take over the whole shebang. Baron Lambert at the Banque Lambert in Brussels got very excited at the possibility of getting established in London through a large shareholding in our company. We would have liked that, but at the last moment his managing director got cold feet and said the Belgian banking commission would make it impossible. Loel Guinness, who was a big shareholder but not a director of Guinness Mahon, was pleased to see movement when James and I went to see him. Kissin had been flirting with the big commodity merchants Sime Darby and they had to be put off. Jacob Rothschild (now Lord Rothschild) intervened and asked Kissin for figures so that they could go together to the Bank of England, but that made Kissin angry and he refused. We asked Warburg to vet the terms of the merger, but Kissin said to me, 'Don't strip in front of Siggy.'

The prospectus was dated 19th December 1972. It was a long, detailed document prepared by Warburg with David Ewart for Guinness, and Peter Dix for Lewis and Peat, but the essence was simple, 'A new group will emerge, combining the traditional merchant banking function of the City of London with activities in insurance broking, commodity, money broking, food distribution, shipping and property development... The merger should accelerate the rate of expansion of both parties to the merger, from which shareholders will benefit.'

The press comment was considerable, but more factual and interested than congratulatory. The point most financial scribes made was that this was the first bank-to-non-bank merger which the Bank of England had approved. The *Daily*

Express said: 'Bid ends closed shop.' The *Investors Chronicle* said 'Putting merchanting into merchant banking.' *The Observer* said, 'The demarcation lines that once divided the City into neat watertight compartments are collapsing and the cartels and restrictive practices which controlled competition are being dismantled. This has been encouraged by the Bank of England.' *The Times* said of me on 2nd February, 'The infectious zeal of this reformer has been rubbing off in all sorts of different directions. A fairly small merchant bank, not distinguished for its ability to innovate in the past, has been transformed into a financial organisation, capitalised at over £50m in the stock market, whose tentacles now stretch from corporate finance to trading in dried onions and dehydrated potatoes. The climax of Villiers' breathtaking reform programme came when Guinness Mahon merged with Lewis and Peat, to form what by any standard is a new form of financial creature in the City. He is wasting no time tidying up the edges. In a few crisp words five directors have resigned and four have been appointed to concentrate skills where effectiveness can be delivered.'

But how to deliver? That became the problem. I had thought that, as in the Helbert Wagg/Schroder merger, the two businesses would dovetail easily and introduce new business to each other but, as we were to find out, there were crucial differences.

First the structure: Harry Kissin and James Guinness were joint Chairmen and I was nominated Chief Executive. I thought I could do that, but I found unexpected snags. Lewis and Peat's major business was in commodity dealing, where they were market makers, taking positions where necessary, very much under control of Harry, who was immensely experienced in this. The Guinness Mahon people, including myself, were market users, going to the markets and using the jobbers and dealers in other firms to quote a price; we were not trained or accustomed to make a price. The same considerations applied to other Lewis and Peat businesses, except

Fenchurch Insurance, which had to go to Lloyds underwriters to get a price.

Secondly, the Schroders merger was, in fact, greatly facilitated by Lionel Fraser's resignation which left Gordon Richardson as the undisputed boss, which everyone accepted. The Guinness Peat merger was confused by the fact that we were twin-headed. The Lewis & Peat companies had been bought, put together and directly managed by Harry Kissin. While Harry was chairman they found it in every way desirable to continue to report to him, not only to get his expert guidance, but also to avoid his wrath if things went wrong. Harry would not allow his dealers or market makers to have desks with drawers; he said dealers will not put their bad contracts in their pockets, but they look for a drawer. If there was no drawer they avoid bad contracts!

Harry lived on the telephone all day long and you could get him at night, too. He was brilliant at managing his companies in this way and he loved it. I used to sit in his room, next to mine in a new building we moved into, waiting for him to finish a telephone conversation; once I walked out and he cried out 'Where are you going, Charles?'

'I'm going next door to ring you up, Harry!'

All this made the job of Group Chief Executive impossible, and I asked to be relieved of it, at a management dinner, so that all the managers would know. Harry insisted that I should become executive deputy chairman and chairman of the bank. Thus I stayed till I went to British Steel five years later. Guinness Peat worked quite well after a fashion, but it never took off as Schroders had done. Even if Harry or I had fallen down dead on Day One I doubt if the survivor could have got the whole act together. The businesses were too disparate. Broking businesses like Fenchurch and, later, Ryans Aircraft Leasing, which have both been very successful, were perfectly compatible with Guinness Mahon. But the commodity and food businesses were of a different order, managed by a quite different type of person, excellent in their own field, but incompatible with the traditional private bankers in Guinness Mahon. I suppose this should have been foreseen, but it wasn't. Things might have been easier if Harry had been chairman of Guinness Mahon as well, but he wouldn't do it. Harry was always a tremendous entrepreneur, which would have been good for the bank, but he would have been very impatient with the 'bankerly' approach. The directors and the staff on both sides made a tremendous effort to put the businesses together, but they just didn't fit. Harry loved his 'telephone' empire, and became executive Chairman of the group.

All this began in the 'Barber boom' years, which turned sour in 1973 and 1974. Our group could not avoid the consequences and I was worried about some of our property investments which began to look sick. Trading in rubber was an important Lewis and Peat activity, but things got so difficult in the Far East that we almost ceased trading there. Nevertheless, the Guinness Peat group profit rose from £1.2 million in 1972 to £1.8 million in 1973 and £3.3 million in 1976, when I left to go to British Steel.

I was succeeded by a sound professional banker and Harry said he was going to semi-retire, which actually meant that he telephoned more from his home than from the office. The Bank of England got anxious about the management of the group and insisted that Alastair Morton, who had been Managing Director of British National Oil Company after leaving IRC, should be installed as Chief Executive of the Guinness Peat group. Alastair negotiated with Harry to buy back most of the former Lewis and Peat companies from the group, with a view to their being managed by his son Robbie.

Three years later, after various set-backs to the bank, Alastair also became chairman of Guinness Mahon. In 1987 he was plagued by an incomprehensible bid for the group by Equity Corp, from New Zealand. In the end the bid succeeded, but Equity Corp went into liquidation. Guinness Mahon fell into the hands of Samuel Montague, another merchant bank, representing Equity Corp's creditors. In 1989, the Bank of Yokohama bought a majority of the shares. Mr. Okura, the President of that Bank, said that Guinness Mahon 'should continue as an independently-managed London investment bank.' Geoffrey Bell, a Schroder man who succeeded Alastair Morton, remained chairman of Guinness Mahon and Alastair is British Chairman and Group Chief Executive of the Channel Tunnel, where he has had far greater problems to deal with.

I continued to leave my few savings in the care of Guinness Mahon, now a city boutique, specialising in things it does well and, as I said at the time of the ill-starred merger, 'concentrating skills where effectiveness can be delivered.' I am glad to think that, as Lord King said, 'The Japanese are very thorough little people.' Good luck to them!

I have called this chapter 'Ireland and Europe' because, at the time I was struggling with the limited problems of the Guinness Peat group, there occurred an enormous political event, initiated by Ted Heath as Prime Minister. In January 1972 Britain and Eire and Denmark signed the European Common Market Treaty, which came into force a year later. Everyone sat up and took notice and with my Institut Bancaire connections I took a special interest and played a small part.

In December 1971 the *Financial Times* organised a conference about the 'the City and Europe.' This was introduced by Geoffrey Rippon who was the Government's chief negotiator of the Treaty. The other speakers included the Governor of the Bank of England, Sir Leslie O'Brien (later Lord O'Brien), the Chairman of the Stock Exchange, Sir Martin Wilkinson, and a few others, including me. Rippon stressed the need in Europe for liberal and free trade policies and for assurances that Britain's interest in these issues would be recognised.

The Governor was very far-seeing and recognised that Britain had embarked on a journey which would, in the end,

141

lead all Europe to a single currency. We could not know how long it would take; that would depend on how long harmonisation of domestic issues and characteristics might take. The £ sterling could be managed so as to enable Britain to take a full part in the progress towards economic and monetary union. Sterling, the Governor thought, 'will become less distinctive.' None of this need, he thought, have adverse effects on the City.

The rest of us made much less significant contributions. The London Stock Exchange would insist on maintaining its accounting and disclosure standards for listing foreign companies. The clearing banks would not spread their branch networks into Europe which is 'already fully banked.' I felt that the merchant banks were being seriously handicapped by the 'impossibly high' requirements for the use of our own cash or paper for direct investment in Europe, which is badly needed for cross-frontier mergers and development. I finished by saying, 'I cannot pretend that the prospects of the City in Europe are rosy.'

My remarks drew a lengthy 'tick off' from the Prime Minister who wrote to me that 'we have agreed to comply in due course with the Community's rules for the free movement of capital... The Chancellor keeps exchange control policy under review, taking good account of practical arguments such as yours.' Compliance took a lot longer than we had anticipated.

My remarks at this conference had been triggered by the difficulties Guinness Mahon were having in completing the purchase of half the capital of Finacor SA, a French money broking business in Paris, but also in Rome, Munich, Brussels, Amsterdam and Switzerland. They were very friendly with Guinness Mahon and one day their partner, Teddy Naggar, asked if we would like to take a participation in the capital of Finacor. We liked this idea and eventually we did get Bank of England consent to buy the shares we were offered. I joined the Finacor board, on which I served till I went to British Steel, and I learned a lot about French business culture and practice.

Finacor was a very dynamic progressive business, largely owned by Pierre Schwed but driven along by Jacques Sides, an outstanding businessman. The other directors were excellent technicians, but none had the flair of Sides. To our horror, in 1973, quite soon after we bought in to Finacor, Sides, while playing tennis, had a brain haemorrhage, from which he never recovered, and led the life of a total invalid until mercifully he died. Finacor supported his family as best they could. This was a fearful blow and although Finacor always made a profit, and we were glad to have the European connection, the company was never able to pay a dividend and when Alastair Morton became Chairman of Guinness Mahon, the participation in Finacor was sold back to the French.

As I was finishing up my job in the IRC in late 1970, I was approached by the Federal Trust to chair a brilliant team of businessmen, academics and bankers (both central and commercial) to try and agree positive recommendations on the monetary integration of Europe. I agreed to do this, but I soon found that my existing workload, together with my ignorance of foreign exchange, made it in every way better for the team to be managed by Professor John Williamson of the University of Warwick and Doctor Giovanni Magnifico of the Central Bank of Italy, the Banca d'Italia, both generally accepted as experts in this field. We reported in 1972; our report is highly technical and I find it easier to work from an article I wrote in October 1972 for a magazine *New Europe,* whose editor was Philip Zec, which tells the story for the general reader. In view of the current interest in this subject, I shall spend a little time in describing the result of two years work on this difficult matter.

What we proposed, in one sentence, was the creation of an alternative currency to the dollar by setting up a European bank which would launch and control the Europa, a new currency. You would not initially have a Europa in your pocket, but it would be used by central Banks and Commercial Banks for the same purposes as the Eurodollar, which is an American dollar held in any bank outside of the USA. At that time Eurodollars were used to denominate many international loans and credit deals.

We wanted to get away from the great and growing bag of dollars which was swinging round the world, seeking better security and higher rates of interest and a capital profit on revaluation of its temporary nest, like some great cuckoo. It was not long before £ sterling was knocked off its perch in just that way.

We wanted also to get away from the endless delay implied by those economists who claimed that a common currency in Europe would be the 'crowning act,' when 'harmonisation' was complete. The most substantial problems raised by these economists were based on the divergent trends of unit costs of production in the countries of Europe, leading to severe regional imbalances. Obviously, unit costs in the Rhineland of Germany were different from those of the six counties of Northern Ireland. What we proposed was an interim period during which existing national currencies could change their parity with the Europa. During this interim period the Europa would only be used between banks and would not reach your pocket.

Another economists' argument was that European businessmen might fear that the Europa would fail to become acceptable (as did the Belga, once the common currency of Benelux) and that business would return to the American dollar. This was a false fear, because the $ was then and is now the currency of a country running a vast deficit on its balance of payments. We strongly felt that the Europa would be in great demand as a reserve currency and as a trading currency.

There is a further argument, much heard in Britain today, that European integration is the wrong policy anyway, and that monetary union is the slippery slope leading to integration in an unstoppable way.

Then came the floating of £ sterling in 1972 and there was a pause in thinking about the Europa while the experts waited to see what happened to £ sterling. Well, we know now; sterling has been steadily devalued. In 1972 one pound bought eight deutschmarks; in 1990 one pound buys only three marks. All this to accommodate inefficient management and greedy trade unions.

We believed in 1972, and I still believe, that we should have gone ahead with the Federal Trust's proposals which were:

1. Preliminary stage. Founding of the European Reserve Bank as proposed by Professor Triffin. Launch of the Europa and its build-up as a market asset, used by international dealers:-

(a) By the issue of loans denominated in Europas by the Community organisations.

(b) By requiring EEC member states to denominate some part of their National Debt (probably Treasury Bills) in Europas.

(c) An obligation on commercial banks to hold some of their assets in Europas.

(d) Willingness of EEC governments to accept payments of taxes in Europas.

(e) The European Reserve Bank should make a market in Europa bills and act as lender of last resort.

(f) Issue by commercial banks of travellers cheques in Europas.

2. In the intermediate stage there would be intervention by the new Bank to defend the rate between the Europa, the US$ and the yen. National reserve banks would intervene as between their national currencies and the Europa, so as to accommodate the divergent cost trends without causing unbearable strain. Further 'harmonisation' of economic condi-

tions, as between the nation states of Europe, would be essential, but 'break down' could be avoided by changes in parity. The US$-Europa rate would have a very wide band to enable the whole European area more easily to absorb hot money without being overwhelmed.

3. The Final Stage would involve full monetary union with a common currency, but only when cost trends in Europe had ceased to be divergent. Only when the economics of Europe had been much more closely interlocked would national currencies give way to the Europa, which at last you would have in your pocket.

Since that date much has happened. We have had the 'snake in the tunnel' (which Britain joined in 1972 and left after six weeks) and now we have the European Monetary System (of which Britain has now become a member). We have had the issue of loans denominated in ECUs, a better name than Europas. But we have had no central European Reserve Bank, and its place has been taken by the Bundesbank of Germany, which has performed with great skill and responsibility.

Britain has been the laggard, fearing, no doubt, the slippery slope and the unstoppable move to monetary union. We have been not only the laggard, but also the sufferer, by mismanaging our economic affairs and allowing devaluation over and over again to bail us out of our chronic desires to pay ourselves more than we earn; a series of own goals!

I cannot resist the conclusion that the Federal Trust group (and Professor Triffin) was right twenty years ago, and that Europe has suffered, Britain especially, from political timidity. If war is too dangerous to leave to generals, currency is too dangerous to leave to the politicians.

One of the joys and delights of the City of London is the variety of jobs and opportunities which come out of it. The collection of enterprise and talent and skill which is to be found there is greater than in any other part of Britain and I was lucky to be caught up in it. Garrett Moore (later Earl of Drogheda KG, chairman of both the *Financial Times* and of the Royal Opera House) had been a friend of Lionel Fraser's and I had met him in Helbert Wagg days. He had, naturally and properly, been asked to take the chair of a group to put together Europalia '73, a biennial exhibition in Brussels of the artistic culture of a member country of the European community. Italy and Holland had put on wonderful shows of their culture in 1969 and 1971, and in 1973 it was to be the turn of Britain. For no very obvious reason Drogheda, as he had become, invited me to be his co-chairman.

The occasion, timed to coincide with Britain joining the Community, was under the patronage of the Queen and of the King and Queen of the Belgians. Ted Heath, as Prime Minister and a fine musician, had said in the House of Commons that his Government was interested in the success of the festival and had asked the British Council to devise a programme in co-operation with a Belgian committee, comprising leading personalities in the artistic world.

The programme was to run for the month of October 1973 and had to cover every aspect of British art, opera, ballet, theatre, cinema, fine arts and two major exhibitions, one from the Tate Gallery and another from the National Trust. A Grand Tattoo would be organised by the British and Belgian armies. An imposing executive committee was set up. The Commissioner was the late Count Michel d'Ursel, a delightful Belgian friend, who chose as his executive secretary our daughter Diana, then working in Brussels in the European Commission, a job she gave up to assist Michel. The so-called 'members' included the Ambassadors of Belgium in London and of Britain in Brussels, Drogheda and me, and representatives of the British Council and many Chefs de Cabinet covering both the French-speaking and Flemish interests. Money was, of course, the problem. The British and Belgian governments made substantial contributions, but Drogheda

147

and I were responsible for finding £100,000 and for persuading galleries, private collectors, orchestras and leaders of the performing arts to lend their properties or services.

This turned out to be an immense task. As I look at the programme I see that there were nearly 100 British sponsors and 70 Belgian and International sponsors, and each one had to be to approached personally and very carefully to ensure that his or her contribution in cash or kind would be forthcoming.

In the event, we had the twelve leading British orchestras and quartets, with ten soloists. Renaissance music, pop, jazz, folk and young people's music were all represented. The English Opera Group performed Benjamin Britten's 'Death in Venice' and Sadler's Wells were to put on 'Semele' and 'Iolanthe.' There were performances by the Royal Ballet, the National Theatre, the Young Vic and three contemporary British theatre groups, well supported by Belgian performances. There were three world premières in the cinema, plus a hundred post-war British films. There were twelve exhibitions of outstanding merit. Of these I do believe that the best shows were the art treasures lent by the Queen, a selection of paintings from the great houses of Britain, lent by the National Trust, forty years of British art entitled 'From Moore to Hockney,' sixty illuminated manuscripts from the Medieval period lent by the British Museum and the Bodleian Library at Oxford, and the treasures of the City of London.

There was much light-hearted stuff as well - 'The Sound of Laughter,' children's books, Pen and Pencil, British Posters and Comic Cartoons; many supported by excellent Belgian contributions. There was something for everybody and it was a huge success.

When it was over I had a letter from Ted Heath at 10 Downing Street, full of congratulations: 'The Festival has been more successful even than we had dared to hope... a large part of the credit is due to you and your Committee and I thank you for the work your daughter Diana did. I have heard from the Ambassador that she contributed as much as anyone to the collaboration which was achieved. Please give her my personal thanks.'

I replied on 14th November, having been 'deeply touched by your thoughtfulness in writing,' but I added a postscript: 'Hard pounding in Britain today and I hope you will pound longest.' On 14th January Toby Aldington gave a dinner for Ted, to which he invited Weinstock, Kenneth Keith (later Lord Keith) and myself. It was a gloomy occasion and as we left Keith said to me: 'Looks like an early election.' And so it was - on 28th February 1974 - and Ted just lost.

It had been a black winter, with the miners' strike, a three-day week, no lighting for display purposes, no TV after 10.30 pm, even over Christmas - and what was the issue? The voters were confused and rather angry at being asked 'Who governs Britain?' The election was a tactical error. Ted could not persuade the Liberals to join the Tories, so Harold Wilson took over with a minority of seats in the House of Commons. In October Wilson went to the country again and got a majority of three in Parliament.

Ted Heath's government did many good things. His great achievement was getting Britain into Europe and no-one can take that away from him. The Industrial Relations Act of 1971 was too comprehensive; you simply cannot take the British into a change of that magnitude at such high speed, and the Trade Unions were just waiting to get their own back. But it was the economy which sank him, like so many of his predecessors and, maybe, successors. He was disturbed by the sluggishness of growth and investment, and he was alarmed by the labour sit-ins and by the consequences of the bank-ruptcy of Rolls-Royce (which from my IRC seat I begged him not to do). So he and Tony Barber pumped up the economy and injected £2 billion into the March 1972 budget. The Industry Act provided £650 million in investment grants (four times more than the IRC had spent). The Barber boom got out of control and inflation increased without increased production. An incomes policy was introduced and there was a standstill budget in March 1972 and another in December. It was clear that the Government had failed to control inflation, to increase production, to reduce unemployment, or to maintain the inherited balance of payments surplus. The sharp increase in the price of Arab oil was the last straw and the Unions, under Jack Jones, Hugh Scanlon and Joe Gormley of the National Union of Mineworkers said 'Got 'im.' Heath played into their hands by calling a General Election. A sad chapter in the history of political economy.

The change of government in 1974 made some difference to life at Guinness Peat. Harry Kissin had, over the years, become a considerable friend of Harold Wilson, who respected and used Harry's knowledge of markets. As Prime Minister, Wilson occasionally lunched with us in the City and I was always impressed with his vitality and ingenuity. He was describing to us one day his problem of housing all the gifts he received in his job, which above a certain value he should not keep for himself. The remainder cluttered his home life and he roared with laughter when one of us innocently suggested, 'Prime Minister, could you not have a jumble sale?' Later he made Harry a life peer and he responded positively when Harry reminded him that I had had no recognition for my work at IRC, which had been very much a Harold Wilson creation. I continued to work with Harry at the problems of Guinness Mahon, and to participate in a number of conferences. Harry asked me to join the Royal Opera House Trust, of which he was Chairman. I enjoyed that, but I was very worried about the economy which I could see was going from bad to worse, with the Trade Unions throwing their weight about, so that people began to think and say that Britain was ungovernable. Harry was not surprised when Harold Wilson resigned in 1976 - Wilson had had enough. I felt the same way about my job - that I was heading for a dead end and I got rather excited about suggestions made to me that I should become chairman of one of the big nationalised industries.

CHAPTER 9

STEEL UNDER LABOUR

My appointment to British Steel was announced in March 1976, a week after Harold Wilson resigned as Prime Minister, to be succeeded by James Callaghan. To understand the political and economic climate at that time one has to go back to the formation of the Wilson Government two years earlier.

The economy then was still sour from the effect of the collapsed Barber boom and the Unions were cock-a-hoop at having defeated Heath's attempts to control the wage explosion. Wilson's government immediately conceded to the miners practically all their pay demands, which represented nearly twice the increases allowable under Heath's pay code. The economy then entered what Joel Barnett, then Chief Secretary at the Treasury and later Lord Barnett, called 'expansive days... leading to five years dominated by economic crises.'

In fact during those early days very serious mistakes were made in handling the economy. The oil price rise of 1973 was just working its way through to prices in the shops and inflationary pressures were building up strongly. At the Treasury Denis Healey then made what he calls a 'venial mistake in the circumstances of the time.' He was let down by what he called 'gross forecasting errors by the Treasury.' Healey continued with Labour's spending programme unabated, because he did not want 'to add to the deflationary effect of the increased oil prices.' The Treasury underestimated the Government's Borrowing Requirement by no less than £4 billion and overestimated company liquidity, so that tax increases brought many companies close to bankruptcy. The effect of these errors was to raise the rate of inflation to nearly 30% before the Government had been in office for a year.

It has to be said that the German and Japanese governments took the opposite view to Healey's. They at once cut expenditure and fared much better. After the 'expansiveness' the remainder of the Callaghan government's life was spent in cutting government expenditure and in imposing incomes policies with decreasing effect, and increasing tension between the right (Healey and Callaghan) wing of the Labour party and the left (Benn and Foot).

The Unions, led by Jack Jones (of the Transport and General Workers Union) at first acted responsibly and the rate of inflation was halved by the first incomes policy, which imposed a £6 limit on all weekly wage increases. Hugh Scanlon and Moss Evans (who succeeded Jack Jones) were, however, unwilling or unable to go on restraining the shop stewards. 'The Winter of Discontent' came after I had been for a year chairman of British Steel and in 1979 we were faced with a demand for wage increases of 20% without strings. We refused to pay and the strike which followed, in which we were supported by the newly-elected Thatcher Government, ended that disastrous sequence of events.

I was pitched into this highly charged situation, first as non-executive deputy chairman of the British Steel Corporation and from 1st September 1976 as its executive Chairman, with Bob Scholey (later Sir Robert) as Chief Executive. It was a familiar approach march for me - similar in many ways to my arrival as managing director of the IRC eight years earlier. I had for some months been discussing with senior civil servants whether I would be available to become chairman of a nationalised industry. They pointed out the need for public service at a time of national crisis, such as Britain was then experiencing. Inflation was at 19% and sterling had lost 12.5% of its value in the previous three months. Unemployment had risen to 1.5 million, at that time an unacceptable figure. Later, Britain had to apply for its maximum entitlement from the International Monetary Fund ($4 billion) to prop up sterling, but the £ continued to fall and Healey had to turn back at Heathrow, instead of flying to a Commonwealth Conference in Hong Kong. He raised the Bank rate from 13% to 15%.

It was not an attractive scenario, made worse for me by the fact that my predecessor at British Steel, Sir Monty Finniston, had not had his contract renewed, due to furious rows he had rightly had with Tony Benn, who at that time was Secretary of State for Industry. Fortunately for me, just before my appointment, Benn was moved to the Department of Energy and Eric Varley became the Secretary of State for Industry, with Gerald Kaufman as his Minister.

I had worked with Tony Benn while I was at IRC, and he was Minister for Technology. I had then found him a first-class operator, who understood the deficiencies of British industry and was willing to go to the limit of his powers. I remember the great Sir Otto Clarke, then his Permanent Secretary, waving his hands about in front of Tony Benn, saying: 'Minister, you can't do that!'

Benn took it all in good part and went to Cabinet with a sensible brief. He seemed at that time always to win points in Cabinet. But during the Heath regime a great change came over him and he wrapped himself up in Trade Union banners and moved leftwards - further, indeed, than most trade union leaders. Perhaps he hoped that with trade union support he would become Prime Minister, in which case he miscalculated. A rather similar case arose at the other end of the political spectrum where Sir Keith Joseph, after the downfall of Heath, discovered he had not been a Conservative at all. He donned the ideological mantle of Hayek and other extreme right wing theorists. Benn and Joseph became isolated from the doing of things.

In just the same way as eight years earlier I had felt I had done what I could for Schroder Wagg, so in 1976 I felt I had done my stint at Guinness Mahon. I could have coasted along, quite well paid, with many outside interests, as Chairman of that small merchant bank, building it up brick by brick, but with no obvious opportunity for a break-through. I was sixty-two years of age and could retire comfortably in three years time to the beautiful property José and I had bought in 1960 on the edge of Windsor Great Park. It was a tempting prospect, but I have to say that I never seriously considered it. I was letting no one down because there would be a six months hand-over period while they found a new chairman for Guinness Mahon and while I got to know something of BSC, as its deputy chairman.

This time round there was no visit to St Mark's Basilica, but a conference organised by the *Financial Times* in London early in March 1976 at which I gave a carefully prepared address entitled 'We all live here.' In this I outlined my political and economic position and an action programme for improving the livelihood of people working in Britain. My argument was as follows:

To make the mixed economy, from which we cannot completely escape, work properly, it must have these characteristics:
  *A capability for creating productive jobs
  *A welfare improving capability
  *A wealth creating society to pay for it all, which means being able to better the international competition.

'We all seem to take for granted that enough wealth will be created. That is not justified. We are not creating as much wealth as we could or should to pay for the kind of life we have come to expect. I say to the Labour Government, How can you spend wealth if you don't arrange to create it? I say to Conservative politicians: How can you be a national party unless you can catch the interest of twenty million work people? The wealth creating society has to be social, fair, and democratic. But, wriggle as we may, we always come back to industrial and business performance as the essential, unavoidable issue, because it pays for everything. If this performance is inadequate our standard of living is inadequate. Always the international competition is nagging at us, inescapable and unforgiving.

'Industrial policy is, therefore, central and should aim for: high investment, high skill, high production, high value added, high wages, high profits; management *of* the shop floor, *on* the shop floor, *with* the shop floor.

This is the nub of the matter.'

I argued that none of this would happen by the massage of the market. It will have to be made to happen. If government sets the stage, businessmen will rouse themselves and make it happen without having government do it to them. If government will conduct the large orchestra which is waiting and ready to play, so that as many instruments as possible are involved, we could perform an Industrial Symphony.

This is a package for a wealth-creating society, not for a herd of sacred cows unable to suckle dependants from shrunken tits. Its success depends upon good management, intelligent trades unions, a Government aware of the industrial problem and committed to its solution. People in Britain are full of common sense and they know our society is evolving in a social and democratic way. I believe they would go for a wealth-creating society, with adequate safeguards.'

I knew also of the report on manufacturing industry dated 5 February 1976 by the National Economic Development Council (NEDDY) to which I was appointed as a member in March:

* The total profits of British manufacturing industry have declined from 10% ten years ago to 6% today.
* Profits retained in British manufacturing industry have been negative in five of the last six years.
* Manufacturing capacity in Britain has shrunk in each recent

year.

* Growth of output in Britain has been dramatically lower than that of France and Germany in the last five years.
* Britain's productivity is one third lower than in France or Germany.
* Industrial employment has been rising for ten years in France and Germany. In Britain it has fallen sharply.

The result has been that the fall in employment has led to resistance by the workforce to improved productivity, for fear of redundancy. Further, more companies increasingly flinch from new enterprise risk.

I felt I knew where British industry stood and where I stood, so I wrote to Sir Antony Part, Permanent Secretary at the Department of Industry, saying,

'Barkiss is willing,' to go to British Steel, provided:

We proceed to a supervisory and executive board system at BSC. We agree a protocol for consultation between BSC and your Department.

We agree debt-equity ratio for BSC.

Meetings between myself, the Minister and Bob Scholey are mutually satisfactory.

We shoot at 25th March as 'impact day'.

The theme of press comment on the announcement was surprise! *The Daily Telegraph* said, 'Next to the retirement of Harold Wilson, the appointment of Villiers to BSC was the biggest surprise of the week. He can never have felt fully stretched at Guinness Peat. So he was keen for a bigger challenge and to be up and away.' 'City reaction ranges from surprise to incredulity.' 'He will bring to the job enthusiasm and banking skill, but little intimate knowledge of the industry.' 'He will get on better with Civil Servants than did his predecessor.' 'Villiers joins the President of Lebanon and the Soviet Minister of Agriculture in the club for people with truly nightmarish jobs.' 'The Government hopes it has found a more subtle executive who can use diplomacy to do what

Finniston couldn't.' Bill Sirs, the leader of the main steel union (ISTC) Iron and Steel Trades Confederation, said 'Villiers' views on labour relations indicate that he would involve the unions in discussions and thereby avoid confrontation.'

There was a lot of sympathy for Monty who, it was widely felt, had done a good job and had been penalised for standing up to Tony Benn. The BSC board said that 'His colleagues have been continually stimulated by Sir Monty's energetic and courageous leadership and have held him in high regard throughout this period.' Monty said, 'I have not resigned, I entered into a contract for three years. I intend to honour that contract and to stay till it ends.'

The Times, in a leading article headed 'More Sisyphus than Hercules,' said, 'The task before Sir Charles is a daunting one, but it is not necessarily beyond the ability of a man with his personal gifts.' Sisyphus spent his life pushing a rock up a hill, which cannot have been much fun. Actually I felt more like Ulysses; Tennyson has him say 'Come, my friends, 'tis not too late to seek a newer world... my purpose holds, to sail beyond the sunset.' Hence the title of this book.

I was encouraged on that day by support from Eric Varley, the Secretary of State for Industry. He wrote, 'It is no exaggeration to say that you now have the key post in the whole of our manufacturing industry. You said it would take a decade or more to make a real impact on the Corporation's problems, and I believe you are right. In the short term you will be subject to pressures from many sides (not excluding me, since we have our problems as well) but I am confident in your ability to set longer term goals and to work gradually towards them. Harold Wilson has asked me to say how delighted he is that you have agreed to undertake the job and he wishes you every success.'

It was not too bad a start - better than I had expected. At the end of that long day I was quoted as saying, 'It's a chance to do all the things I have been talking about for years... I feel

157

I am serving my country in the way I know best, through business. I have never been interested in party politics. It's not my bag... I want to see a thrusting, thriving, thirsty steel industry in Britain.' I guess we all felt thirsty by that time.

The first thing I did was to establish an efficient 'private office' at Steel. Christopher Beauman, a director of Guinness Mahon, came with me on Day One and stayed to the bitter end. He is enormously intelligent and perceptive and has an incredible way of getting people's confidence. He is loyal to the core and I would have got nowhere without him, though the length of his hair did attract some comment from Bob. Barry Cheetham, a real steel man, was invaluable for detailed knowledge of the steel industry. He drew up the 'proformas' with which I tried to measure the performance of the plants. He gave me wonderful service during his stint. I inherited Ian Coulter, as press man, from Monty and he did well till Ron Melvin took over from him. Ron is still in post and has been ideal in that job. Sheila Burns was my magnificent secretary, and without her I would not have the papers, diaries and scrapbook with which to write this story.

I then set off on a tour of the BSC's establishments and met with an astonishing reception of good will, interest and inquisitiveness. I made some terrible howlers. At Scunthorpe's blast furnaces I said to the Keeper, 'I've got it; the steel comes out here.' 'Iron, Chairman,' said the Keeper, 'white hot iron.'

But I avoided the traps set for me at a first visit to Shotton in North Wales, which was a marginal steel producer. I then gave no future commitment, but unwisely I did later. I got it wrong at Bilston, a small steel works in the Black Country. I felt enthusiastic about the excellent people who worked there and I gave them the impression that they were safe from closure. But they weren't and we had to close Bilston in the end; they never forgave me. At Ravenscraig, outside Glasgow, I said that I was a gardener and might have to do some pruning. 'You mean you're going to cover us with manure,' came a voice from the back of the hall. It would not be true to say that it was all good, clean fun. Men were ever so worried about their jobs and rightly so. I had to be careful not to give hostages to fortune.

But Benn's legacy remained. He and Frank Beswick (later Lord Beswick) had insisted that Labour's promise not to close uneconomic steel works must be honoured. Beswick saw the economic argument, but he was a Labour politician and he refused to agree to these old plants (Beswick plants they were called) being closed at once. He extended the life of each by several years, to the fury of management, who saw Beswick's intervention as a direct challenge to their right to manage. One of my first tasks was to negotiate BSC out of the Beswick trap.

I learned a great deal about British Steel during the six months I was Deputy Chairman. I came to understand the long, complicated process of steel making and I came to see that the old plants, left with open hearth furnaces, could never compete with the modern Basic Oxygen System which made more, cleaner and cheaper steel. I saw the new plant Monty had built at Redcar and the new investment he had made at Port Talbot, Llanwern, Scunthorpe and Ravenscraig. I saw also the mistakes - a direct reduction plant at Hunterston, overly modern coke ovens and a second monster blast furnace at Redcar, which was never completed.

Above all I got to know the management of British Steel. Bob Scholey took me round eighteen plants, patiently explaining the processes, the problems and the people. He has spent his life in the steel business and knows it inside out. His managers respect him, and fear him when he is in 'Black Bob' mood. They look to him for promotion, and he was and is undoubtedly the dominating personality in British Steel. Although our ideas on management differed greatly, he once said of the two of us, 'We come from different stables, but we get on well enough.' We came unstuck at one point in my chairmanship, but that was probably my fault, as I shall tell. Bob had a dozen or so managing directors reporting to him.

They were hand picked by him and were absolutely first class; I have nothing but praise for their professionalism, commitment and loyalty to British Steel. I have to describe their attitude towards me as 'protective,' for which I have always been grateful.

And I had to get to know the unions in steel, none of which had been in the orbit of Sir Leslie Cannon, who taught me so much about trade unionism when we were at IRC. The Iron and Steel Trades Confederation was the leading union and its General Secretary was Bill Sirs, a magistrate and a keep-fit enthusiast, a most respectable, moderate and respected man. I went to see him in his office early in my steel days and we had a friendly chat. I mentioned my desire to have a supervisory board for steel, as in Germany, and the possibility of Trade Union representation on it. He was coy about this and said I would have to convince his Executive Council on the desirability of such a board with Trade Union representation. I felt he was very much under the thumb of his Executive Council and I agreed to attend one of its meetings. The main speakers were from South Wales and said BSC needed an 'industrial relations strategy to cope with modern conditions, as in European Countries.' I said 'amen' to that.

Most whole-time officials were satisfied with their relationship with the BSC management. I had the uncomfortable feeling that these men were more concerned with their union (by which they were paid) than with BSC or even than with their members. Indeed, Bill said in his book, 'Hard Labour,' 'I regard the trade union movement as the most important and influential voluntary movement in the whole of the world.'

The other unions in BSC were the National Union of Blast Furnacemen (NUB) a small union, then led by Hector Smith who had been a sergeant-major in the Welsh Guards. He had to make a great effort not to stand to attention when I spoke with him. His union was very friendly and co-operative, but very closely aligned to the ISTC. The craftsmen in BSC belonged to fifteen different unions, but they had been brought together in the National Craftsmen's Co-ordinating Committee (NCCC) of which Eddie Linton was the convener. They tended to go along with management more readily than did the ISTC.

I became convinced that BSC had to come to a better relationship with its unions and the workforce and by September 1976, when I became chairman, I had worked out what I called The Steel Contract. The Steel Contract was a proposal made by BSC to the Trades Union Congress Steel and Iron Consultative Committee (TUCSICC), known as the TUC Steel Committee, based upon partnership between the industrial and staff grades in BSC on the one hand and the Directors and Managers of BSC on the other, through their respective representatives. The proposed partnership was intended:

1. To achieve not only consultation and understanding, but also active participation and the positive involvement of both partners in the development of BSC as an expanding exporting and profitable organisation.
2. To extend from Departmental level to BSC main Board.
3. To cover all subjects, including pay, work structure, consultation representation, disputes, investment and closures.
4. To operate continuously and to include the planning function.
5. To ensure that employees and Management would commit themselves to the implementation of all agreements.
6. To include all the Unions in TUCSICC acting in concert, who are now invited to nominate a person to negotiate the proposed steel contract with Mr Bob Scholey for BSC.
7. To reach agreement in principle on 23 January 1977.
8. To achieve either a National Joint Council or a National Joint Consultative Council by 31 December 1977.
9. To be announced, as a matter of firm intent as soon as

TUCSICC and the BSC Board jointly agree and after the interested parties and HMG have been informed.

Sadly, only item 8 was ever agreed and that only much later. A very great effort was made by BSC, particularly by Gordon Sambrook, at that time the BSC managing director responsible for personnel and industrial relations, and by Dr David Grieves, who followed him, to meet and discuss and negotiate this agreement. A national working party was already in existence, covering restructuring and manpower reductions by 40,000 by March 1978; and by May of that year the approach to single status by way of harmonisation was fully prepared by BSC. A preliminary conference had been held at Windermere in September 1977 and we were all set to finalise the main lines of the contract at Selsdon Park, where the full TUCSICC would meet the full BSC negotiating team on 11/12 July 1978. We had failed to get Bill Sirs to Windermere, and he was reluctant to attend at Selsdon Park, where he led for TUCSICC. Bill Sirs turned the Steel Contract down. The Blastfurnacemen and some of the craftsmen would have gone on with it, but Bill Sirs had more members and that is what counts in trade union life.

It was a great disappointment; we had really hoped for a break-through and had expended endless time and effort upon it. We never got Sirs to say exactly why he turned aside from this opportunity, but putting two and two together I surmise that he felt the Steel Contract would limit the Union's freedom to do what they thought was good for the Union, whenever they liked. Secondly, he probably felt that the Union would be committed to reacting to movements and prices in the market for steel: this he had always said was a matter for management. Lastly, he would undoubtedly have become, with management, responsible for redundancies and that was just too much for him. The discussions lingered on thereafter on specific points, but the main thrust of 'the Steel Contract' was lost. We did not give up. We tried a different approach.

We had, of course, kept Government, our sole shareholder, aware of our intentions and progress. Government had, indeed, published its own White Paper on Industrial Democracy. In August 1978 the BSC Board was reconstructed by Eric Varley and six employee members were appointed to it, together with two BSC managing directors, plus two Civil Servants, Sir John Buckley, chairman of Davy International, and Alastair Morton, at that time managing director of the British National Oil Company.

This was the climax of a plan I had had in mind from the moment of my appointment to British Steel. My idea was to follow the German example (initiated I believe by British Trade Unionists) of a Supervisory Board of mainly non-executive members, including representatives of the Trade Unions, and an executive board of managing directors, chaired by the chief executive officer. At BSC the Chief Executive's Committee was already an executive board.

I had been to Germany to spend a day with Hermann J Abs, who was Chairman of twelve supervisory boards, to get from him all his advice and thoughts, which he gave generously. In consequence, our Employee Six, who were paid by BSC, not by their Union, went on a five-day course at BSC's college at Ashorne Hill to understand how and why:

* BSC must become viable, to get money for development.
* BSC must be competitive, to keeps its customers.
* BSC must get people involved, to get productivity up.

They responded very well to this training and they soon picked up enough board-room jargon to follow what was going on and make useful contributions. They never really grasped the idea of being individuals on a board; they remained representatives of their own group and as time went by they came, step by step, to see the force of management's arguments.

163

In BSC we had had worker directors on local boards, usually at plant level, for some years and it worked well. Most of the six who came on to the main board had had this experience from which they had benefitted. The trouble was that their mates were suspicious that they had 'gone over to the enemy,' their unions feared that they were doing the Union's job and their board room colleagues did not think that they knew enough about business to be of much help. All these opinions were unjustified. When I handed over to Sir Ian MacGregor I found that he did not really approve of worker directors; he let them finish their contracts, but these were not renewed.

It has to be admitted that this experiment, like the Steel Contract, failed and it is, I fear, the 'them and us' inherited industrial culture which prevented success. This is very serious, because unless we can get an industrial relations structure in Britain which is at least as successful as the structures in Germany and Japan we are going to remain at a disadvantage and we cannot afford that. Britain's best hope, I now believe, is to establish just such an atmosphere of trust between managers and the workforce on the shop floor, and that the unions' function is reduced to identifying grievances at an early stage and to solving or reducing them quickly - this means local, not national, action. Industrial relations certainly have improved in Britain, but we should not think that they are nearly good enough.

I have dealt at some length with our efforts to improve industrial relations at BSC. These were not immediately successful, but although the crunch point, the 13-week strike in 1980, was still to come, I have no doubt that an atmosphere for better industrial relations had been created.

To portray the full problem I have now to describe the operational and financial problems with which we were faced. I had in July 1977 to present BSC's accounts for the year to April 1977, although I had been chairman for only the last six months of that period. They were the months when, as I said, 'the favourable trend stalled and the steel industry of the world went into depression.' BSC made a loss, after all charges, of nearly £100 million. We needed external funding of nearby £1 billion to cover investment and all other out-goings. That money had to come from the Government in the form of Public Dividend Capital and long term loans.

I reported our view that the demand for steel would grow much more slowly than previously expected. In Japan and Europe steps were being taken to cut out old and expensive steel making capacity. As I said, 'This is very painful. BSC has been doing this for some time, and is continuing to do so on an agreed programme.' Nevertheless, we intended to continue with the investment programme which we then estimated would cost £5 billion of Government money. I went on to say that we were aiming at a liquid steel making capacity of 30 million tons per year. We were then producing 20 million t.p.a and employing 208,000 people. I finished by saying that the year to April 1978 would show a substantially greater loss.

The press comment was objective: 'Steel's hopes melt away;' 'Steel heads for a £250m loss;' 'British Steel could lose £500 million;' 'Pay explosion could break British Steel;' 'Cash loss gloom;' 'No simple solution;' 'Steel's commanding depths.'

By September 1977 market conditions had got much worse. We had switched Gordon Sambrook from being managing director, personnel, to being the commercial director. After he had had time to look round that patch he commented to Bob and me, 'If this goes on we won't be able to sell a ton of steel.' We were in a 'cost-price' squeeze, where costs were rising and prices were falling. Clearly, drastic action was necessary. Our industrial relations initiatives were slow moving. Our decentralisation plans were only just beginning to work. Our improved marketing could do little in a cost-price squeeze. Our investment would take years to complete and pay off. We had to do something at once.

165

Bob suggested, and I readily agreed, that we should have all the managing directors for a day-long conference at Blacknest, our home on the edge of Windsor Great Park. Excellent statistical material was prepared and we came to dramatic decisions:

1. To cut the target for liquid steel making capacity from 30 million tons per annum to 15 mtpa.

2. To start giving effect to this forthwith, by closing old plants.

3. To face Government with the prospect of heavy redundancies.

Some of these old plants were Beswick plants (Beeswax, we always called him) and his reprieve from closure had to go. I managed to get that agreed with Varley and Kaufman, who got it through Cabinet. I felt somewhat better about these closures, knowing that our subsidiary, BSC (Industry), was ready to go to work in the steel closure areas, helping to start up new businesses and expand old ones, thus creating new jobs.

The first plant to go was Clyde Iron. Its workforce went to the BSC Scottish director, Jake Stewart, and said that they knew the plant was clapped out; they asked how much compensation they would get if they agreed to closure before Christmas. Dr David Grieves had become personnel director and he at once saw the importance of getting closures started on a quickly agreed basis. My recollection is that the man with an average number of years service got a year's pay, those with more service got more and those with less got less. The plant at Hartlepool applied for closure on the same terms, provided it was paid before Christmas!

The going got worse in 1978. The East Moors plant in Cardiff, employing 3,000 men, was in the constituency of Jim Callaghan, then Prime Minister. He asked me to see him when he was opening an extension to Capital Steels, a steel user next door to East Moors.

'What are you going to do about East Moors?' he asked,

'We are going to mothball and probably close it,' I replied.

'If you do that, I shall oppose you in private and in public. You are taking on the Prime Minister. Do you realise that?'

'What do you think I should do, Prime Minister?' I asked in some anxiety.

'You should ask the men,' he said.

I had the works manager with me and he replied,

'The men know the plant is clapped out and they want to take the money and go.'

The Prime Minister turned away and left the room without another word. We heard that he was asking the men all round and was getting the same answer. We closed the works a few weeks later without a squeal from anyone. I heard later that other Members of Parliament complained to him about steel works closures in their constituencies and that he replied, 'That bloody man did it to me and he can do it to you.' I think that may be apocryphal.

In January and February there arose an extraordinary series of events arising out of evidence I had given in October 1977 to the Select Committee on Nationalised Industries. I have read the questions and answers over again and I would not have answered differently today or on any other day. We were in the middle of discussions with Government about steel works closures and with TUCSICC about the Steel Contract. Both these issues were dynamite and at that time quite unsettled, especially the closure of Beswick plants. The Select Committee wanted to get in on the act and to act as 'a friend at court.' They reported on 11 January 1978 that the 'BSC either turned a blind eye to the real danger or deliberately avoided revealing the true situation.'

As I wrote in a letter to *The Times* on 13 January 1978, 'This is completely unsustained by the evidence given to the Committee and published by them.

BSC said that the immediate future was a down-turn and a further down-turn. All our public statements predicted a worsening trade and financial situation. There can be no

167

excuse for the Committee failing to realise this.'

The Committee also complained that I had refused to discuss with them in October 'the options we were reviewing, or to disclose our preferred option.' I replied, 'If it was of value to you to have Mr Varley and me together, and he agreed, I would play my part, but I am one of the parties to an agreement to try to solve this huge problem and, honestly, I am not going - short of the Tower of London - to break that agreement. The present case indicates the extreme difficulty of trying to serve two masters.'

The Prime Minister wrote to me, 'In my view, the BSC has been treated unfairly in this matter and, unusually for a Select Committee, this Committee has not taken an objective view of the situation.'

There was a tremendous rumpus in Parliament and the Press, calling for my resignation and that a cover-up should be exposed. Varley was in the dock with me and I must say that he proved a good man with whom to go tiger shooting. Apparently it was the new Tory leader, Margaret Thatcher, who decided to force a full parliamentary debate on the Select Committee's report. This took place on 8 March with Keith Joseph opening and Gerald Kaufman closing. I listened to every word of the debate without ever feeling anxious. The crunch point came when Eric Varley quoted Neil Kinnock (a member of the Select Committee) as saying, 'This is the most stupid and incompetent abuse of the purpose of select committees and it is the most insensitive and contemptible disregard of the real needs of the steel industry, to use it for stupid and superficial party political purposes.'

Eric Varley followed this up with quotes from a letter written to me by Ray Emmitt, the Coopers and Lybrand partner who audited BSC's accounts. He wrote, 'I have discussed the situation with some of my partners and they support my view that in the circumstances in which BSC found itself at the time, an adequate disclosure of the deteriorating trading prospects was given in the documents... I do

'No, no, Sir Charles, when I de-
manded you reveal all ...' (Repro-
duced by permission of *Daily Mail)*.

not think it realistic in all the circumstances to have expected that you (that's me) could have said more than you did at the time, pending detailed assessments of the prospects, which were then in hand.'

Nicholas Ridley then jumped up and asked Eric Varley to invite BSC to change its auditors who had devalued their reputation by writing such a disgraceful note. The debate seemed interminable to me sitting up there. Everyone seemed to have a go; Tebbitt continually intervened and Foot called him 'a polecat.' The debate covered 100 columns of Hansard. In the end the Select Committee's report was negatived by 302 votes to 254. Afterwards, Varley extended my contract as chairman of BSC by another year, to 1980.

We won the battle, but we did not win the war. BSC generally and I myself personally were damaged by this entirely politically-motivated event. If there was non-political fault it was mine. It would have been possible for me to have accepted the Select Committee's offer to go into secret session and to have told them of the options which we were discussing with Government and on some points with the Unions. I had been warned that Select Committees generally, and this one in particular, were 'leaky sieves' and could not keep secret information to themselves, whatever they might promise. I simply did not dare to take the risk of spilling the beans to them, thereby risking the extremely delicate negotiations which were going on with Government and the Unions.

In March 1978 the Government at last came to our rescue. We had been in discussion with Gerald Kaufman ever since the Blacknest meeting. We found him completely understanding of the problem and he respected our intention to do all we could in various ways to ease the pain of plant closure. The White Paper, 'The Road to Viability,' whitewashed BSC for the closures at Clyde, Hartlepool and East Moors and went on, 'Further rationalisation will be necessary in future, but this should be considered on a 'step by step' approach, with later developments in the market situation taken into account. It is necessary for capacity to move in line with demand. BSC should seek to negotiate closures in close consultation with TUCSICC and the loyal workforce.' This was really all BSC wanted.

My deal with Eric Varley was that he would put in the 'step by step' formula, if BSC would undertake to inform him of intended closures and enter genuine consultation with the local workforces. This worked perfectly except for a bad hiccup at Bilston where the local BSC plant manager 'jumped the gun,' which caused a bad delay. Shelton was closed and the workforce re-employed in the Potteries without problems.

The closure of Ebbw Vale came at the same time, but only after great travail. It had been the constituency of Aneurin Bevan and then of Michael Foot. The population was intensely loyal to the locality and to the steel works. The suggestion of going to work in the Hoover plant, eight miles away at Merthyr Tydfil, was regarded like a proposal to emigrate. Michael Foot fought alongside the steel workers, but when he saw we were determined to close the hopelessly uneconomic steel plant, he got the men's leaders to negotiate for the best possible closure terms and in the end the plant closed quietly. The BSC tin plate works at Ebbw Vale continued to operate with increased investment and has been a success.

In April 1978 we issued 'Prospects for Steel,' in which we said, 'It may be we have not yet reached the bottom of a recession in the demand for steel... it is unlikely that the high loss situation can be immediately turned round... the current year will be very difficult.' In July I had to report a loss of £443 million. I said, 'The whole of this bitter experience was outwith steelmakers' normal experience and expectation ... The task has been to preserve the business through the crisis ... Within two years BSC will have new low-cost steel making capacity coming on stream, especially at Redcar and Ravenscraig. The problem will then be to load plants fully and economically, since it is the level of capacity utilisation which determines BSC's costs, competitiveness and profit.' It was then that I disclosed BSC's policy to get to 'breakeven' in the profit and loss account by the end of March 1980.

But the new style supervisory board was put in place. The Davignon plan to reduce steel overcapacity in Europe was starting to work and BSC's borrowing powers were raised yet again. I felt we were coming through the worst of the steel crisis. I was wrong: there was worse to come.

In March 1979 there was a great row about importing coal from Australia. I had been with Eric Varley on a trade mission to China where we had offered them a huge credit to buy British goods. There was a lot of song, but no dance. I made a big pitch, along with John Buckley, to reconstruct the old Russian-built Capital steelworks, just outside Peking, which our subsidiary British Steel (Overseas) together with Davy would have very well been able to do. We all got on well with Eric, who is a most excellent man, but I had a shock when we got home.

I received a rather pompous summons to see the Secretaries of State for Industry and for Energy, together with Sir Derek Ezra, the Chairman of the National Coal Board. I guessed what that was about. BSC found that the new ultra modern blast furnace at Redcar, the biggest in Europe, would only work efficiently using a special volatile coal, rank 301 (known as Morrison Superblend) of which the British supply, from Durham, was rapidly running out.

I had been to see the Morrison washery where it was mixed and the manager told me he could only promise supplies for another few months. In Australia there was an unlimited supply at £10 per ton cheaper. There was plenty of coal left in Durham but of the wrong quality, which would have caused our new blast furnace to seize up. BSC had not given much notice of its changed requirement of rank 301 coal. 'We want you to go on buying Durham coal for Redcar,' said Varley.

'There is not enough of the right quality,' I replied.

'We can get the quality right,' said Ezra.

'It would be politically wrong to buy Australian coal,' said Benn.

'The NCB people have been working with BSC on this quality problem for years. BSC says there is no solution,' I replied.

'Anyway,' said Benn, 'we want you to use Durham coal with an election coming up.'

'Unless you give me a written directive to do so, I shall have to start buying suitable coal from Australia,' I said.

'Now, now,' said Varley, 'BSC is a nationalised industry and should help the Government. I am sure a directive is unnecessary.'

'I have to look after BSC, not the Government,' I said.

'Are you going to give me a directive to buy the wrong sort of coking coal, which will cause us to lose the new blast furnace at Redcar?'

The Secretaries of State gathered their papers together and left the room.

'I know what I would do,' said Ezra.

'Well, you would, wouldn't you?' I replied.

I enquired the next day from the Civil Service whether a directive was being prepared. The answer was 'no.' Next day, at a meeting with the BSC managing directors, I authorised Frank Holloway, our supplies director, to order the coal from Australia. The National Union of Mineworkers and Labour MPs yelled like hell, but after the General Election I heard no more of it. The Redcar blast furnace has worked admirably since, on a mixture of Durham and Australian coal, converted to coke.

Throughout these difficult three years I had plugged on about improving the quality of our steel, which had become poor. I had many meetings and dinners with customers and listened to their complaints. On the whole they were amazingly patient with us and we were able to keep our market share at around 55% of the home market. I promised better steel and I am thankful that in the end BSC was able to deliver

173

it.

The Labour Government fell at the General Election on 3 May 1979 and, along with the other nationalised industries, I felt Harold Macmillan's 'Wind of Change' blowing round the Civil Service and their attitudes to BSC. Varley and Kaufman had been first-class ministers and I really do believe that their long-sightedness enabled us to save the British Steel industry - much reduced, but still alive and kicking and capable of the splendid recovery which my successors at British Steel have achieved. We had to wait a few more years for that.

The 'Winter of Discontent' in 1978/79 had been a dreadful experience for everyone in Britain. As Denis Healey said, 'It had destroyed the nation's confidence in the Labour Party's ability to work with the unions, it had also turned large numbers of working people against their own trade union representatives.' As Joel Barnett said, 'The first three months of 1979 were the longest in the whole five years.' The tanker drivers' dispute in January caused shortages of heating oil and fresh food, and 1,000 schools closed. Callaghan, returning from a conference in Guadeloupe, asked, 'What crisis?' The railway unions started one-day strikes. The public employees started strikes in hospitals and schools, turning away patients and young people. Dustbins and rubbish were piled up on the streets. Hundreds of thousands of workers were laid off. Some cemetery workers in Liverpool refused to dig graves.

Union leaders told the Prime Minister that they could not control widespread, unofficial and paralysing strikes in protest against the 5% limit on pay rises required by Government. Pay settlements had been between 15% and 20%. The Union pact with the Government, setting out long term plans for reducing inflation, was branded by Mrs. Thatcher as 'a boneless wonder.'

The Trade Union leaders, especially Moss Evans (Transport and General) were determined to break the Government's pay policy and at the same time to restrain secondary picketing, which frightened them. As Joel Barnett comments, 'It was only natural that some of the unpopularity of the unions should rub off on the Labour Government that had tried to work so closely with them over the previous five years.' Callaghan, having missed a favourable opportunity for an election in 1978, eventually went to the country on 3 May 1979 and the Tories under Margaret Thatcher emerged with an overall majority of 43.

CHAPTER 10

STEEL UNDER THE TORIES

I had great anxiety about BSC under the Tories and I was resigned to my own dismissal. BSC was still going to be a great user of government money to fund losses and to keep the investment programme going. It was doubtful if we could meet the target of working at break-even by April 1980, which we had set in 1978 as a challenge to the managers and workforce in BSC, and it would be disastrous to stop investment in mid-stream with new works and plant half finished. For myself I was under no illusions. I had been 'abolished' with the IRC in 1970 and anyway, all governments like to change people appointed by their opponents: they suspect them of being 'unsound' or 'unreliable.'

When Sir Keith Joseph (now Lord Joseph) was appointed Secretary of State for Industry, the net was closing round me; he had spoken against the IRC and had opened the Commons debate on the Select Committee report which criticised me. He had constantly harried the Labour Government for the 'financial incontinence' of the Nationalised Industries. On taking up his job at the Department of Industry he had asked his staff to read Hayek and Schumpeter, who regard government intervention and spending as 'the road to serfdom.' My days at steel were numbered.

Our first meeting was scheduled for 20 May 1979. The Permanent Secretary at the Department of Industry, Sir Peter Carey, one of the great Civil Servants, had assured me that all would go well and that Joseph would understand the immense problems of BSC. He was with Joseph at the meeting and Christopher Beauman was with me. We met in the excellent new Civil Service building, Ashdown House in Victoria Street. I could never go into it without thinking of the idyllic days at 'Cherry' and walking with Grandfather in Ashdown Forest. 'God butter my soul,' as I thought Grandfather used to say, seemed more appropriate now than then.

Joseph was, as is his wont, extremely polite and his introductory patter about 'this Department should not exist and I should not be here' was part of his act; but his soubriquet of 'the Mad Monk' did flash through my mind. However, he soon got down to the key question of ending BSC's losses. We had lost £300m in the year just ended, less than in the previous year, but I was extremely anxious about the financial year just beginning. The 'Winter of Discontent' had severely damaged BSC and the first projections of the current year's annual operating plan were not good at all. We wanted £500 million for investment. We had an overall cash limit of £700 million set by the previous Government, but I was very worried lest contingencies should cause us to need more than that. Then Joseph intervened to say, 'You will have to get to break-even by March 1980 because there is no way we will fund your losses thereafter.' So!

We moved on to the closure of Shotton steelworks which the Labour Government had been simply unable to face. Joseph was clearly in favour of closure but he felt he had to consult colleagues because there would be a great uproar. He also took on board our idea of forming a joint company with GKN (in the private sector), codenamed 'Phoenix,' to take over much of the rod and wire manufacture of both BSC and GKN. Carey started muttering about the Monopolies Commission but Joseph liked the scheme and said he would try to comment within three weeks. He approved our purchase of Australian coal.

Finally we came to the major reconstruction of BSC which I had codenamed 'Jaguar,' to make each works accountable for its own finance, supplies, manufacture, marketing and personnel. This would mean a big change and a reduction of personnel at Head Office, and a layer of Divisional Staff would go. Joseph supported me in principle and I heard afterwards that he was pleased with the meeting. My diary commented that the meeting was a plus, but that we would have to wait for the next meeting to see how far we had actually got.

Back 'on the ranch' and serious doubts about the validity of our plan to break even by March 1980 began to sink in all round. These gloomy prognostics were cheered up by the Prince of Wales coming to lunch with the board of BSC. He stayed for a meeting of BSC (Industry) which was busy starting new companies and thus creating new jobs in the travel-to-work areas of closed steel works. He was obviously very interested and we started a correspondence which continued for many years. As we shall see, he was of immense help in promoting BSC (Industry) as a useful social tool in the battle against unemployment.

'Jaguar,' so called because it was in my company Jag that Christopher and I had the idea, was a complete revolution in the management of BSC. I began work on this on 7th April 1979, before the General Election, and the diary that day reads, 'I see now that BSC will never get better on an 'as is' basis. I sketched a first draft of a new system, with 18 works reporting to Head Office but competing in the face of the customer and being responsible for all functions. I shall start by rejecting this year's annual operating plan which estimates the loss this year at £260 million.' Two days later I noted, 'If we nurse the works all the time and do their work for them they will never get that sharpness and independence and real motivation to make them successful. I doubt if this can be done under the present management structure; a different system will have to be introduced before I go, so I shall have to move quickly!'

By April 26th, on a drive in the Jag to Sheffield with Christopher, the whole picture suddenly came into focus on the basis of 12 works reporting to Head Office through 'co-ordinators,' cutting out the divisional managing director layer. On May 4th I put the Jaguar scheme to the non-executive directors. All were pleased with it except Mark Littman, who felt we would not be able to overcome the difficulties.

There was a pause in this activity during the post election period. I spent a week visiting steel works in America and some days on the business of Eurofer, the European steel cartel, masterminded by Vicomte Davignon, 'Steevie' to everyone; then to Shotton, where José opened the new coatings complex which has been a huge success.

On 5 June Queen Elizabeth The Queen Mother opened BSC's ore terminal at Hunterston. It had cost £100 million and was the largest in Europe, supplying iron ore for the steel works at Ravenscraig, up the Clyde. Unfortunately, there had been an inter-union dispute about who should unload the ore carriers, so when Queen Elizabeth sailed up the Clyde in the Royal Yacht not much work was going on. Her Majesty gave a great dinner on board the night before the opening and I was able to brief her about meeting Arthur Bell, the leader of the ISTC in Scotland, whose wife was ill and unable to attend. Next day at the presentations, when her Majesty got round to Arthur I whispered in her ear, 'This is the chap.' Queen Elizabeth responded at once and asked about his wife and his work and the dispute and finished by saying, 'I know how influential you are here and I do hope you will be able to bring this dispute to an end soon.' Alas, that did not prove possible.

On 11 June I felt able to send to Peter Carey a draft press announcement of the reorganisation of BSC 'aimed to eliminate trading losses, an aim which has become even more difficult to achieve.' The reorganisation would group profit centres in a way to test the financial viability of each of them and make their own performance the deciding factor in their own survival. Each centre would be accountable for its own P & L and cash flow and would have responsibility for and control over its business decisions. Each centre would report

179

publicly its results each quarter.

The centres would be in three groups:

Flat products, Long products and Special products. Each centre would report to an executive vice chairman, who would be a member of the office of the chairman with full operational authority and responsibility delegated to him for his group. Each executive vice chairman would report directly to the chairman.

The office of the chairman would be served by a staff covering finance, personnel, technical support, commercial supplies and transport, R & D, secretarial.

These changes marked a further step in decentralising BSC and in strengthening profit awareness at all levels, and were intended to contribute to the fastest possible recovery of profitability.

I told Carey that I expected to lose a managing director and that I could not see exactly where Bob Scholey would be fitted in.

On June 20 I had a long session with Keith Joseph, who tried to persuade me to finish my career with reaching break-even at BSC and leave organisation to someone else, thus avoiding the difficult repercussions which he said he could foresee. I could not accept that, because I saw that without the drastic measures I proposed it would not be possible for BSC to reach the break-even point. I told him I thought I could swing the Board of BSC in favour of my proposals, but if I failed we could still carry on 'as is' and he could look for another chairman. Joseph said 'What on earth am I to do about your successor, who might not like the new system you are proposing?' I said, 'I am proposing a system widely used in big business today.'

'Why have you waited so long to move?'

'I regret having been dissuaded from such a change by the senior executives, who said they had just had one change and could not take another so soon,' I replied.

'Surely you could wait a few months,' he said.

'Every week counts,' I said. 'BSC lost £80 million in the last three months and we lost another week when you postponed this meeting.'

Joseph then got up and went to another appointment, saying he would be in touch. At 6.00 pm that evening Peter Carey rang to say that Ministers had decided to support me and would do all that was needed to help, and that I must get on with it as soon as possible. That was quick work and I went over much of the detail with Carey; we feared trade union and worker-directors opposition and I agreed to hold an informal 'pre-board' meeting to test worker-director reaction. They had been very loyal to me for having got them on the board, but I did not know for sure what they would do when the fundamental 'no change' culture was challenged. If they opposed the changes, and were supported by Bob and the other executive directors, we could not get the reorganisation through.

On 27 June I submitted my proposals to the informal pre-board meeting. I was supported by Counsel's opinion that these changes were within the Act governing BSC. The changes were, however, totally opposed by the six worker-directors on the grounds that they would disturb regional arrangements and existing management, and that they were against them altogether. I knew that there had been consultation between the worker-directors and their regional managing directors, and between Bob Scholey and Jimmy McLaren, the leader of the worker-directors who, like all trade unionists, instinctively opposed change. The existing top executive management had decided to resist the changes (which adversely affected them) and had persuaded the worker directors to vote the changes down.

My diary note says, 'At this point the proposals were in fact lost. After 2 hours of debate it was clear to me that the proposals could not be put to the Board on the following day. I refused to consider resignation because that would add to BSC's problems. We must form a group to think about the future and get on with our business in the meanwhile. This met with general approval.' I learned later from Bill Sirs' book that Bob had in fact approached him to advise the worker-directors to vote my proposals down, which he, with some hesitation, had done. Fair enough. I had, of course, lobbied the other directors in my favour.

This was a bad set-back and I would have to sit out the rest of my time at steel 'as is,' hoping that the other things we were doing would take us to break-even point. I would have to mend my fences all round, which would not be easy. Ride it, cowboy! At the main board meeting next day, having accepted the decision of the majority, I did not put the reorganisation proposals.

I wrote to Keith Joseph saying, 'I failed to carry my proposals through the Board of BSC... my resignation is in your hands to use whenever you want it. Meanwhile all is quiet and there is great determination to succeed... the executive team will act with me to run the business on an 'as is' basis. The objectives are clear and so are the consequences of failure.'

Of course there were leaks. On 2 July the headlines were 'Steel boss faces sack;' 'No time to split ranks;' '£1m a week loss may sink Shotton;' 'Steel board rejects change.' On the next day I had to announce a loss of £309 million for the previous year. I had a lot of explaining to do.

On the reorganisation issue I said, 'Decentralisation was introduced by me as a policy when I became Chairman; we have made some progress and we have had some benefit. Clearly, we could go further and the Board would like to do this. The debate was about 'when'. We have decided to proceed under our present organisation. The Board is united in a vigorous approach to the grave problems which face us.'

On the overall losses I said, 'Last year was bad, but better. Last year demand for steel was at its lowest point since 1962. The current year is very difficult. Inflation is swelling our costs. The market for steel is flat. Prices, due to overcapacity in Europe, are weak. The strong £ sterling smothers any attempt to increase our exports and invites foreigners to step into our markets. The loss for the first half of this year will be £150 million. The target of break-even by 1980 remains, although conditions are worse than when it was set, demanding still greater efforts.'

I rubbed in hard that there would be no more cash available from Government to pay for losses after March 1980. We had a tough press conference, but Mark Littman said it was a 'tour de force.' The press believed there had been a split on the board and they did not believe we could get to break-even in 1980. They were right on both counts and they were not surprised to hear from the unions that we were negotiating to close steel making, after endless delay, at Bilston and, from now on, at Corby and Shotton. There were a hundred journalists at the press conference, which was followed by seven TV interviews, four broadcasts and an hour and a half's grilling by Tory MPs in the House of Commons. I finished the day at the Chinese ballet and was glad to see the end of it!

Next day I had a bad time in the press, with most papers calling for my resignation and making pretty wild guesses at my possible successor. I noted in the diary that, 'We shall settle down again, having given everybody a sharp shock which is what was required. I remain convinced that it would have been better to carry the reorganisation through and be in better shape for next year, which will be even more difficult than this one.' Unfortunately, that had proved impossible. I was 'hoist by my own petard.'

One of the unexpected consequences of this crisis in BSC's life was the harmony with which Bob, Frank Holloway (Financial Director), Gordon Sambrook (Commercial Director), and I worked from that moment on. I do believe that the four of us (the 'Big Four,' so called) had the interest of BSC at heart more than our own personal interests. We all knew the immense difficulties and that only a miracle could get us to break-even in nine months' time. We all knew that by then there would be a different chairman. The executives wanted Bob, but it was unlikely he would be promoted at that stage. They were grateful to me for not pressing the reorganisation to the point where the split in the board would have been damaging in the longer term.

I am sure I lost Keith Joseph's confidence at that time, if I had ever had it! I am not surprised; I had pressurised him to no avail. He got his own back in the end. The Civil Service, especially Carey, continued to support me while looking for a replacement. I have no criticism of anyone who opposed me. I tried to go too fast, in view of the worsening financial and trading situation. That never works with Brits; they like time to get used to new ideas and change of any sort.

When in 1980 Ian MacGregor (later Sir Ian) succeeded me as Chairman, he had McKinsey look at all the organisational options. He came down firmly on a scheme very similar to my 'Jaguar' proposals. The difference was that he became Chairman and Chief Executive Officer and made Bob the Chief Operating Officer, an American device to overcome exactly those difficulties I found in the 'one over one' relationship. Time had done its work and the reorganisation went through without a ripple.

On the trade union front things were far from sweetness and light. Bill Sirs was very annoyed that 'things' had taken place at BSC without his being consulted and because the further inevitable closures would leave him with fewer members, reduced income for the ISTC and less clout in the TUC. All that was to boil up into a major explosion in six months' time. Meanwhile, the blastfurnacemen's union, NUB, had asked me to get Davignon, the Commissioner for Industry in the EEC, to speak at their annual conference to be held in Torquay. He was a great success and it is worth looking at what he achieved.

In 1978 it was clear to the EEC Commission in Brussels that an internecine war between European steel producers was breaking out, in which each country would feel bound to support its own steel industry to avoid major loss of employment opportunities. This would certainly endanger the Community spirit needed if the integration of Europe, so much desired by Brussels, was not to be snuffed out by trade war over steel. Davignon, a very senior, but still young, member of the Belgian Foreign Service, was made Commissioner for Industry and was enormously successful in checking the trade war by persuading the steel companies to reduce their steel making capacity and by bullying the governments concerned to reduce the subsidies they were paying steel companies to continue their uneconomic production.

To do all this Davignon set up a European steel cartel, to which all the major steel producers were invited to belong. The smaller producers (less than 1 million tons of steel a year) were left out, to their great satisfaction. The cartel was called Eurofer and the chairmen of the big steel companies took it in turn to take the chair, a thankless task. When it came to my turn Jim Callaghan, then Prime Minister, vetoed my taking this job on the grounds that I was much too busy coping with the problems of British Steel to waste time 'farting around in Europe.' My place was taken by Emmanuel Tesch, the very diplomatic chairman of Luxembourg steel complex.

The idea was that we would all reduce capacity, stick to minimum prices for steel products, and invest in badly needed modern plant, according to a plan worked out by Davignon's staff, under a most able Belgian - Defraigne.

BSC maintained in Brussels an ex-diplomat, to watch the BSC interest in these very important plans. This was what was needed. The trouble was that many of the largest companies paid little attention to what was agreed. Inspectors were appointed, but that did not seem to make much difference. The dear old law-abiding BSC stuck firmly to what was agreed at the meetings, except on one occasion over steel tubes where we made a genuine mistake.

One of the chief offenders sat next to me at Eurofer and I drew from my pocket an invoice of his steel sold in Britain at

185

far below the agreed price. He snatched the invoice from my hand and swore it would never happen again. 'It had better not,' I said, 'or I will crucify you with dumped steel' - a mixed metaphor, but effective. Other offenders were on a larger and more important scale and Eurofer imposed fines (with EEC authority) but these were watered down, 'between friends,' so that they were largely ineffective.

There was a lot of special pleading by countries and companies. One meeting, which I was unable to attend, was electrified by Bob Scholey's comment on one such pleading which echoed round the meeting, he having forgotten to switch off the instantaneous translator: 'What's the French for bullshit?'

I eventually remonstrated with Davignon that the British were the only people who stuck to the agreements.

'You are the best boy in the class,' said Davignon.

'This is a class in which I would like to be at the bottom,' I replied.

'You are not communautaire, Charles,' he said.

'What on earth is that, Steevie?' I asked.

'Well, we know we cannot and will not keep the agreements, but we do the best we can and that is better than doing nothing,' said Steevie.

That is about as good a description of Common Market culture as I ever heard. It explains a lot!

Eurofer was an added burden on time and effort, but it was well worth doing. With my IIEB experience and schoolboy French and German I quite enjoyed the meetings and hospitality we were offered. Bob is chairman, as I write, and I have no doubt he makes an excellent job of it - less bullshit, anyway!

Eurofer was certainly important for BSC on the macro-economic scale, but we still had fearful problems with our own steelworks. In July we were losing £1 million each day, so we had to add Shotton in North Wales to the active closure list. We estimated we could save £80 million a year by closing Shotton as well as Corby. I was wrong-footed in the Shotton case because I had said we hoped to keep the steelworks going till 1982, which proved too optimistic, and the Unions were able to throw 'broken pledge' at me in their defence of 6,000 jobs in all. The announcement of closure was very well handled by Peter Allen, our managing director in Wales, who pointed out that the steel coatings complex at Shotton would continue to operate, using steel from Ravenscraig or Llanwern.

Barry Jones, the Labour MP for Shotton (East Flint), got a debate in the House of Commons to try to stop the closure; the Government won the vote and that was the verdict on Shotton.

Although we had started consultation about the closure of Corby early in 1979, the workforce there was proving very violent. On 17 July we had five hours of argument with the militants, who called me a murderer. We said Corby steel making was costing us £40 million a year. They said to 'Villiers the villain,' 'You are not thinking about Corby, only about BSC.'

'Right,' I said, 'because we have to take out the capacity, which does not justify further investment.'

The first National Steel Conference came next, the only tangible outcome of the Steel Contract. It was attended by 140 people and was opened by Bob. Frank Holloway, the financial director, described the past year, and Bill Sirs then went into a long political speech whose content was really quite wrong. I responded, saying that I was happier about BSC than before, because all the points just made by Bill Sirs were capable of solution by joint consultation and that was the way we would go about it. Throughout there were facts and questions, but the real interest came when we discussed absenteeism and overtime!

After the summing up, Bill Sirs said to me, 'You have been able to get your point of view across, and that is a good thing.'

We planned to repeat this conference when the whole situation got clearer.

187

A few days later we went to Shotton and met the local councils and Trade Unions. Those who represented the workforce were resigned to closure, which had hung over them for so long, and were prepared to take their money and go. The Councillors were, I noted, 'in a terrible state,' moaning about unemployment. There was never any hard, rude speaking; it was sad and unhappy. We saw Brits faced with an inevitable situation ('sitiation,' we always say in BSC) and being unable to mount a viable counter argument. The meetings seemed to go fairly well. No-one can say the BSC did not communicate.

I noted that it was 'a month since 'Jaguar' had failed and the cash limit imposed. These things have had an astounding effect and gone right the way through. There is a new spirit and the profit/loss reporting centres are drawing together, focussing on performance, efficiency and profit. If you want to turn a great elephant like BSC round 45° you have to try to get 90° in the hope that you finish up at 45°.'

July finished with a BSC board which was able to draw together all the different strands of our work. On the face of it all the activity of reorganisation, cash limits and closures had settled down, but I feared that trade union resentment smouldered beneath the surface and I was sure Government was looking for a replacement as chairman of BSC. A good feature was the close co-operation between the 'Big Four' at BSC, the foundation of our hopes for future success. A joke feature was a Neddy meeting, following Joseph's description of 'the six poisons in the British system,' one of which was the Trade Unions poisoning British industry. The 'Neddy Six' trade unionists fairly pitched into Joseph, who responded, 'Oh well, I've said it many times before.'

'Well, don't say it again,' said Len Murray, General Secretary of the TUC.

Overall I didn't think the Government or the BSC board or management would let us down, but BSC was going to have very great problems with the unions. Bill Sirs was 'lost' to us, joining other trades union leaders in opposition to Government policy and thus to plant closures.

By September we were at it again, considering the closure of a small works, Normanby Park near Scunthorpe, and of Consett near Durham and even of Llanwern in South Wales. Since 1973 costs had multiplied three times, but prices only twice and we were still miles from break-even. We had to take a hard tough line, but as we did not have the money, what else could we do?

I got into a bit of trouble by telling managers 'to be bastards to bad workers.' I had seen that sins of omission were a habit in BSC and that managers tended to forgive them for fear of rousing the wrath of the Unions, who took the line that the man on the shop floor was always right and that the manager was always wrong. We called this 'the Union buggeration factor.' Labour MPs in support of the Unions shouted for my removal and there were some witty and relevant cartoons in the papers. The BSC management got the message and saw that unless we were tough on what are now called 'sloppy procedures and practices' we would never get back full control of our business. I suppose I was somewhat ahead of the times, but I was driven there by the urgency of our commercial and financial position, which was not improving but deteriorating.

By mid-September 1979 it was certain that, due mainly to the cost/price squeeze, we would not get to break-even by March 1980. All our costs were rising: coal, oil, transport, electricity and, of course, the cost of labour were shooting up in the inflationary atmosphere and we could not pass these costs on to customers who would buy foreign steel instead of British steel. Already the price of British Steel was the highest in Europe. We reckoned we would lose £125 million in the last three months of the current year and over £200 million in the following year. We would have to come off the break-even target, perhaps when we announced the half year's results in November. We had a very nasty situation in front of us.

If finance was bad, so was production. The continuous steel caster at Teesside had broken down. Ravenscraig steel output was well down due to the inter-union dispute at the Hunterston ore terminal, and when we compared ourselves with the other major steel companies in the world, despite our enormous investments during the last five years we were not getting value for money and we came out at the bottom of the list. The most sinister feature was that BSC was making less steel per man than any other big producer. We knew what that meant - we employed too many people. But how could we get the numbers down, apart from closures, without precipitating a strike which would maximise all the difficulties? I asked managing directors what were the ideal manning levels at their plants, but they turned aside, saying it was too dangerous even to calculate because the enquiry would leak out and bring their plants to a standstill: so strong were the unions then.

Conventional means would not get us out of the mess and I noted, 'We shall have to apply shock treatment. If we closed a major works it would apply a tremendous shock to the whole system but how could we then provide steel for 'tubes' at Corby and for 'coatings' at Shotton? Credibility would join viability and technicality as a major problem.'

The omens were not good for Margaret Thatcher's proposed visit to light the new big blast furnace at Redcar, or for our next meeting with Joseph. I noted that Michael Edwardes at British Leyland is in the same bind, closing 12 factories and making 25,000 people redundant. We are both caught by rising costs, falling demand and the strong £ sterling. But the real fault was overmanning and poor performance. Davignon told me the French and Italians had the same problems as BSC, but the Dutch, Belgians and Germans had moved up towards profit.

On 20 September we called off the Prime Minister's proposed visit to Redcar because the blast furnace was not ready. We saw the loss for August, £45 million, but none of the managing directors wanted to give up the target of break-even by next March. They showed me estimates of loss as low as £8 million for the month of March - I was entirely sceptical, unless the losses of plants scheduled to be closed were excluded from the calculation. Could I get Joseph to agree to that?

In the following week, on 27 September 1979, I met Joseph alone. He seemed very sick, with blotches all over his face, shielding his eyes and speaking in a very nervous and jerky way. He said he saw the need for management change in BSC and would go along with whatever the Board wanted, but he could not intervene because he had no powers and anyway intervention was not his philosophy. I felt very sorry for him, but reminded him that shareholders do have to be involved in major management problems, which require shareholders' resolutions. 'No,' he said 'I don't accept that. It may be so, but I cannot do it.'

'We had been considering a man,' I said, 'who could be very valuable to BSC. What will you do if he says he will come?'

'I will ask you to come over and talk about it,' said Joseph.

'What would you say to me?' I asked.

'That would depend on circumstances,' he replied.

'It is you who are ultimately responsible for this vast business, and if you say that top management is nothing to do with you, you are backing out of your responsibilities,' I said. Poor chap, he was in a very sick state and just talked about his philosophy.

We met again in the afternoon and Joseph looked even sicker. He said he had not read the papers. We said the profitable works would make £130 million next year; we estimated that the other plants would lose £175 million. We wanted him to finance those intended to be closed next year.

'No,' said Joseph, 'you are just asking for more money. I don't have it. Nobody has any more money.'

'What happens if we run out of money, which we could well

191

do?' we asked.

'You will just have to exist. What is your core business? Let me have a note on that,' he said.

On the way out he said to me, 'What is really worrying me is the underlying direction of the economy.'

I recount these conversations as I recorded them, because of the intense frustration they caused at a time when we needed professional understanding, as one would get from big shareholders or bankers. I do not believe that professional politicians are the right people to deal with these situations - Civil Servants would be better; a Quango set up for the purpose would be better still.

That night we put the state of the game to all the main board directors at an informal dinner meeting. The non-executives, businessmen of long experience, were very critical of the whole situation, but did not have anything constructive to suggest. The worker directors said, 'If we put this to the unions, they would have to call a strike throughout the steel industry.'

'What good would that do?' we asked.

'The union leaders would not be able to help themselves; they would just have to call a strike to keep their jobs.'

This was getting out of hand and I said, 'Well, if any of you has no stomach for this fight, now is the time to leave the Board.'

Perhaps that was a mistake and Jack Tweddle, one of the best of the worker-directors, blew up and said he had never been so insulted because he had never shirked a fight in all his life. I apologised and they promised to be with us when we came up to confrontation with the unions over closures, redundancies and pay.

I warned Joseph next day that we might well be faced with a steel strike, joined perhaps by other unions, such as the dockers, which might bring the country close to standstill. It was clear that Joseph was not going to bail us out and that the 'Big Four' at BSC would just have to pick our way forward as best we could, step by step, carrying an enormous weight of responsibility, greater than ever before.

The steel workers' pay round was about to begin and instead of giving it all in a flat percentage increase to everyone, we intended to say there was very little money available for the percentage rise and anything more had to be earned by productivity at plant level. This was revolutionary in BSC and, it was feared, would produce a great explosion. None of this was helped by the top people's pay review body awarding me a 22% pay rise after three years of no increase. I tried to refuse but I was begged to accept to facilitate finding my successor! In the event he required rather more than that.

I can remember a great sense of foreboding at this time. All round Britain there were plants and businesses closing down, some temporarily, some permanently - ITV, The Times, Rolls-Royce, ship builders and engineering companies. I went down the Clyde and there was practically no activity there of any kind. Gormley of the Miners Union called for a day's strike each week. Callaghan was fighting for his political life at the Labour party conference. Lord Mountbatten was killed by an IRA bomb. Iran took the first American hostages. Oil prices doubled, increasing inflation and depressing industrial output in Britain. Only Seb Coe cheered us by setting three middle-distance running records.

We were wondering, I noted, whether Margaret Thatcher could hold on to her policies or whether she would have to do a U-turn like Ted Heath. 'For the moment,' I wrote, 'the Tories are sitting tight, but Adam Butler, one of Joseph's ministers, admitted to me that if there were compelling reasons, the money to keep BSC going would be found.' Following my 'be bastards to bad workers' speech, production of steel in the preceding week was a record. This was followed by a visit to Port Talbot, where I banged on about four policies:

* Joint consultation
* Cuddle the customer

* Decentralise as far as you can go
* Good performance.

The Chairman of the Works Council said they now understood exactly what had to be done and would take it to the shop floor. I would not have got that response two years earlier.

On 26 October we did in fact lay the foundation for the subsequent strike. The unions had asked for 20% pay rise without strings; we decided to offer 2% for consolidation of a previously earned bonus, plus whatever works directors could concede for productivity with a maximum of 10%, after joint consultation locally. This formula, which was honed and refined in practice, cut across all BSC and ISTC tradition. Works directors would only improve on the 2% consolidation if they could see an advantage by reducing the number of men they employed, or by improving productivity in other ways. The General Secretary of the ISTC, Bill Sirs, could negotiate round the consolidation figure, but the bigger part of the pay package would be negotiated locally, not nationally. One of the main functions of the Union's General Secretary was thus removed and we knew he and his Executive Committee would fight like tigers to retain it. The BSC management, including the worker-directors, came to the conclusion that we had to try this formula; there was no alternative as we did not have the money to pay a national claim of any size. We decided that if we were taken to arbitration and told to pay more nationally, we would refuse on the grounds that we didn't have the money; then BSC would grind to a standstill. We were playing for high stakes.

I noted that as the winter began and I moved into my last year at steel the trading conditions were getting worse again. We found the home market for steel shrinking and we would have to reduce capacity by at least another million tons. The price of electricity and oil and the cost of labour were mounting. I had to see the Prime Minister and describe the situation; she saw the difficulties but was not sympathetic. Bill Sirs launched into a diatribe against me for not communicating with him - I listed four recent occasions when we had spent the day together. Carey told me he had been unable to recruit a successor for either Bob or me. This opened a dreadful prospect as I moved towards my 68th birthday.

'What,' asked Carey, 'do you really feel BSC needs?' 'Above all,' I replied 'it needs shock, continuous pressure and change, through a new chairman.'

And that is what happened.

It seemed to me at the time that we were living in what Geoffrey Howe called 'a dreamland'. I met most senior ministers at a reception for Chairman Hua of China. Margaret Thatcher I saw as spry, quick, alert, healthy, strong, powerful. Poor Keith Joseph was a little shadow of a man, darting about, avoiding eyes and not looking up. Peter Carrington looked tired after negotiating the necessary, but unpopular, Rhodesian settlement. Geoffrey Howe seemed very confident and quiet, feeling the abolition of exchange controls in Britain, just announced, was absolutely right. I was surprised to find what a good reception and sense of identity I found with ministers at that time.

By the beginning of November the CBI predicted that we were just entering the worst recession for many years. BSC was on collision course with the unions, particularly over the closure of Corby. At Shotton opposition to closure had died down and the terms of severance had been agreed. The closure of Consett was just coming up. I wrote, 'This will be the story of a strike we tried to avert. We have had masses of consultation but when the emotions and ambitions of the Unions are aroused, no amount of consultation can overcome it. Michael Edwardes at British Leyland is also asking whether consultation and participation is really worthwhile. He says the workforce voted for his organisation plan, but 98% of the shop stewards voted *against*.' My own feeling at BSC was that our workforce was willing to go along with us and that maybe we would have to put that to the test.

Almost every day a new event created new problems for BSC. On 20 November the miners settled for a 20% pay rise and the Prime Minister congratulated them on their moderation. We came to think we should 'slim line' both Port Talbot and Llanwern, by mothballing half of the production of each works, which would probably result in overkill, but that was what we had to have. There was some good news. The Steel Committee of the TUC (TUCSICC) refused to back Bill Sirs plan for confrontation, overtime ban and non-cooperation with BSC, but I feared this would prove temporary. We got the big new blast furnace at Redcar lit and the inter-union dispute at Hunterston was at last settled. *The Times* was back in publication after being 'out' for many months. José launched the BSC ore carrier 'Ravenscraig' in Belfast. *The Guardian* said I was British industry's most tormented leader. There was nothing to look forward to and one just had to be deeply dug in, doing one's duty as one saw it.

We knew we had to take out another five million tons of steel-making capacity - $2\frac{1}{2}$m in Wales, 1m at Corby, 1m at Consett and the rest at Scunthorpe. The worker-directors, knowing everything, were very determined that BSC had now to move to what they called 'the last bastion.' They told me that if I could guarantee that this would be the end of closures, the men would go along with it. I could not guarantee, because there were so many external uncertainties; British Leyland was on strike (after the sacking of the shop steward Red Robbo) and if that company went down, we should have to cut production again. These excellent men felt a heavy burden, but they knew they had to go through with it and realised that they could not represent just their own sectional interest; fortunately they all, except one, came from ongoing plants. They refused to take orders from their union or to say what Bill Sirs wanted them to say. This was confirmation of the value of worker-directors.

On 30 November we had to announce the loss of £145 million at the half year, with the expectation that losses in the second half year would be larger still. The target of break-even by March 1980 had to be abandoned. Since 1975 BSC had lost £1 billion. The collapse in demand for steel had created the need for further plant closures and heavy redundancies. 'There are more terrible years in front of us.' I said. 'Home demand is likely to fall by another 1 million tons and we are seeking consultation with the unions in steel to manage this situation, which is very, very serious. *The Times* wrote, 'BSC is being carried downward on a tide of adversity,' and I responded in a letter to the Editor:

* In the last two years BSC has reduced its workforce by 25,000.
* We have given notice of closure of steel making at Corby and at Shotton.
* We have put new plant, costing £800 million, into production at international manning levels.
* We have held our home market share at 55% against increased competition.
* We are moving to a 'core' which we can defend with confidence.

I had a talk with Joseph and rubbed in: 'The most terrifying thought is that politicians might pull the rug out from under us.'

'I promise not to do that and I am pleased with the way you all are grasping the nettle. How is Bob handling the unions?' he asked.

'Very well,' I said. 'He is the only person who could do that and he just might bring it off.'

'Right,' said Joseph. 'I shall back you to the hilt.' He did.

On 4 December Bill Sirs publicly rejected our pay offer of 2% plus local productivity payments of up to 10%. He said it was 'ridiculous' and 'highly insulting,' and that the unions were 'livid' at the 'miserable' offer. On 8 December a total steel strike at all BSC works was called for 2 January 1980, the first such action since 1926. We responded, saying it was tragedy and the only winners would be our overseas competitors. The *Sunday Times* ran the BSC story under the headline 'Is this the end for steel?' All Bill Sirs could say was that his members would have to give up every fifth pint of beer. I diaried, 'Having a strike, which I hope we can defeat, may sharpen the whole management and make our victory secure.'

On 14 December Bill Sirs and his President came to see Bob, David Grieves and myself. Bill disagreed with our analysis and actions, which he said were all due to my ignorance of the steel industry. On pay he said the 'up to 10%' was no good to his members, who could not be sure of getting it, so it was pie in the sky and he had discarded it. Bill had to preserve himself and his union. We had to preserve the BSC. I did not feel or sense any animosity at this meeting. In the evening there was a fearful debate in Parliament on steel, which aroused deep passion, and the Speaker had to intervene on several occasions, but the Government had a majority of 57. Next day The *Daily Mirror* took my side and the *Financial Times* took Bill Sirs' side. We were both at work on hearts and minds.

On 19 December I attended a dinner at the Bank of England, given by the Governor, Gordon Richardson, at one time my chairman at Schroders. The chairmen of all the nationalised industries were present. Most of them were fat cats putting up their prices in the home markets. I lay low at first but when Gordon turned to me, I said 'Mr Governor, I am sitting among my natural enemies. You, Mr. Governor, have put up base rate to 17% and you hold the £ sterling at $2.20. The rest of you are charging me more and more for electricity, gas, coal, rail and GPO services. I cannot pass on any of these charges in the face of international competition, effective here in Britain. All I can do is shrink the business and give nothing for nothing to our workforce. None of the rest of you are doing it. We are the people who cannot pass the buck.' Gordon did not look best pleased.

Just to make things easier, the IRA sent me a parcel bomb from Brussels to our home at Blacknest. It was on the living room table with our grandchildren all round. José, with some heaven-sent instinct, was suspicious and carried it out into the garden and rang the police, who came at once and safely defused the bomb. José's presence of mind certainly saved our family that day and she had a wonderful reception on TV and in the press next day. Her great qualities came to the fore, but she greatly resented the total press invasion of our privacy which this event caused.

On the next day we met with Len Murray and the 14 General Secretaries of the unions in steel. We had all our team and Bob led for us. Bob offered to raise the 2% to 5% if the guaranteed working week payments were suspended, but this was howled down.

Bill Sirs says in his book that Bob and I were at loggerheads at this meeting. I think Bob feared that I was taking over conduct of the negotiation from him... not so. Len Murray said we should raise the 2% to 10%, but we could not possibly do that. Len did advise the unions to stop and think again, but the ISTC people had worked themselves up into a great state. We parted at 6.30pm on the Friday before Christmas with heavy hearts.

Just before Christmas Len Murray proposed to Government, through the Civil Service, that we should pay 10% basic plus 10% for productivity. That evening I took Christopher with me to see Joseph at his London house; Joseph was perfectly steady, whatever he may have been before. When Jim Prior (Minister for Employment) rang up, Joseph very firmly shut him up. I asked Joseph if he was going to pull the rug out, after all. Joseph said, 'No. Go ahead with what you think is best, in complete confidence. Do you think you can stop the strike?'

'Very unlikely,' I replied. 'In the past there have been many attempts to buy off trouble, and they have always made things worse.' We left Joseph, feeling safer, but all knew that many

Ministers were very unwilling to face a steel strike.

Christmas Eve 1979 was given up to a BSC Board meeting and members were alarmed about the meeting with Joseph the night before. To be honest, the worker-directors were the most steadfast. Len Murray rang to propose further negotiations. Len, plus the 14, came round to BSC to meet the Board. There was a good debate between the two sides. The trade unionists wanted to get the flat rate up from 2% to 8%. Murray said the 14 must be shown to have got something out of BSC which was not previously on offer. So we met again on 28 December, which was a long, sad day; we made some technical concessions and the unions considered them for a couple of hours. Then the unions came back and said our concessions were not enough and that there would now certainly be a strike.

The next two days were devoted to efforts in the media to get our story across; there was not much union response. Len Murray said it was a one-man strike which Bill Sirs had engineered and that he must be left to sweat it out. From Margaret Thatcher came great congratulations to Bob and myself, and a promise of 100% support in our search for viability and competitiveness.

The changes in political economy which came with Thatcher's government had begun to take sharp effect and nowhere more so than in the nationalised industries. Steel had been nationalised, denationalised and then renationalised. The unions in steel had become very strong and for them strength meant numbers. The post war policy of full employment had given them the excuse to build up those numbers and the shortage of steel, which lasted till the mid-seventies, had enabled the companies to pay for what can only be called gross overmanning. This happened in most countries in Europe and in America, but not in Japan.

As we saw it in steel in 1979, the first inherited policy casualty was full employment, a sacred cow since World War II. Thatcher's government was prepared to see unemployment rise to unprecedented levels in order to achieve their other objectives.

Secondly, the government was reflecting a national mood, being utterly fed up with the 'over mighty' attitude of the unions. Thatcher refused to do deals with them over beer and sandwiches in Number 10, and in their industrial disputes they lost all government sympathy. They first learned that in two cases - British Leyland and British Steel. Anti-union legislation was to follow.

The third policy change came with the end of 'financial incontinence,' a phrase of Joseph's which described a condition which had become widespread. Another way of describing it was a decision not to 'buy your way out of trouble,' a practice which started to come to an end with Thatcher.

The fourth change was the attempted withdrawal of government intervention, financial or otherwise, from every area of national life. That tooth was very deep rooted and more difficult to extract.

The fifth change was that the market must be allowed to solve all problems. The 'invisible hand' of competition, so called by Adam Smith in 1766, was considered to be a better guide to economic success than human planning, which had proved very faulty.

The sixth change was that enterprise was to be encouraged by cutting the rates of taxation by deregulation, where possible, by freeing capital markets, by reducing industrial subsidies, by abandoning incomes policies and by reducing inflation.

David Henderson, of OEC called this 'a blitz on intermediate sources of authority between the state and the individual.' Caught in the blitz were unions, local authorities, employers' associations, universities and the Church. You have also to add in the nationalised industries. Certainly, both the unions and the employers in steel were caught in this blitz. The unions were mortally wounded; the employers knew the blitz was necessary, so they adjusted to it and survived. In steel, the critical year was 1980.

CHAPTER 11

STEEL STRIKE, JANUARY-APRIL 1980

'We'll cripple the country,' said Bill Sirs.

'There is no more money,' said Keith Joseph.

'There is more money but it has to be earned,' said Bob Scholey.

'I will not recall Parliament,' said Margaret Thatcher.

'A telephone call would get us back into discussion,' I said.

Bill Sirs replied, 'Unless there is more money on the table, there is nothing to talk about.'

'A fight to the finish,' screamed the *Sheffield Morning Tele-graph*.

BSC's offer was a bonus consolidation of 2% plus up to 10% to be earned by increased productivity, negotiated at plant level. How could we get the productivity deal across?

The New Year of 1980 began thus. On 1 January both Margaret Thatcher and Keith Joseph on TV made what was taken to be a declaration of war on the steel unions and the word got around, quite wrongly, that the Government wanted this strike to make an example of the unions. I believe that all the Government wanted was to stop inflationary wage payments and 'financial incontinence' by nationalised industries. If that led to a strike, of which I had warned Joseph, it was just too bad, but I could not see that the Government had made any preparations for it. On 2nd January the unions in steel, led by ISTC, called out all their members working in BSC on an indefinite, national strike. My diary noted, 'The only way we are going to get a win here is by convincing the men that there is more money to be got locally by improved performance and that they would do better to go for that than to follow this strike.' The employee-directors were helpful at a meeting on 4 January, saying the men were used to the national pay round and were unaccustomed to local productivity deals, which would take more time to get across.

During the next days there were a number of feelers put out by the unions. Len Murray tried to get the big unions to restrain Bill Sirs, but he was on 'a high;' he did however suggest that the 10% for productivity should be split into 5% now and 5% when earned. That, of course, was exactly what we did not want, first because it cost more of our precious cash and second because the extra productivity was what we wanted more than anything else. Len Murray and the other General Secretaries came round to see us and it was clear that they wanted 13% flat now, because that was the increase they had decided they wanted for all trade unionists in Britain. Both sides agreed to say nothing to the press, but Bill Sirs roared out, 'We have got them up to 8% and we are doing well.' I rang Murray who was furious with Sirs, and Murray apologised, but the damage had been done. Thatcher did not help by saying on TV, 'I don't like the way British Steel and the unions sit in their trenches and growl at one another.' I diaried that Government had tried to intervene and tell us what to do, but we had not done it and their interference had not been effective.

By 7 January the BSC offer was 8% across the board for a good nationally-agreed productivity agreement, plus a minimum of 4% for extra productivity, agreed at plant level. All day we wrangled round this with the unions, who put up a variety of deals, always shirking the idea of more pay only when earned, which they called 'pennies from heaven.' At the end of that day the steel unions, ISTC and NUB, turned our offer down and there was nothing left to talk about, so we broke off. Bob was excellent on the 8 o'clock news next morning and the propaganda war continued.

My diary noted, 'This is a terrible position to be in... maybe we are coming up to the day of confrontation. I thought it would be British Leyland which would start it all off, but it has turned out to be us... an unenviable and unhappy position... but we must make our case as widely known as possible, so that this process of change from flat to productivity payments does eventually come to be accepted.' The union pickets were out for the first time and I had to remonstrate with the worker-director, who had been active on the picket lines in Sheffield before coming to the board meeting. He felt the two roles were compatible, but he gave up being the union's public relations adviser!

On 8 January I wrote, 'The two sides are drawing apart now. There are four weeks steel stocks in most businesses, but the strike could last a great deal longer. There is now a good deal of criticism of management, being too optimistic in setting 'break-even by March' as a target. But the Government seems to be firmly behind us. *The Times* is busy criticising both sides.'

On 10 January there was a Neddy meeting chaired by the Prime Minister. The Neddy six trade union leaders took the first opportunity of telling the Prime Minister how wrong she was not to accept responsibility for the nationalised industries and that this was bad and irresponsible. She replied, 'I am as sorry as anyone that the talks have broken down. I hope they can be resumed. There are well-established institutions for negotiations. Next question.' That did not stop Duffy of the Engineers' union shouting across the room at me, 'That's the man over there who ought to pay people more.'

I diaried that day, 'The trouble is that when a worker or a union feels frustrated, or angry, or wants to make a fuss, all he can do is to go on strike and that does harm to everybody. We do have a most senseless system. Perhaps out of this something sensible will come.'

The *Daily Mail* devoted its middle page to an interview with Bill Sirs and me on 11 January. Bill Sirs was seen every night, smartly dressed and groomed, quiet voice never rising to accusations. The article said, 'He plots for the nation - how his union can knock out a large slice of British Industry by stopping steel going to the factories. He is like a doctor telling people they have only so much longer to live if they don't take their medicine.' Sirs had grown into someone who wanted the good life for everyone, especially for those who worked. There was nothing left-wing about his expensive two-garage house in Hatfield, where he ran early in the morning and saw the lights go on in the homes of the stockbrokers who were his neighbours and who liked him for what he was. His grown-up family respected him. His dream was a great yacht in a marina, now he had only a *Mirror* yacht stored up somewhere. He was not the sort of man you would expect to find leading something so deadly. Outside was a chauffeur-driven Rover.

No smile was ever on his face. There was only one side to his character. 'What we are seeing now,' he said, 'is union solidarity the like of which is unknown in modern times - it's fantastic. Steel is a dangerous business. Last year £2m million was paid out in compensation for accidents. These boys are being asked to take a $15\frac{1}{2}\%$ cut in their living standards. They are being asked to buy five eggs instead of six. But when it comes to paying rent they have to pay up all the way. The steel workers have been picked out by Government for a low wage rise. If I had tried to persuade my people to compromise on a wage rise which is practically nothing, I would have lost my credibility. What it all means is that we are being asked to give up tens of thousands of jobs and eventually get nearly nothing for it.'

There would not be time for a game of squash that night. Fit as he was, Bill Sirs was beginning to look tired. 'I try to think,' he said 'of poor old Charles Villiers. He's naive, you know, not wicked. It's the people around him who are doing this. Charles doesn't even know what day it is.'

The *Daily Mail* then turned on me. 'It's tempting to cast Villiers as the Cavalier with Militant Commoner Sirs as the

Roundhead, but the analogy breaks down on the detail. Charles drives his own Ford Escort and winces at the word chauffeur. He asks for the duty driver. He comes over on TV as often as Sirs, but as the Archetypal Boss... pinstriped, plummy, curiously dated, a leaner, tougher cousin of Captain Mainwaring of Dad's Army. Tough he is, but not rooted in the past, despite union sneers. "I'm trying," he says, "in my little way, to make Britain better. By better I mean more understanding, more clever, more successful, richer." Sir Charles seems very much the Grenadier Guards Colonel who had had a "good war" - Dunkirk, parachuting into Yugoslavia, getting half his face shot away.

'He is a life-long Tory radical who has never voted Labour but was given a medal by Tito, a Communist dictator. He is a proud man in his understated way. He could have fled the present storm by refusing to extend his chairmanship of what he calls the "steel." "I was brought up on duty and service," he says "and I'm much too old to give them up. I'm an optimist; what we're trying to do can be done. Maybe like Moses I'll never see the Promised Land."

'Sir Charles has an old-fashioned hatred of throwing good money after bad. "It isn't more money that's needed, it's more efficiency." Villiers won't play the traditional union game - "beer and sandwich peace parties at Number 10 do no industry any good in the end." In fact Villiers is far more of a stubborn puritan than the flamboyantly down to earth Bill Sirs. "I'm sure," he says, "the workforce knows that we can't go on in the old way. But they are reluctant to take the initiative. Someone has to take the hard decisions for them." He looks down at his blotter and murmurs without regret, "It just happens to be me."'

It was about that time that I began to feel doubtful about winning the propaganda battle for hearts and minds. Bill and I were on Panorama together and I was told that Bill came off second best, but one never knows. I had a long session on Granada TV with Kaufman, which went well, and Bill's habit of telling half-truths was exposed. The next morning Bob had an excellent letter in *The Times* which compared BSC's case with the union's case very objectively. But somehow people were not convinced that we were right to challenge the old habits.

The Times asked Bill Sirs and me a number of questions:

Q1. Is this strike due to failure of presentation or to deep seated reasons? Bill answered, 'You have to bear in mind what has been happening over plant closures and the injustices we had to face. We just could not let these things happen. There was a feeling of frustration that BSC thought we were insignificant.' I answered, 'The strike is due to one fundamental deep-seated reason: that is, the unwillingness of the unions to accept BSC's dire financial situation. We should have been negotiating improvements in performance rather than improvements in pay.'

Q2. What kind of collective bargaining should be adopted? Bill answered, 'BSC tried to change the system. Our system is a model for other industries. We have many decades of hard bargaining and peaceful negotiations. The system should not be changed.' I answered, 'BSC needs collective bargaining at national and local level, allowing local pro-ductivity bargaining to happen on a multi-union basis. The system must take account of the financial circumstances.'

Q3. Can unions and management resolve this dispute? Bill answered, 'I think it will require third-party intervention.' I answered, 'The dispute should settle at a level which will allow BSC to get to viability by improving efficiency and costs. We do not want intervention which would upset that process.'

Q4. What kind and size of steel industry shall we get? Bill answered, 'Money was easily available in 1972. They were throwing it around like confetti. Now they are ruining us, sheltering behind an iron hard government.' I answered, 'There is a limit to taxpayers' patience. Funds for BSC can only be justified if both management and workforce are committed to viability through international competitiveness.'

All this time an emotional feeling was growing that the unions had been wrongly penalised for matters which were not their fault, but were largely due to management mistakes and government intervention in the past. The unions were the underdogs and had been ignored and maltreated, and what could they do but strike? Of course, there was something in this, but the fact remained that we were overmanned and had too much capacity and were in danger of being driven out of the market; but that was not a very exciting argument to put to the man or woman in the street. Besides, there was more bad news to come.

The executive of BSC had started to concentrate on the problem of too much steel capacity in South Wales. Llanwern and Port Talbot employed 22,000 people and made 5 million tons of steel a year, of which we could only sell a half. Either we closed one of the plants or reduced the output of each by one half under a plan we called 'Slim-line,' worked out by Peter Allen, our excellent managing director for Wales. Any plan would be bitterly resisted. It would be extremely difficult - 11,000 men made redundant - but as both works were on strike, we had the opportunity to decide how we would eventually restart steel making there. We put it to Nicholas Edwards, the Secretary of State for Wales. He gave us good support in this and in the steel debate. The BSC board approved 'Slim-line,' but we were heavily criticised in the Parliamentary debate. Joseph was strong on our line, but Prior (at the Department of Employment) was not. 'Oh, well, you are bound to settle some day; settle now and get it out of the way,' was his Department's line. We feared Thatcher would settle for the 'quiet life brigade.'

We went to see Jim Prior in his office, for breakfast on 18 January. Joseph was present. I noted Prior's words, 'You really must settle. I know you think I am an old softie and that my department is wet, but you won't get all you want and you must settle this week.' Joseph then took me by the elbow and marched me to a corner where he said, 'You must hold out... This is the really important issue... BSC must not weaken... I will support you to the hilt and I agree with all you have done so far.' So there was the government split. Many Ministers agreed with Prior, who was trying to negotiate a moderate Trade Union bill with the TUC.

The BSC board had no intention of weakening. We were meeting with the conciliatory service, ACAS, but they were taking the teeth out of everything and we would be left with grey words and just go on as before. Bob and I got very anxious and felt we had only Joseph for firm support. The Prime Minister was going to see Bill Sirs and Hector Smith; we feared beer and sandwiches again.

On 20 January Brian Walden in 'Weekend World' had Keith Joseph, Bill Sirs and me for a long, carefully prepared session. It came out pretty pro-Bill. I was presented as a purple faced bully, but Joseph was firm and fine. I had a sense of negotiations going on all over the place, trying to find a formula for getting the steel men back to work, without the improvements we had staked all to get.

On 22 January the Prime Minister was to see Bill Sirs and Hector Smith in the morning and Bob and me in the afternoon. This looked like the approach to a watershed. We had a single sheet of brief for the PM at Number 10 by 9.30 a.m. that day. Bill Sirs described his meeting that morning in social terms - the Prime Minister's dress, the furniture at Number 10, the tea and Joseph taking honey in it instead of sugar. He says she was reasonably well briefed and was surprised to hear that Consett was 'condemned to total closure.' He thought the PM had 'intervened behind the scenes to prevent payments being made to steel workers.' Joseph had said there would be no more money for wage increases for steel workers, but in the end 'we did win more and I would like to think our meeting with Mrs Thatcher had some slight impact.'

Bob and I and Christopher were met by the PM at the door of the Cabinet room where we sat down facing her across the table. She was flanked by Joseph and Prior and her Secretary Lankester, a friend of Christopher's. The last time I had sat there was with Frank Kearton, asking Harold Wilson and Roy Jenkins for more money for the IRC. This time the PM pressed hard on how we were going to spend the £450 million previously made available. We showed that it was, in fact, already overcommitted to investment, redundancy payments and trading losses. I rubbed in that there would also be a loss in the following year, for which Government had made no provision. Joseph was very strong in support throughout. The PM asked excellent questions which Bob and I were able to answer confidently and we felt we had established some rapport with her. No doubt Bill Sirs and Hector Smith felt the same, because she said to us, 'You must talk the same language as Mr Sirs.'

'No, Prime Minister,' I said, 'we cannot do that.'

'Why not?' she asked.

'Because we talk about productivity, which is a word Mr Sirs won't use.'

'I see,' she said. 'Well, what should I do?'

Prior then intervened and said, 'We have to think about the damage you are doing to the whole economy and the wider implications of running out of steel and the harm that is being done to industrial relations and all that sort of thing.

The PM shut Prior up by saying, 'Don't you tell Charles how to run his business or he will tell you how to run yours.'

'He does that already,' said Prior, sourly.

The meeting finished by Joseph saying, 'Prime Minister, I think we have to be very grateful to Charles and Bob for the enormous amount of difficult work that they have done in the past three years.' The PM appeared to endorse that heartily.

Bob and I were very reassured by that meeting. The PM had obviously taken the side of Joseph and rejected Prior. If we could avoid silly mistakes and slipping on banana skins we would certainly win the strike, but we thought it would go on for many weeks to come. Bill had been to a meeting in Sheffield with Scargill of the miners' union, who had had a rapturous welcome. Bill had been coolly received, which he hated, and we felt he would harden his position to get popularity.

There was still plenty of steel about in the economy, and Bill's attempt to call out the steel workers in the private sector was very unpopular. He was under more pressure than we were. Geoff Owen and Malcolm Rutherford from the *Financial Times* came to see us and we gave them the single sheet brief we had given the PM. They were rather impressed and we hoped they would use it, because our arguments would come better from the *FT* than from us. Next day I had to address the Grand Council of the CBI; Bob and Gordon Sambrook spoke too and I noted, 'The whole affair was quite a success.' There were many side meetings at this time with Len Murray, the ACAS people and the Steel Craftsmen, many of whom wanted to settle. Another kerfuffle had arisen because the private sector steel bosses tried to get an injunction to stop ISTC calling out their workers on strike. Lord Denning, always a maverick, granted the injunction, but the ISTC had appealed against it. Bill Sirs refused to obey Denning and called out the private sector steel workers. He went to a meeting in Wales and burst into tears saying that he could go to prison as a martyr for the whole working class. All this was very distracting, but the major problem gnawing at me all the time was that BSC was rapidly running out of cash and that we were effectively bankrupt. To make things worse, the Law Lords overruled Denning, so the ISTC could now call out on strike their members in the private sector of steel making. Bill did not really want to do this, but he was overruled by his Executive Committee, who were very militant and by then were running the strike.

There were endless interruptions to this job. One of the

211

men who shredded discarded papers of the BSC started reading them and decided to pass them on to Granada TV who made a film for 'World in Action' showing BSC in a totally inaccurate way. I went to Manchester to comment live on the film, not having seen it beforehand. Fortunately for me the presenter was a young man who knew little about steel or the strike and I was able to put him down at the beginning, so that he was barely able to finish his programme. Granada asked me to have a second innings. No thanks!

Next day Tiny Rowland, whose company Lonrho owned a small steel works, Hadfields in Sheffield, marched into my office saying 'You are responsible for my losing money and I demand you have my man, Derek Norton, as 'a softener' on your negotiating committee.'

'First,' I said, 'we are not responsible for your losses. If the ISTC calls out your men that is not our fault. Second, we don't need a softener, but a hardener.' We had a very angry meeting and Rowland stalked out saying to the Press: 'Villiers is quite impossible.'

There were pickets on the door of our office and José drove me there in her little car which was not spotted till I got out and went in. The pickets then cheered José whom they knew from her many visits to steel works.

José got a lot of excellent coverage at this time. 'Lady Lifeline' they called her, for her work in the Belgian resistance movement, organising the escape of British airmen who were shot down over Europe. She couldn't bear to watch the TV serial Secret Army: 'It was so painfully real and brought back such distressing memories.' She was described as the 'lady with the secret past.'

On 15 February we heard of the 'terrible time Keith Joseph had in Wales, where they pelted him with eggs and he could not get into the plants as he wanted.' I had to go to Teeside that day, to speak at the Cleveland Institute. Pickets from Consett were gathering there and the police were anxious about safety. There was a big crowd, shouting and throwing things. I got hard pears on the face and a woman poured a bucket of bad fish over the policemen who were trying to get me through the crowd.

Another woman came along behind with a brush and a pail of water to wash the policemen clean after the bad fish! The police got hold of me and rushed me through to the hall where I was to speak. I saw a delegation from Consett but I could offer them nothing except good severance terms, the same as elsewhere. By the time I finished my talk the pickets had gone. 'A noisy reception outside, a sad talk with the Consett people, whom I knew personally and a warm reception inside,' the diary says.

A few days later there were headlines like, 'Villiers to be retired;' 'Villiers to get the axe;' 'US Whizz kid sought for British Steel;' 'Villiers stays and gets a pat on the back.' It seems that Prior at a confidential meeting with reporters had told Routledge of *The Times* that Ministers had decided to sack me and hire an American industrialist.

I really was quite relaxed and said, 'I'll wait for the whistle to blow.'

The Prime Minister said in the Commons, 'There is no question of undermining the authority of the chairman of BSC. I take this opportunity to express my confidence in him and I hope he and the steel unions will get together to sort out this strike. We would be irresponsible if we were not already looking for someone to replace him.' James Callaghan replied, 'The position of the chairman of BSC must not be undermined. He and the union leaders have the job of settling this dispute and we have every confidence in him to do so. It is the job of Sir Charles and the BSC management to run the Corporation.' I asked Peter Thorneycroft, chairman of the Tory party, what to do. He said, 'Talk with Joseph and leave Number 10 to him'... good advice, which I took.

Next day I was due to talk at the Cambridge Union and the Corby lads came and threw stink bombs in the hall. I picked them up and threw them back and then finished my speech.

Back in London quite a stir arose about bungled government communications and about a Cabinet split between 'wets' and 'drys' on how to handle industrial strikes. The 'heavies,' *The Times* and *Telegraph* (but not *The Guardian*) have swung back to support of BSC. Indeed, John Junor of the *Sunday Express* asked me to write a piece for the following Sunday.

The PM weighed in on 25 February during an interview on Panorama with Robin Day, who asked her why she had not sacked Jim Prior for undermining the chairman of BSC in the midst of negotiations and a strike. 'You don't just sack a chap for one mistake,' she said. 'If you are going to kick up a fuss over one mistake... and it was a mistake... Jim Prior was very, very sorry indeed... he was very apologetic.' Prior said, 'I will be bloody careful in future.'

Prior was, of course, a dove over the steel strike, as were several of his Cabinet colleagues. The hawks were the PM herself, Joseph, Howe, Nott and perhaps Biffen, but that did not stop many trade union leaders saying that if the strike went on long enough the government were bound to find more money, as they always had done in the past. Joseph was excellent and I saw a great deal of him at that time. There were, of course, endless feelers being put out by authorised and unauthorised people. Bob and I often saw Bill Sirs on TV and radio programmes and we were friendly and perfectly comfortable together. None of us felt that the crunch of the strike had yet come, but it was obviously getting nearer and BSC's position was being undermined by Prior and Ministers who wanted a quiet life.

Just at this time Michael Edwardes of BL rang me up. 'Why don't you have a ballot,' he asked, 'about the question: Would you accept a ballot result?' We had had meetings with the Electoral Reform Society, but until then had judged it too early to move. But Michael's suggestion rang a bell in BSC minds and we had a ballot-about-a-ballot ready within the week. We told the TUC Steel Committee we were going to do it and nobody seemed to be against it except Bill Sirs, who advised his members to ignore it.

Joseph was good enough to say in the House that he had full confidence in BSC and Adam Raphael wrote a piece for *The Observer* in which he said of me, 'He's like Tito, indestructible and cold, he's taken so much shot and shell. We are stuck with him and so is the Government.' That was not at all how I felt and, indeed, I told Joseph that if he sacked me, which I knew one day he would, I would sue him for improper dismissal! He just giggled. Bill Sirs, however, had just sacked from his union 600 members who refused to obey his orders to come out on strike at Sheerness, a private sector steel maker.

As we moved into March we felt sure the unions knew they had lost the strike. Steel was pouring into the country from overseas through nearly every port. The private sector steel workers were going back to normal. Those on strike in the BSC were feeling the pinch and getting fed up. The strikers started picketing BSC's customers, which was deeply resented. But, best of all, 69% of those who completed the ballot paper voted to say that they would accept the result of a ballot. Bill Sirs argued that because only 65% of the strikers bothered to vote, only 44% were in favour of a second ballot (*sic*). 'Humpty Dumpty Sirs,' I called him, 'living in an upside down world.'

There is no doubt that the ballot put the skids under him, because he feared the result of a second ballot. The *News of the World* called him 'Silly Billy.'

By 12 March we were in fact negotiating with the unions again, not about pay, but about productivity and how to measure it and about job loss, which the unions were still resisting. Bill was acting as the great national leader, but the others were just trying to get the best deal for their members. We started preparing a second ballot, but we had to be careful; it could backfire.

Ten days later was the red letter day. The unions came to BSC at 2 o'clock and stayed till 9.00 pm, by which time we

215

had agreed a remit on which to go to a court of enquiry or to an arbitrator. Bill tried to get out of it but the other unions were determined to settle. As I diaried, 'Bill hates this; he wants to be flying free, challenging everything and making a lot of trouble, but the other unions have penned him in; they were paying out strike pay and ISTC was paying nothing.' The end of the strike was in sight. The arbitrator was bound to make us pay a bit more, but the strike changed everything and the men said 'never no more.' They would not come out on strike again and the power of the union was broken.

On 26 March all parties agreed that, at the suggestion of Woodrow Wyatt, Harold Lever should be chairman of the Committee of Enquiry, plus Richard Marsh for BSC and union leader Bill Keys for the unions. The ISTC strikers still had some stamina in them. The confidential polls taken by BSC on two occasions showed them ready to go on for another three or four weeks, but the craftsmen's leaders said they would accept the award of the Enquiry, which began four days later. We were rather scared that Marsh would be rolled by Lever and Keys, who were trained and experienced nego-tiators, so we said we would go to a second ballot if we could not live with the Enquiry's award.

The award came on 1 April. BSC had to pay an extra 1% to get the productivity agreement and a further $\frac{1}{2}$% on the guaranteed minimum of the lump sum bonus scheme, making a total of 15.9% with strong productivity strings. This com-pared with the unions' demand of 20% without any strings and BSCs original offer of 12% of which 10% was tied up in productivity. The next day the ISTC accepted the award by 41 to 27 on the negotiating committee, and the strike was over, the longest national strike since World War II and a watershed in the history of BSC and, one can dare to say, in the history of industrial relations in Britain.

The militant steel pickets flared up into violence and spat and kicked the ISTC Executive as they left their union headquarters after accepting the Lever award. There were 'walk-outs' in South Wales and in Rotherham and Sheffield, but after the Easter weekend on 9th April all the plants were back at work; the only one damaged was a chilled hearth at Scunthorpe. The men lost £1,300 a head, which would never be regained. The militants were very low everywhere.

Bill Sirs had gone to ground. He had made many mistakes: the 'virgin striker' they called him. In his book Bill said, 'The strike, to the surprise of the Government, the Civil Service, the media and the public was 100% successful. Every single member of ISTC supported it.' Well, I have to comment that his union members at Sheerness did not. Hector Smith of the blastfurnacemen's union made a shrewder remark: 'We didn't get much out of it, did we?'

Bill Sirs claimed that I said before the strike began: 'Bob is the hawk and I'm the dove.' There is much in that. Bob had been in the trenches opposing the growth of trade union power for years. I, still a pupil of Tubby Clayton, longed for rational discussion to bring people to sensible collaboration, in which to this day I passionately believe. Hitler was demoniac and we had to fight him. The steel workers were the salt of the earth and I simply loathed having to fight them. They were worked up by their leaders, as Brits easily are by those they trust, and the leaders saw that our proposed local productivity deals would undermine the authority of the unions and of those who led them. They feared to be personally diminished and it was that that caused the strike. Bill had said he thought the trade union movement was the most important and influential voluntary organisation in the whole world. That was his credo and BSC had to challenge that false value, which had led to 'overmighty' presumption and to the 'winter of discontent,' only twelve months behind us when the strike began. No doubt BSC had been clumsy at times. The opening of 2% was for consolidation of a previously earned and paid bonus. Bill knew that, but he ignored it and insisted that it was a flat rate pay increase. BSC thought the 2% would help. Actually nothing for nothing would have been better. In the

217

negotiations there was a lot of wasted time. On the other hand our rather boring economic case was well handled by Bob and by David Grieves, who led the negotiation. The strike was in fact a classic set-piece confrontation, with sympathetic action and mass and flying pickets. TUC rhetoric and heavy trade union expenditure were involved. Subsequent anti-trade union legislation would prevent much of that happening today.

I must say that Margaret Thatcher's performance as Prime Minister during the strike was impeccable. She saw everyone who wanted to see her and she heard their story; she gave an impression of understanding, without giving hostages to fortune. She supported her responsible minister, Joseph, and the responsible executives, Bob and me. She slapped down Prior, who was simply out of date. Keith Joseph too, once he had got the measure of the job, of the economic problem and of the chief players, was utterly loyal, supportive and shrewd in what he said and did. I suspect he hated the strike as much as I did. Joseph's role owed a lot to Sir Peter Carey, his Permanent Secretary, who knew it all and steered us all through massive difficulties. Government as a whole was divided and wobbly. The TUC and Bill Sirs knew that, which prolonged the strike by several weeks. BSC could rely only on the PM and Joseph.

They did not seek or engineer the strike, but once it was inevitable they kept out of the detail and backed their management. They applied the cash limits, which gave BSC the reason to resist a wage claim, which would have increased the inflation spiral. They saw the productivity need and stood up to all the parliamentary and media flak to get us through. British industry has reason to be grateful to them. I had bitterly to learn that collaboration with traditional style unions at national level is fruitless. Above all, Government kept the investment programme going. What private sector shareholders would have behaved like that? If BSC had not been nationalised it would have been reduced to one or two unmodernised plants and another large chunk of British industry would have disappeared. There are occasions when national-isation plays a vital, indeed essential, role.

For the BSC management the strike was the turning point in our fortunes. The market for steel remained terrible for some years to come, but management was able in an under-standing way to decentralise control and de-man the plants, so that they became internationally competitive. Further, management was able to get the trust and confidence of the remaining workforce. True, we 'put the frighteners on 'em,' as steel people say, but at times you do need sticks as well as carrots.

BSC had a strong management team under Bob Scholey. Peter Allen in Wales closed Shotton and slimlined Port Tal-bot and Llanwern without a murmur. Derek Saul in the North East closed Consett and John Pennington closed Corby. Jake Stewart was fair and firm in Scotland. David Grieves in London quickly got the new productivity bonus scheme go-ing. Gordon Sambrook got BSC's home market share back in no time. Frank Holloway was able to blame the strike for much of BSC's heavy losses. Strong management and col-laboration with the workforce direct at local level replaced attempts to collaborate with unions at national level. The local productivity deals on a plant-by-plant basis worked even better than we had imagined. The workforce watched the output, the quality, the cost, the cobbles and all in terms of what they could get out of it, and they got a lot when everything was going right. The men wanted that cash bonus more than they wanted the good offices of the union. The union was helpful at local level, but had been disarmed by the strike at national level.

BSC learned that they needed the customer more than the customer needed them. In most years, post World War II, there was a shortage of steel, which had to be allocated. After 1977 there was a surplus and steel had to be sold in compe-tition with steel from Japan, Korea, Germany, France, Bel-gium and most other European countries. Ours had to be as good as theirs and delivered right first time and every time. It was a fantastic challenge and in time Bob and his executive team got on top of it. They have done many other good things, such as technical training and investment, extending their market and constantly improving quality. All that followed the strike which broke the power of the unions in steel. Sad that that had to happen but that power was due to years of government intervention with political purpose, (instead of economic common sense) and consequent management weakness. The decisions we took at British Steel while I was chairman led to 70,000 redundancies. Another 60,000 redundancies arose from the productivity measures set in train after the strike.

I have a cartoon illustrating BSC as Burning Sterling Continuously. Now, British Steel makes a handsome profit and enjoys a cash cushion against the return of a downturn in the cycle of demand for steel.

On 17 April 1980 Government announced that they had found new chairmen for the Post Office and for British Steel. I knew that our new man was to be Ian MacGregor, an old acquaintance. This was a very good choice and he would do the job excellently. Bill Sirs might not like it, but BSC had to press on with reform at top speed and I felt sure Ian would do that. He had to get into the hard core overmanning and cope with inflation, over-capacity of steel in Europe and the strong £ sterling.

Ian would, I felt sure, get on well with the BSC management. His style was more 'macho' than mine, which tended to be 'Guardee', but never macho. I had in fact lost the confidence of BSC's managing directors, who thought, like Bob, that the steel contract and worker-directors and decentralisation made their job harder. They were probably right. I was aiming 'beyond the sunset,' at the management philosophy of Germany and Japan and, as throughout my life, I was way ahead of my time. My diary noted, 'I feel sure it is time for me to go, for the sake of BSC and, indeed, for myself.'

But Ian MacGregor was hard to get and he did not come cheap. On 23 April I told Solly Gross, the Civil Servant from the Department of Industry on BSC's board, 'Solly, there is no way I shall extend my contract, whether the new man comes or not, and if he comes and is ready to become chairman on 1 July, I will certainly make way for him before my contract ends in September.' I set up a team of Hugh Parker of McKinsey, Hodgson (chairman of ICI) and Pennock (president of CBI) to advise the in-coming BSC Chairman on organisation.

On 29 April I paid a farewell visit to Joseph. He was rather embarrassed and said a lot of nice but feeble things. He came down in the lift with me and said good-bye at the entrance. I noted, 'After four years at steel it was a very weak ending.'

Next day I had a good, positive meeting with Ian and I felt certain he was the right man to take on BSC. His 'transfer fee' from his old job at Lazards in New York was £1.8 million which raised eyebrows everywhere. Joseph described him in the Commons as 'a Scottish-born business man, phenomenally energetic and successful.' On 7 May at a big CBI lunch Joseph paid tribute to our 'long hard struggle which was very largely successful.'

During May I went round the steel plants with Ian and I was amazed at what a good reception we got. Clearly, everyone wanted to forget the strike and start again. We also went to America and visited our offices and customers there. Bob Knight, 'our man' in New York (he was also chairman of the Federal Reserve Board in New York) gave a dinner for Ian and me to meet steel people. To my surprise they started to congratulate me. After dinner Ian said, 'Would you stay on as chairman of BSC Industry, which is doing so well creating new jobs where steel works were closed?'

'Sure, Ian,' I said, 'but only till you find someone younger and better and I don't want a salary, as I don't know how much time and trouble that job will take.'

'You must be paid,' said Ian.

221

'I'd rather not,' I replied.

This was endorsed by the main board and I stayed at BSC Industry for the next nine years, by which time its original job was pretty well completed. Steel does get into one's bones.

We had to go on managing till my last day as chairman of BSC which was fixed at 30 June 1980. The closure of Consett was the last decision I took with the management and board. A very sad event, but a new Consett has sprung from that closure, with 200 new companies operating there as we shall see in the next chapter.

My final meeting with Joseph was on 26 June when I had to tell him that we were probably going to exceed our cash limits and would need more money from Government. He faced a hostile House of Commons with this news and blamed it on me. He did in fact say to the House that I 'had not proceeded with sufficient speed and vigour.' Oh well, it had to be somebody's fault and under the rules of the game that somebody had to be me.

My final act as chairman of BSC was to announce the results for the year to 31 March 1980. They were terrible. We lost £545 million of which over £200 million was due to the strike. We had, but only by a whisker, remained within the cash limits set by the government. We would need much more government money in future. We had that year closed steel-works plant at Corby and Shotton and obsolete plant had been taken out at Redbourn, Cleveland and Hallside. The great new blast furnace at Redcar had been successfully lit and the Shotton coating complex had been opened, as had the ore terminal at Hunterston. Finally I said, 'The outlook is grim. We are still in a cost-price squeeze. We shall lose more money this year than last. My successor will have his work cut out, but he has all the qualities needed for his enormous task.'

He had, indeed, but even larger losses were incurred and six more years were needed and three more chairmen were appointed before that task was completed.

I did not feel downcast. I had done what I saw I had to do,

without fear or favour; one cannot do more. As I finished my stint as chairman a new era in British Steel, and perhaps in British industry, began. It was based on the work done by Bob Scholey and me and the executive team and board at Steel, supported by both Labour and Tory governments. I do in fact feel very proud of what we all have done and am happy to have played a part in it.

The main lesson that came out of this experience was the necessity for 'collaboration within strong management,' and the success which follows this formula. I tried to introduce the Steel Contract and worker-directors and decentralisation in order to achieve that. Where we got collaboration it worked. Where we failed to get it we ran into trouble. We had good collaboration with government, with customers, with other steel producers at home, in Japan and eventually in Europe. We had in the management a coherence which stood up to severe strains. Even the workforce, as the post-strike experience shows, knew what we were trying to do. It was only with the unions, and chiefly with the ISTC, that we failed to establish a basis for collaboration - and it was not for want of trying.

British trade unions had in fact been spoiled by all political parties ever since World War II. Governments of whatever stripe and, perforce, management, had become afraid of the unions and the unions knew it. They thus came to develop exaggerated ideas of their own importance, which obsessed them and caused them in the end to overcall their hand. It was inevitable that one day they would be put down. Heath, Wilson and Callaghan tried to do that, but they failed. Thatcher succeeded. The steel, motor industry and finally the coal strike made it clear to all that trade union power had been curbed.

That, it seemed to me, was the most significant change in the political economy of Britain during the eighties. It left British management with the opportunity to manage firmly and to extend the process of collaboration, thus to compete on level terms with the Germans and Japanese. Sadly, that opportunity was not firmly or fully seized across the industrial board. The early nineties started by witnessing a return to inflation, which gives the trade unions their opportunity. As in the seventies, they protested that their members were being unfairly impoverished by wage increases below the going rate of inflation. If inflation is not checked, we in Britain may have to repeat the performance, described in this chapter, all over again.

CHAPTER 12

THE HAPPY ISLES

I fired only one Parthian shot over my shoulder from my new saddle and that was at *The Economist,* which wrote, 'Only Villiers was allowed access to capital to construct new steel works.' That was too much and I replied, 'In my time at BSC we cancelled the doubling of Port Talbot, arc furnaces at Hunterston and a plate mill on Teesside. We finished four schemes already begun, but we closed steelmaking at Clyde Iron, Hartlepool, Cardiff, Ebbw Vale, Shelton, Bilston, Glengarnock, Hallside, Corby, Shotton and Consett. We mothballed half the steel works at Port Talbot and Llanwern. We cut capacity by one half and took decisions which made 70,000 of the workforce redundant. I was not a steel plant builder, but the Chairman who had to do the dreadful spadework.'

All this spadework had distressing consequences on communities who lived in the travel-to-work areas of the closed or mothballed steel plants. That had been foreseen by my predecessor, Sir Monty Finniston, who had set up a subsidiary company within BSC, which came to be called BSI, British Steel (Industry), to regenerate these areas. It was passive when I went to BSC in 1976 because the Labour manifesto of 1974 had postponed steel closures. BSC was trying to make too much steel in too many small and old pots. By 1978 we had got free of the restriction through the Government White Paper, 'The road to viability.' It was already clear to me in 1977 that a huge closure programme would have to begin and I became chairman of BSI in addition to chairing BSC. The first chairman of BSI, Ron Smith, a former trade union leader (Union of Post Office Workers), retired and I had to change the first chief executive of BSI, who was an economist and a planner, in order to get the most energetic entrepreneur I could find.

I was helped in this by my friend John Broadbent Jones (JBJ), who was the best consultant and recruiter I knew. He gave me a short list of some six or seven people to choose from. They were all excellent 'as is' people, so I turned them down. JBJ then said:

'But of course there is Paddy Naylor.'

'Who's he?' I asked.

'You'd better see him,' said JBJ.

Paddy was out of a job at the time, having left both the Plessey Company and Redland. I could have checked him out with them, but I didn't. I saw at once that Paddy was the man to get BSI on the road by hook or crook, without respect for persons or compliance with bureaucratic restrictions.

Paddy was 43 years of age at the time and a real enfant terrible. The job he took on at BSI was ideal for him. It was urgent, important, human, and above all new. No industry since 1918 had actually tried to get hundreds of new companies and thousands of new jobs started in areas left desolate by its industrial closures. Many people thought it could not be done, especially during the deepest post-war depression, which was coming upon us. Paddy was hyperactive and the staff he recruited round him looked upon him as a mini Napoleon. I had other preoccupations with BSC at the time and I turned Paddy loose to get on with the job, reporting to me on 'surprises' or difficulties and to the BSI board quarterly.

BSI had money made available to it through BSC, but that money came from government, and civil servants did not want to see it used in competition with their own pet schemes. So Paddy said, 'OK. We'll do the deals you don't want to do

- bad deals, if you like, but we'll see if we can make them succeed.' And many of them did succeed. Paul Usher, in his book 'Putting Something Back' (published by the Planning Exchange in 1989), says, 'Paddy involved himself with intuitive ease, and the underlying thrust of discussion with him was to challenge ready-made assumptions, to break up the ground, so that some fresh seed - some new idea - could be planted. Paddy had the ability to enhance expectations, to create a buzz.'

Paddy often came to me and asked - 'Chairman, how can we find a "plus," something other people can't offer those wishing to start up or expand?' Paddy tried many ingenious plusses such as free consultancy studies, giving guarantees, subsidising customers' costs and purchasing or leasing equipment on friendly terms. In the end 'soft,' unsecured loans at below the market rate proved the solution for bigger companies, and for smaller companies accommodation was found in workshops created out of unwanted BSC buildings. These were made over to BSI to rebuild and let to small businesses under the direct supervision of a workshop manager or manageress. The leases were in fact licences, which enabled the tenant to get out quickly if he became bankrupt. 'Cheap, quick and easy' was the way BSI offered its facilities to those who wanted to start up in Wales, Scotland or the North of England - not at that time the first choices for most entrepreneurs.

The principle we established was that our money was to be used for job creation in the steel areas and that our success was to be measured, not by conventional financial profit, but by the number of new job commitments which had been obtained. Now, this was no part of Thatcherite industrial policy, rather the contrary. Her policy was against subsidies to business for any purpose. Her Government did not intervene against us because we were clearly and successfully creating new companies and new jobs in areas of traditionally high unemployment at a time when the national unemployment figures were mounting alarmingly, in excess of 3 million. We made no secret of our subsidy in our advertisements, which were the main source of enquiries; of these, one in ten turned into a real business on the ground.

The BSC was very generous to BSI. When I was Chairman of both companies it was, I must confess, quite easy. But when MacGregor succeeded me at BSC he saw the point and kept the financial support and property transfer to BSI going strongly. Indeed, when in 1983 he handed over the Chair of BSC (en route for the Coal Board) to Sir Robert Haslam (now Lord Haslam), he said, 'I hope you will continue the support I have given to BSI. Their work has helped me greatly in industrial relations.' I sat there purring and Bob Haslam did all he could for BSI. Over the twelve years I was at BSI we received some £40 million in cash, property and kind from BSC and £10 million from the European Commission in Brussels. Bob Scholey never took much interest in BSI and when he became chairman of BSC I wrote, 'BSI is the well-heeled cousin once removed from Dear Octopus, a play by Dodie Smith, in which Dear Octopus is a large possessive family, and I think it should so remain.' It did.

BSI had a small London staff and what we called 'co-ordinators' in the steel areas. Apart from Paddy they were, at first, all recruited from within the BSC. They were paid BSC rates, stayed in the pension fund and had the right of return when their stint in BSI was completed. They were an unusual lot of men plus one or two very unusual women. Most of them had done non-steel jobs before. They were well above average in intelligence and motivation, and came from a variety of backgrounds. I was surprised that Paddy, when he arrived with us, retained the enthusiasm of almost all of them and built them into a creative and imaginative team which helped to raise a high profile and a strong image from nothing in a short time.

The BSI Board (it was a private limited company) consisted of Dr David Grieves, the personnel managing director of

BSC, a clever and energetic man; a senior industrialist from Ravenscraig area; another from South Wales; and the former chief executive of Clwyd in North Wales. I invited a partner of Deloittes, the accountants, to join us, and we had Bill Sirs of the ISTC and Eddie Linton, the convenor of the Craftsmen in BSC. Paddy Naylor, Tom Young and later the financial director were also members. It was a very coherent and enthusiastic group. Every member had his own favourite area, industry or function, but I think that over the years we managed to satisfy most of them.

At a very early BSI board meeting I agreed to the infilling of what is now the Deeside Industrial Park next to the Shotton steelworks, built by the Summers family in North Wales. It is a huge area, too big for us, and we sold a half of it to the Welsh Development Agency. But before we could do that we had to raise its ground level to above the level of the River Dee, which flows alongside. We got Peter Summers, one of the Summers steel family, to be our co-ordinator there and he was performing very well, but Paddy on his first visit to the site said: 'You're nothing but a bloody amateur civil engineer, Summers. Why the hell don't you get out there and bring in some punters?' 'Punters' was the word Paddy used to describe the clients or customers who we hoped would come and back themselves by starting a business on our properties. As Peter Summers readily admits, he got the message. In 1990 the Deeside Industrial Park is fully occupied with new, flourishing, high technology businesses and the former BSC Shotton workforce is either working in the steel coating complex, (which has doubled since it was opened by José in 1979), or in one of a hundred new businesses started up on the Park from scratch, in many cases at BSI instigation or with our help.

Paddy reckoned at the start that the cost of one new job in an old steel area would be £2000. His target in 1979 was 3,000 new jobs = £6,000,000. In 1980 BSI hit a target of 10,000 new jobs and we continued at about that rate for each of the next ten years, but by careful housekeeping and using other sources of funding we got the costs to us per job down to £500, which made the whole operation feasible.

The Managed Workshops scheme started in 1978 when BSC had closed and was demolishing the Clyde Ironworks at Tollcross near Glasgow. Paddy came to me and said, 'You must stop demolishing all the buildings at Clyde. We could convert them to workshops for small businesses.' 'Do you really believe you could do that?' I asked. 'What evidence?' 'No evidence,' said Paddy, 'just a hunch and it wouldn't cost much.' 'OK, Paddy, I'll stop the demolition and you get on with the workshops.'

It was the first workshop of its kind and it has been copied all over the world. Paddy had sniffed out that there was a market for space with a roof, a water tap and an electric light point, at a very low rent and in an area which could be managed collectively with telephone and secretarial services. Those requirements have moved up market through time, but cheap rents, and 'easy in and out' have been the hallmark. In 1990 we had nine of them in the steel areas: some made money, some lost, but in the aggregate we were all square. Between them they contained at any one time nearly a thousand small businesses of which a third went bankrupt and disappeared, a third stayed as they had started and another third grew and prospered and moved out into bigger premises. We called the workshops the seedbeds and we have always been very proud of them.

What Paddy did was to introduce a new and special culture into BSI; we were on the side of the entrepreneur, not to make money out of him, which we never did, but to help him succeed and thus employ more people and in that way 'Put Something Back,' as Paul Usher said. I remembered Tubby Clayton saying, 'Never knock something down unless you can put up something better.' Well, the companies we helped to start or expand were better than the old clapped-out steel-works they replaced and they offered more variety, so that the old steel towns no longer depended on a single industry like steel, which was subject to deep cyclical changes.

Paddy wrote an 'accountability report' in 1979. 'We gave ourselves,' he said, 'two hundred weeks to come to grips with the job-creation task, to complete it and then self-destruct. We are nearing the mid-point.' Something was happening to Paddy; I could see he was getting itchy feet. One day in 1980, I think it was 22nd January, just as the steel strike was getting really difficult, Paddy came to see me.

'Charles, I've come,' he said, 'to hand in my resignation.' 'But you have another year to go to finish your contract,' I said. 'You can't hold me to that. I would be browned off,' he said. 'What are you going to do?' I asked. 'I'm going to start my own business, Job Creation, and I'm taking the best BSI people with me.'

I was furious, but I knew Paddy, the entrepreneur, 'OK, Paddy, so be it,' I said. 'Thank you for what you've done, but you be buggered for quitting.'

I turned away and rang up JBJ for a replacement. Paddy's new venture did not eventually work out well, but as far as BSI was concerned he got the show on the road.

While JBJ was taking a trawl to find a replacement for Paddy, I had a very interesting meeting with Lord Thorney-croft, who was then chairman of the Conservative Party. I had been his fag in the same house at Eton and had followed his distinguished, but 'greasy pole' career (as Disraeli called high office) with much interest, because I felt his motivation was not very different from my own. He asked me if I would have time, when I finished as chairman of British Steel, to investi-gate what would be best for the Tory party to recommend and for the government to do, to encourage the growth of the small business sector of the UK economy, which seemed to have been neglected by the Labour Government. I had been in-volved in the small business world as chairman of BSI, be-cause it was mainly new, small businesses that we were able to attract to our steel closure areas in the North of England,

Wales and Scotland. So I accepted Peter's offer and started researching into the problem with the Members of Parliament and institutions and lobby groups I had met and who were likely to have thought about the development of this sector, which, I believed, comprised about a quarter of the British economy. Graham Bannock had done the staff work on the Bolton Report on Small Business in 1971 and so I started with him and with Michael Grylls, Tory MP for North West Surrey, who I knew had raised a number of points about small business in the House of Commons. They were both extremely helpful and got me into the small business 'daisy chain' of experts and interested parties.

Peter Thorneycroft had suggested I should make not more than six proposals and I was ready to do that in December 1980. Reading my report again I don't feel very proud of it. It was too long, too complex and probably too concessionary. I suggested a 'subordinated loan,' to be issued by the Government's Development Agencies. I followed that with the proposal that there should be an English Development Agency to match the existing Welsh and Scottish agencies. My next proposal was that, for the first five years, new small businesses should pay no tax on profits retained in the business. Lastly, I proposed a Minister of State responsible for propagating the needs and opportunities for small businesses.

I had borrowed a good deal from experience in France, where the small business contribution to the economy is more successful than in Britain and I was asked to discuss this with Robert Armstrong (now Lord Armstrong) who was at that time Head of the Civil Service and Secretary to the Cabinet. The French have an organisation called DATAR for regional development, which then reported to the Prime Minister, and I thought this was relevant to Britain, but Robert did not think Margaret Thatcher would be sympathetic to that idea. There is now a Minister of State for small businesses in Britain and a Government guaranteed loan scheme and there have been tax concessions, but I cannot claim that my report was directly responsible. Nevertheless, it brought me into contact with many people who were trying to get changes which would stimulate the growth of small business in Britain; with them I have had a rewarding relationship for the last ten years.

The first new friend I made in the small business world was Bill Poeton. He had his own highly successful business which gave him the time and resources to devote himself to the British and International world of small business. He told me of the White House Conference on Small Business, convened by President Carter in January 1980 with the introduction, 'I came to Washington as a small businessman with an abhorrence of unnecessary paper work and regulation, a sense of the need to help small business to obtain capital and a determination to strengthen the word 'free' in our free enterprise system. I was determined to make sure that your voice would be heard.'

The conference, in which 50,000 small businessmen from every state in the USA participated, was a great success. No less than sixty strong recommendations were sent to President Carter; fifteen were given priority status and in one way and another most have become part of American business law.

I felt sure that we should do something like that in Britain: say, a Downing Street conference on small business. A great deal of support came from Barry Baldwin and Brian Jenks, both very senior accountants in famous firms and in turn advisers on small business at the Tory Central Office. We put up what we thought was a good case, but we were unable to persuade the Prime Minister who felt, so I was told, that the conference might make proposals of which she would not approve and so it would all be a waste of time! Some years later we were able to organise an International Small Business Congress in London, but that was not quite the same thing.

I did however in that way see a lot of Graham Bannock, then managing the Economists Advisory Group, which had been commissioned by Shell (UK) to make a proposal for a Small Business Research Centre. This was presented in 1981.

The proposal said 'There are great gaps in our knowledge and a small business research centre could act as a collection and diffusion centre for information, carry out research and at the same time develop means for stimulating the efficiency and growth of individual small business.' Shell put John Moorhouse in charge of this project and allocated a budget for its implementation. John was a dynamic Shell manager and really got something going.

Bannock and Moorhouse roped me into their discussions where I met for the first time Stan Mendham, who had started the Forum of Private Business. This was rapidly becoming a leading 'lobby group', promoting and overseeing legislation affecting small business. In due course Moorhouse was promoted to Shell in Aberdeen and Bannock had to devote more and more time to his own business, which is concerned with projects and research into small business matters. That left Stan Mendham and me at the heart of what became the Small Business Research Trust - SBRT.

I want to say a word about Stan, who is the most dynamic of all those good people who are promoting the small business sector of British industry. He is a big man in every way. He goes straight and at once to the point he wishes to make in any conversation or meeting. Some people are disconcerted by his directness, but all immediately see his genuine conviction of the importance to Britain of small business. He is an engineer by training and an inventor by instinct. He is punctilious and correct in business matters almost to a fault, and I have trusted him completely.

Some who know Stan well say that at times he gets carried away by his own enthusiasm, and that may be so. Perhaps for that reason he asked me to be Chairman of SBRT and later of the International Small Business Congress, which was held in London in 1986. Stan was always the driving force of both these organisations and I am delighted that in 1990 I was able to hand over the chair of SBRT to him, as an established and useful body carrying out the functions very much as originally suggested by Graham Bannock and the Economists Advisory Group. SBRT's problems were general, in that the sector had been neglected by government and by public interest and the problems were particular in that we had to find both management and money. Stan felt he could manage the Forum from Knutsford in Cheshire and SBRT whose HQ we all felt should be in London. Stan would have, I felt sure, the inclination but not the time to do both jobs, so we started to trawl around for management. We made a false start but then we ran into a series of excellent people who helped us greatly, but only on a temporary basis. Finally, in 1985 we had the great good luck, at the suggestion of one of our trustees, David Watkins of the Manchester Business School, to recruit Professor John Stanworth of the Central London Polytechnic and Colin Gray, a most enterprising researcher. With these two men plus Gilly Barker, our indefatigable projects manager, we set off on firm ground, which has stood the test of time; they have made a success of SBRT.

Money is always a problem with new ventures and in 1984, when Norman Tebbit, then Trade and Industry Secretary, launched the Trust and we felt we were established, I wrote to all the chairmen I had got to know in the City of London and in British Industry asking for their support. They responded in an amazing way and every year for the first five years their donations, plus what the Trust was able to earn in fees, exceeded the costs of running the Trust. The people who ran it took minimal remuneration and the Trustees, who were really the directors, took nothing but gave immense service. Three of them I must mention. First, John Bolton, author of the Bolton report on small business in 1971; secondly, Charles Green, a very senior executive of the National Westminster Bank; and thirdly, Russ Wilson of NatWest, who kept us on the 'straight and narrow' financially.

NatWest became, indeed, our chief supporter and has sponsored the Trust's Quarterly Survey of Small Business in Britain which is now regarded as the best indicator of the state of the sector. The Trust has gathered together a group of researchers who between them during the last five years have published sixty reports on various significant aspects of Small Business in Britain. We have had many congratulations on these careful, detailed studies, including a letter from Norman Tebbit saying, 'Your surveys are helpful to us in our work and provide a valuable addition to knowledge of what is happening in the sector.'

From the start of SBRT we had been worried about the lack of organisation in the small business world in Britain. In Germany, America and France the sector is carefully organised, which enables it to speak with a single, authoritative voice to government about its needs and problems. In these countries, small business makes a much bigger contribution to the whole economy than it does in Britain. Besides, every company was once a small company and unless we have many seedlings and saplings we will not have enough great trees in the future to succeed the forest giants of the present.

We therefore decided to organise a council of SBRT which would be a forum for joint consultation and, hopefully, of agreement and action by bodies representing small business. We invited twenty organisations to come and talk with us quarterly. We had the four so-called 'lobby groups', four academics, the Chambers of Trade and Commerce, the CBI, the British Institute of Management and the Institute of Directors, three very big companies and a scattering of others whose interest in small business was well established. Before long these sorted themselves out into a smaller group who attended regularly and helped to fix the work programme of SBRT.

On the wider issues and where Government was involved we found it most difficult to get agreement. Every member of the council had or represented a slightly different view, which made that member 'special' in the eyes of those he represented. Agreement would tend to make the member or his organisation redundant and none of them wanted that; be-

236

sides, representing the 'special case' was for some their livelihood which they obviously did not want to lose. Falling back
on merchant banking and IRC experience, I tried to get some
of them to merge, but after several two-by-two meetings I gave
it up as a bad job, as others had done before me. I believe that
this is true of British culture generally. We are centrifugal: that
is, we tend to fly off when revolving round a centre, not
centripetal, which is tending to move towards a centre. I am
sure that comes from the Protestant culture which insists that
we each have our own direct line to God and a duty to develop
our own individual talents. The effect of this culture is to
proliferate numbers of small organisations, all with ideas,
functions or products slightly different from each other, run
by people who, with religious tenacity, cling to their particular
line of country. This culture was of immense value in the early
stages of industrial development but it makes life much more
difficult in later and more sophisticated stages, where collaboration is clearly called for but very hard to bring about. It
remains my hope that in time SBRT will provide the basis for
a coming-together of the small business community in Britain. That was the motivation of Stan and myself at the start
of SBRT.

In 1988 the Trust moved its operations to the Open University at Milton Keynes, where we have been made welcome
by the Vice Chancellor, Andrew Thompson. This move was
initiated by Colin Gray, showing his usual entrepreneurial
flair. In 1990 Stan's organisation, the Forum, agreed to
underwrite the Trust's expenses and Stan became chairman.
I remained associated as President.

I do believe that SBRT has been a useful body. Much more
is now known of the small business sector, which was a kind
of 'secret garden' before it was opened up. The Council has
achieved a wider understanding of the sector's needs and
problems, even though agreement on wider issues has so far
escaped us. Lastly, SBRT has been one of the agencies
spreading the Enterprise Culture in Britain where we have

helped to bring what was dimly perceived into sharper focus. All parts of the media have helped to spread these ideas. Most newspapers have a small business column at regular intervals and all TV channels and local programmes have run stimulating series which have had an educational content.

The growth of small business in Britain in the eighties has been phenomenal and the sector is certainly twice the size it was at the beginning of the decade. In 1990 one thousand five hundred new businesses were being registered each week.

Stan did not confine his efforts to the Forum and SBRT: he was also a member of the steering committee of the International Small Business Congress, which had held twelve meetings in world capitals, but never one in London. The steering committee would not agree to any congress being held without a firm invitation from the government of the country concerned and a guarantee that the costs would be covered.

Stan asked me to be the chairman of the organising committee for a congress in London and I agreed, although I did not immediately see how we could get the necessary permits. I felt that we should get the guarantee before seeking the formal governmental invitation. As we had failed to get Margaret Thatcher to agree to a British small business conference, I was by no means sure that she would invite the international fraternity.

We had, through SBRT, established an excellent relationship with the NatWest Bank and I felt that we should try to persuade that bank to 'underwrite' the expenses of a Small Business Congress of about 400 people interested in the subject, to be held in London in October 1986. We started, as is best with banks, at the operating level, with the manager of the Small Business Section and he responded somewhat cautiously: but we did some lobbying higher up the hierarchy and finally the chairman, Lord Boardman, agreed. I quote his letter after the Congress: 'I know how successful the Congress was and I can assure you that we were delighted to be associated with you in every way.'

With the costs underwritten we had no difficulty in getting the Government to issue a welcome and, indeed, the Prime Minister was most helpful in getting the Queen Elizabeth II Conference Centre in Parliament Square made available. She wrote, 'I entirely agree that the Small Business Congress would be an admirable use of the new centre and I wish you every success for the occasion.' We were on our way.

Everyone concerned wanted the Prince of Wales to open the proceedings. He was already internationally known as a great supporter of the small businesses which had been started up with funds from the Prince's Trust and he had just become President of Business in the Community, so he was just the man. Unfortunately, he was already fully committed on that day, so I asked if he would do a video, answering questions, which we could show as the congress opened. We used Nick Daw's excellent small firm to make the video and Prince Charles was in top form in the garden of his house in Kensington Palace, answering my questions for ten minutes with great sincerity and enthusiasm. The opening ceremony was performed by Lord Young, then the Secretary of State for Trade and Industry. He faced some stiff questioning (organised by the committee) with which he dealt with complete equanimity and knowledge of detail.

The organising committee was taken in hand by Stan and they used their brains, experience and energy without stint to make the three-day congress a pretty good success. Before speaking, every speaker was put through his paces by Brian Jenks and the visual slides were often greatly improved at that stage.

The theme of the Congress was 'Enterprise Route '86' and most of the presentations lived up to it. As usual, the most valuable meetings were the twelve workshops where small business owners conducted seminars about their own experiences. These often continued past the advertised time. Simultaneous translation into English, French, Japanese and

Spanish was provided at all sessions. The whole conference benefitted enormously from the skill of Pat Davies of Conference Associates.

Sessions were conducted by the Director General of MITI's small enterprise agency, by an official of the EC in Bruxelles, by John Bullock from Deloittes, the accountants, by David Trippier, the British Minister for small business, by John Bulloch of the Canadian Federation of Independent Business, and by Victor Kiam, President of Remington Rand, a tremendous enthusiast.

Her Majesty's Government gave a reception in the 600-year-old Guildhall, in the City of London, which was very impressive. The highlight was undoubtedly the Banquet at Grosvenor House, hosted by the financial firm 3i, which has done so much to stimulate and finance small business in Britain over the years.

We had arranged through John Sloan, President of the National Federation of Independent Business in Washington DC, that Malcolm Baldridge, Secretary for Commerce in President Reagan's Cabinet, would speak and answer questions for half an hour on a huge screen direct from the White House after the dinner. This was sponsored by John Sloan's NFIB and British Telecom. It was a most ambitious undertaking in view of the state of the art at that time.

Mr Baldridge was a hard-hitting, fast-talking man who never pulled his punches. He was a great horseman who performed in rodeos. Sadly, at a later date he was thrown from his horse and died of his injuries. When he spoke to our congress he was in great form, speaking freely about America's opportunities and problems in trade. He gave a great boost to the small business sector world-wide and the audience in Grosvenor House gave him a tremendous round of applause.

When he came to answer questions I had to choose from about 50 which had been sent in advance. They were all polite and rather boneless, but one delegate rose from his seat and asked, 'When, Mr Secretary, is America going to eliminate its huge deficit in trade with the rest of the world?'

This was a fair but delicate question, but Baldridge was not a delicate man. He knew he was talking to an international audience, but he replied, 'When the Japanese stop dumping goods on us.'

At that point the Japanese Ambassador, who was present with his wife, got up, looked round and started to leave the room. All the other Japanese present followed him out. The rest of us sat tight and stayed, to be enchanted by the marching and playing of the band of the Royal Marines; later we danced to the music of the 'Moonlight Serenaders'. Next morning the Japanese turned up at the Congress quite unperturbed, saying that they had had to leave because their bus had come for them earlier than they had expected!

But the Congress was not all pomp and ceremony; we tried to balance that with hard and serious work on problems of the small businessman throughout the world. These turned out to be remarkably similar the world over; problem number one was identified as the availability and cost of finance, and the next greatest problem was shortage of skilled people. There was much discussion of the role of government in relation to small business and whether large companies hindered or helped small business. The success and failure rates of small business were constantly discussed. Enterprise agencies as a route to success was an important topic in a large workshop. Small business in twelve countries was described and much was learned from these comparisons.

Forty countries sent representatives and many of these brought their wives or friends, for whom there was a good social programme. The cost per head was quite high and I suspect that most of the delegates were sponsored by organisations keen to pick up new ideas for use in their own environment. Many came for a short holiday in London!

I have no doubt it was all worth doing, both internationally and as a stimulus to small business in Britain. We worked out a 'bursary' scheme so that those who could not afford the full cost got a substantial discount. The Congress was well covered by the media and the global problems of small business came to be better understood. Many good linkages between people were made and there is no doubt that a good deal of real business was done.

For myself the lesson was once again that other nations organise themselves better than do the British. We still prefer to 'go it alone' while other countries get organised and collaborate. In the small companies where I am still a director I try to stimulate collaboration at the right level for continuous improvement; that is the point.

I have been for years Chairman of the Theatre Royal, Windsor, a most successful enterprise started by the late John Counsell. We work closely with other provincial theatres to the considerable benefit of all. The Anglo-American 'successor generation' project is all about collaboration and after six annual conferences we feel proud of that. The European Investment Company in Switzerland, of which I was a founder member, has had a success repairing hi-tech companies in difficulties in Europe; this requires infinite collaboration with all parties involved in each venture. The Norris Institute in Minneapolis has started close and detailed collaboration on very hi-tech matters with similar bodies in Moscow. I love the world of small business, so long as it collaborates for continuous improvement. No part of it have I loved more than BSI, to which I must now return.

Back at BSI, JBJ had found two outstanding candidates to replace Paddy. In the end I chose John Dunbar who had just returned from the Middle East where he had had a highly remunerative job as financial adviser. Sadly, one of his daughters, Catherine, was sick with anorexia nervosa, so he returned with his family to London and was looking for a congenial job. His first job had been with IBM, who are superb business trainers, and thereafter he had a successful business career of considerable variety. He was less of an entrepreneur but more of a professional businessman than Paddy. I knew that Paddy had left a raft of loose ends hanging about unfinished and potentially dangerous to BSI. John Dunbar seemed to me just the man to convert the exciting but untidy BSI into a controlled but still growing business unit, which would stand up to inspection from outside. I always thought that one day BSC would start asking awkward questions for which BSI must be ready. As I hoped, John was just that man and more.

John was a good match for Ian MacGregor, who had taken over from me at BSC at just the same time as John took over from Paddy. As Paul Usher says, 'MacGregor was more interested in the hard centre than the soft centre;' what he wanted was 'BSI as an auxiliary component of BSC; a well-lubricated machine with all the parts checked and working.' But Ian was very conscious of and concerned with social responsibility and education and training. We saw at once that he would be a good friend and a bad enemy. If BSI could match up to his standards of efficiency, he would be our friend. I am not sure that Paddy could have achieved that. John did. He took over in June 1980 when BSC had 50,000 redundancies in the pipeline and the national unemployment figures were moving up to 3 million. We did not know it, but even then we were not at the bottom of the recession and things were going to get worse. John weathered the next five years with success and was awarded an OBE for his good work.

John set an ambitious target: 20,000 job opportunities to be created by March 1984, with another 15,000 anticipated if the new businesses developed according to plan. Add in the results of Paddy's efforts and you would get a total of 46,000 new job opportunities since 1978. John would tolerate no increase in BSI's staffing. Everyone would have to work harder. MacGregor would contribute from BSC what was already earmarked for BSI, but there would be no more funding after 1984, by which time BSI had to become self-funding.

John constructed a detailed plan with which to meet these objectives. The main thrust was to use 'other people's money,' mainly that of the banks, to get new ventures going, using BSI's core capital as a catalyst to entice other financial agents into the projects. 'It should be possible,' John wrote, 'to finance job creation on a self-funding basis, using BSI's capital as a permanent fund, yielding enough to cover our expenses and to provide on-going financial support to BSI areas.' These areas were to be turned into self-funding job-creation trusts as soon as possible. John and I saw that we must use the energy being created by the Local Enterprise Agency movement, which just at that time was being born.

There is some argument as to which area was the first to start a Local Enterprise Agency (LEA). I was certainly talking with Brian Wright, the Chief Executive of the London Enterprise Agency (LENTA), early in 1981, but the first LEA I saw in action was in March that year at St Helens in Lancashire, where Pilkingtons had set up a trust under Bill Humphreys to start up new businesses, with a view to absorbing the redundancies arising at Pilkingtons glass works, following a major reorganisation by the chairman, Sir Alastair Pilkington, a man of huge intellectual and social capacity.

Bill Humphreys was a great character and I spent a helpful day with him. He insisted throughout that money was not important in his work. The St Helens Trust had been given unwanted properties by Pilkingtons and had started to use them in the same way as we were using the workshops at Clyde. Bill said he used no money, but I found that Pilkingtons were behind him, as BSC were behind us. Nevertheless, he insisted that he was a 'poor friar' and that everything came from his customers, clients or 'punters,' as Paddy would have called them. Bill took me to lunch with the St Helens Borough Council and there I saw the foundation of the Trust. The Mayor and the Deputy Mayor were, or had been, Pilkington employees and they were supporting the Trust in a number of ways, as were some of the businessmen on the

Council. That gave me the clue that LEAs had to have the active support of the local council and the local business community; then the Agency's chief executive could play the 'poor friar' act. That is what BSI should do. I see from my notes that I called Bill Humphreys more a Robin Hood than a poor friar; perhaps Friar Tuck was the best name for him.

But there was more to St Helens than that. Alastair Pilkington had picked up the idea of the Agency in America and he got Michael Heseltine, then Secretary of State for Employment, to organise a conference at which the idea was developed and a Civil Servant detailed to propagate the idea widely in the industrial areas, where hard core unemployment was heaviest. Michael was, therefore, starting to do through the LEA movement what BSC had been doing through BSI. John Dunbar and I felt certain that we should try to start up LEAs in all those steel closure areas where they did not already exist, to take some of the heat and cost off BSI. I do not see that this is incompatible with 'stand on your own two feet,' as described by Margaret Thatcher. Indeed, after a while she came round to being an enthusiastic supporter of LEAs and business subscriptions to LEAs were made deductible for tax! We found that not only Pilkingtons, but Marks and Spencer, Shell and BP and the big four banks were strong supporters of LEAs, and other companies, many locally based, were drawn into the movement.

The LEAs have proved a success. The one-time Minister for Small Business, David Trippier, started one in his own constituency at Rossendale in Lancashire. I believe that to date some 300 LEAs have been started. They don't always work well; success depends on the people who are running them. Sometimes the local council, if doctrinaire left wing, prefers to do the work of regeneration itself through its industrial development officers, rather than through despised capitalists. That happened to BSI at both Scunthorpe and Ebbw Vale. In Scunthorpe we had to start a South Humber agency in nearby Brigg and at Ebbw Vale we agreed to put a

BSI man in alongside the development officer. At Ebbw Vale that worked so well that the Mayor of that very left wing town gave a public civic dinner for the chairman and executive of BSI, to thank them for what they had done to regenerate the area after the steel works closure. That was a good trophy, wasn't it!

BSI policy in 1980 was to convert the steel closure areas, of which there were then thirteen, into LEAs in which BSI would try to obtain a majority shareholding and funnel our support for new or growing business in the area through them. Our support had become by then more and more specialised and sophisticated. The workshops on our own property would remain our sole responsibility and, hopefully, remain self-financing.

A great boost for BSI came from the Prince of Wales' visit to our workshops in South Wales in June 1982. This had been suggested by Prince Charles' then assistant secretary, Francis Cornish. It was just at the critical moment of the Falklands War in which Prince Andrew was serving as a 'chopper' pilot, and Prince Charles must have been worried, but he went flat out all day and delighted everyone. He arrived at Port Talbot by chopper and opened our new workshops there. He was indefatigable and insistent in his questioning of everybody as to what they did and with what materials and how and how much and how long. He laid a foundation stone, subject to correction by the bricklayers; 'You have to do these things properly,' he said. 'Are you all right?' asked one well wisher. 'Yes,' he said, 'but I keep on spitting out bits of teeth I broke playing polo yesterday.' We drove round together and all the time he had his car window down so that he could shake hands and take in the flowers. He loves 'pressing the flesh,' I noted, just like the Pope.

We flew on in the chopper to Ebbw Vale and he visited all the firms in our workshops at Brynmawr where the Mayor apologised for the rain! 'Just too bad,' said Prince Charles. A man standing near to me said, 'I think he is a great fellow; he's got the common touch.' All this is well known now; at that time it was something of a royal revelation.

We went on to a meeting in Ebbw Vale of the Prince's Trust for young and disadvantaged people. They had all sorts of clever ideas for self-employment and were passionately enthusiastic when he told them how his Trust was giving £1000 to help any young person who had a plan to set up in business. Later that Trust merged with another, the Youth Enterprise Scheme. The joint effort is now called the Prince's Youth Business Trust and it has given £1,000 to no less than 10,000 'bursars' as the recipients are called. The Government matches voluntary gifts to the Trust and the total now available for 'bursars' is over £80 million.

Shortly afterwards Prince Charles suggested that we bring a band of, say, twenty senior businessmen to meet him, perhaps in the North East, so that he could ask them whether they could follow BSC's example and do more for those they made redundant or who were locally unemployed. The national unemployment figure was then over $2\frac{1}{2}$ million. We suggested Consett as a good place to meet and he was delighted. I wrote off to twenty-five business leaders whom I knew personally. It was amazing how many of them had board meetings on the day suggested for the meeting - they knew what they would be asked and did not want to say NO to Prince Charles. Many sent their personnel directors, who said they would report to their Boards. Only Tim Bevan of Barclays Bank was entirely positive and they started a workshop complex in the North East in response.

As we approached the meeting place in Consett steel works, a number of out-of-work skinheads cheered and shouted. Prince Charles at once went over to them. 'What are you yobbos doing behind that fence?' he asked. 'I'm on the dole,' said one. Prince Charles took him by the hand. 'He was just like one of the lads,' said another. 'He's genuine and really cares about the unemployed,' said a third.

But the meeting with the businessmen did not go very well.

247

They were out of their ground and did not want to be quoted. I felt sure their bosses had told them to keep their heads down. I tried to make the best of it, but Prince Charles was a bit disappointed. He tried again at the annual jamboree of the Institute of Directors, in front of an audience of over 1,000 in the Albert Hall. 'Why,' he asked, 'do you not do what Villiers does with British Steel Industry to re-employ redundant and young people?' There was no applause and people in the Hall looked at me as though I was the man from Mars. The industrial culture of the 19th century dies hard.

Prince Charles visited most of our workshops and LEAs, some of them twice, and one day I said to him at breakfast in the train: 'Sir, don't you really need a bigger piano to play your wonderful and helpful music?'

'What on earth do you mean?' he asked.

'Well, Sir, there is a new organisation called Business in the Community, which does what BSI does, but nationally across the board. Perhaps you would not like it, and I won't mention it again unless you raise the matter at breakfast tomorrow.' We were travelling from Kilbirnie to Workington and I had been told by Stephen O'Brien, the Chief Executive of Business in the Community, that they would love to have the Prince of Wales as their President. All day I heard him asking people about Business in the Community. I was rather anxious because some BSI people thought that this new organisation was speaking about 'our' LEAs without knowing much about them. It all turned out well. Prince Charles talked about it next day and I said that O'Brien would get in touch with him.

'Good,' he said. 'I know Stephen and I'll see him.' It was not long before Prince Charles became President of Business in the Community and it seems that it is one of his favourite organisations, able to carry out many of his carefully thought out social plans.

BSI benefitted enormously from Prince Charles' visits. Enthusiasm and energy rose wherever he went and the local people referred to them for years after. He always told me that he was the one who was benefitting most. I think those visits gave him the opportunity to meet people, especially young people, in the rather sad parts of Britain where people felt forgotten, deprived and dustbinned. All he had to do was to be his own splendid self and the people he met responded positively and immediately to him.

Ian MacGregor took interest in our work and I recall a BSI board meeting which he attended; he said, 'In the steel towns of Britain young people expect to follow their fathers into the steel works. Where we have closed these works they won't know what to do. The most important thing BSI could do would be to open the minds of these young people to the enterprise culture, so that they think about starting their own businesses or behaving like entrepreneurs in the job they are doing.' Ian said, 'If your friend is hungry don't give him a fish, teach him how to fish.'

Ian said that in 1980, and it was not until 1985 that we were able to launch a national and optional curriculum for schools called 'Going for Enterprise.' We immediately saw the point of Ian's comment, but how could we do it? John Dunbar had been impressed with a talk given by Alan Gibb, the head of the Durham University Business School. I was keen to involve the Royal Society for Arts which was launching a similar project, 'Education for Capability.' After talks with both organisations we settled on DUBS and voted them an initial grant of £25,000, which was matched by a grant from the Department of Trade and Industry, to do a feasibility study. Our colleague Tom Young, a Chartered Surveyor who had spent most of his life in the steel industry, joined the working party and Alan Gibb detailed one of his staff, Cliff Johnson, to take charge of the study. Two excellent young headmasters of local secondary schools joined in and we had a good team to work on the idea, 'Education should develop in all students at least some of the skills and attitudes associated with successful enterprise.' The aim was to educate young people away from an 'employee' to a more 'entrepreneurial' attitude. We decided to use Consett and the North East of England as a test bed for a new schools curriculum, a summary of which follows:

THE ESSENCE OF ENTERPRISE
The ENTERPRISE method at its simplest can be expressed by a series of interlocking modules:
ASKING QUESTIONS
PRODUCING RESULTS
FINDING IDEAS
MAKING PLANS

Asking questions: Am I enterprising? This includes a number of questions about the nature of enterprise. It focuses on the key qualities associated with enterprise and with starting a business and relates these to the young person's self-assessment.

Finding ideas: How do I generate ideas? This introduces a variety of idea generating techniques, normally in a small group context. This is fundamentally a creative process. Ideas emerge, are evaluated and refined and become owned by groups who then proceed to validate them often in the field.

Making Plans: What will I need to start-up? This means planning to turn an idea into reality by identifying resources and customers in detail - in business terms, formulating the business plan. This will involve anticipating areas of difficulty as well as assessing cash, profits and costs.

Producing Results: How do I put a plan into action? This is the most exciting part but also where there is most risk. It means setting up and running the business or project. Adults from outside the school may be used extensively. It means coming to terms with success and failure and perhaps going back to the drawing board. Everything is immediate, practical and critical.

The use of these modules in teaching is participative, project-based and calls for work with small groups. All the materials contained in the ENTERPRISE teaching books are designed to fit these requirements.

THE ENTERPRISE EFFECT

What qualities does ENTERPRISE seek to engender in young people? It encourages them to be:
* more self aware * more independent * more socially skilled
   * more self confident * more creative * more flexible
* better communicators * better decision makers
* better problem solvers * more determined * better planners
* better leaders * better informed about business * more skilled.

These extracts from the 'Going for Enterprise' brochure show how the original idea had been developed by the team. BSI planned to use the material first in the schools in the North East of England, then in the 500 schools in the steel closure areas. We supplied the material plus financial and training support to the Education Authorities. It turned out in the end to be attractive nationally and internationally as well.

Altogether BSI subscribed £100,000 to the preparation and publicising of 'Going for Enterprise.' We paid also for the cost of introducing the scheme into 500 schools in the steel areas. Hundreds of schools used the material after it was fully launched in August 1985. Many other schools adapted the material to suit their own purposes. In BSI we came to think that 'Going for Enterprise' was perhaps the most important long-time initiative we took.

The launch of this initiative coincided with the move of John Dunbar back to the private sector, where he has proved a successful managing director of a group of industrial companies. He did us well in BSI. He was the right man at the right time and his work stands up well today in this changing world.

John was succeeded as chief executive of BSI by Roger

Thackery, brought up in Bradford and educated at the Quaker School in York; he graduated in business studies at Edinburgh University and got his practical business training in Marks and Spencer. He was running a major North Sea Oil service base in the South Shetlands when he answered an advertisement for the job of chief executive to start up a new LEA in the South Humber area, where BSC's Scunthorpe steel works are situated. I watched him doing that job and was very impressed with his qualities and performance. John Dunbar agreed that Roger Thackery would make an ideal successor, so I offered him the job.

The 'first aid' period of BSI's life was over by 1985 and we were into the economic regeneration of the steel areas on a longer timescale. Unemployment was still horrendously high, but as one moved around Britain it was obvious that people had begun to expect and anticipate revival. In BSI we felt that, rather than creating any new job at any price, we had to get down to helping to form a strong, diversified and quite new and different economic base in the steel areas. As far as possible we would do this through the 19 LEAs we had helped to form, also through our nine workshops which were buzzing with activity, and through the use of our funds, which were still substantial, due to John Dunbar's careful husbandry. Job creation had lost its prime position to wealth creation.

Regeneration was the word we most used in connection with education, technical training, quality and technology, which we saw as the essential base for a revival of British industry. We were not alone in the field, as we had been in Paddy Naylor's time. Indeed, there was a plethora of agencies all doing slightly different tasks and offering a confusing number of options to would-be entrepreneurs. As Paul Usher says, BSI was not a 'me too' body: we were always looking for the gaps, the jobs other people could not or would not do. Government was offering a loan guarantee scheme to small businesses and the Business Expansion Scheme looked very ingenious and helpful. Neither scheme has been able to maintain its initial promise mainly because of restrictions placed on them by the Inland Revenue.

Roger Thackery's first order of the day to BSI was, 'We must look at the quality of new job opportunities and how long they will last. This includes ways of helping businesses to survive in the long term, of improving their management skills and helping them to find new technologies, products, processes and markets.'

Obviously, 'Going for Enterprise' was going to be an important plank in Roger's platform and he threw himself into the task of propagating the Enterprise Culture with zeal. He also energetically supported the expansion of the Prince's Youth Business Trust and the Youth Business Centres in the steel areas. Young people had suffered most in unemployment and from lack of training, where Britain trails the world. Recent government schemes will help in the long run, but in the eighties the lack of training was abysmal.

Advanced technology was always an objective for BSI and Roger gave it a high priority. In almost all the steel areas there were one or two high technology firms which we had tended carefully over the years. They were high risk businesses which did not easily attract commercial capital. Roger and I worked out an Accelerated Business Development scheme. This linked training in appropriate skills to the provision of finance on advantageous terms, which we offered to businesses which had established a sound base for expansion. Roger moved on to a Seed Capital Development Fund to support bright people and bright ideas. These schemes were directly in line with government's White Paper, Cmd 278 of January 1988, which strongly followed up all BSI's recent initiatives.

The initiative I especially liked was to establish the hi-tec training firm MARI in our workshops at Hartlepool. This firm is commercial, but dedicated to teaching computer skills to young people. Those who were accepted for training there were immediately offered good jobs. As we move into the computer age there is a great shortage of hands with the skills to use them. I hoped that MARI would come to operate in all our workshops.

But time was closing in on Roger and myself. He was wanted for a senior, important and difficult job in BSC, where I am sure he will prosper fast and far. In all my experience I never came across a chief executive with so many qualities needed for leadership in modern Britain. And Bob Scholey asked me to come over for a chat and I knew what that meant. He reminded me that, as I approached my 77th birthday, I would be miles over the BSC retirement age. I felt that the job I took on in BSI was pretty well completed. We had supported over 3,000 companies which had created some 95,000 new job opportunities in the steel areas, where the atmosphere was by then hopeful and positive. The extract from an article in the *Financial Times* on 2 June 1990 describes the amazing change which has come over Consett during the last ten years. We did not do it all, but BSI was the trigger, the catalyst of change. I feel proud and happy about the result, which is typical of the results of collaboration at the right level under strong leadership.

CONSETT SEES CLEARER FUTURE

FINANCIAL TIMES SATURDAY JUNE 2 1990

The red dust no longer hangs in the air of Consett. It used to be one of the most famous features about the Durham town, caused by pollution from the steelworks, which was the other famous feature. The dust disappeared when the steel works closed 10 years ago that September. After its steelworks closed, Consett had the worst unemployment in Britain. Pessimists said the town was finished. Optimists said it would take years of painful effort to rebuild the wrecked economy of the one-industry town and the lives of its people.

Its population had fought a losing battle to preserve the steel industry in an area where iron was first made in Roman times. But developments since then have significance beyond the region. Local and central government agencies and the European Community invested heavily in the redevelopment. In addition to £11m spent on demolishing the steelworks and reclaiming the site, £17m was invested in building factories and industrial estates, without which there could be no hope of reviving the local economy. A further £13m was spent on roads and other infra-structure and environmental improvements.

British Steel (Industry), the corporation's job-creation arm which was active in Consett after the closure, has calculated that the public sector investment will be offset within the next few years from tax revenue raised by businesses established in Consett since the closure, combined with savings in unemployment and social security benefits. Also, about £50m has been invested by private sector venture capitalists and banks to help new business start-ups.

The story since 1980 begins with the dust. For the first time in generations, the closure permitted an unpolluted view of the area of outstanding natural beauty to which, in 1840, the Derwent Iron Company had added the incongruity of a steelworks. 'Once the works closed, there was a collective determination in the town that we were not just going to join everywhere else in the north in trying to attract new jobs,' recalls Mr Neil Johnson, chief executive of the local Derwentside District Council. 'We wanted to shape a different, more modern sort of society out of the closure. Consett went from high levels of pollution to having some of the cleanest air in the country. We decided that this, combined with the glorious surroundings, was how we must market the new Consett.'

The council bought the redundant steelworks and demolished it in what became Europe's largest environmental improvement programme. Mr Johnson said Consett did not want to attract low-quality, dirty businesses that would have spent years picking over the remains of the works.

While demolition was going on, the council took a brave decision. In spite of a male unemployment rate of 33 per cent, it made it clear that Consett had no place for incoming industries which would bring fresh forms of pollution to the new industrial estates being built around the town.

In the past 10 years at least 4,000 new manufacturing jobs have been created - slightly more than the number of people working at the steelworks when it closed. These include a few well-known names such as Derwent Valley Foods, which makes Phineas Fogg snacks, and which has grown from small beginnings in the town.

Other companies to have set up in the town include: Security Laminators, which needed clean air for its glass production processes; Integrated Micro Products, a high-tech company founded by two former Open University researchers, which chose Consett because of the skilled industrial workforce, its location close to two universities and the attractive surroundings; and Blue Ridge Care, a business start-up, manufacturing disposable nappies, which has expanded rapidly and employs about 200 people.

By last year the 20 leading companies in Consett - most of which were not in existence when the steelworks closed - had a combined turnover of £110m.

Some businesses have been established by redundant steelworkers such as Mr Mike Heyward, who began making home-brew kits when the steelworks closed and now runs the Rowley Wine Company, employing about a dozen people. 'Things were very difficult when the works closed, especially for some of the older men,' he says, 'but many of the younger ones have found jobs in the new factories, and we really do have a more varied and stable industrial base now.'

But the past 10 years have not been a one-way street to success for Consett. Many new jobs do not pay as well as those in the steel industry and overall spending-power in the local economy has been reduced. The unemployment rate is 12.3 per cent - an improvement on 33 per cent but above the northern average and high by national standards.

Consett does not intend this to be the end of the story. The landscaped, 700-acre site of the former steelworks is set to become Europe's first truly green, fully environmentally friendly, comprehensive development. Wind farm and hydro-power from artificial lakes will provide the site with its own low-cost, clean energy. Workshops and offices of companies involved in recycling and environmentally based activities will be accommodated alongside high quality housing develop-ments. Research and educational organisations concerned with environmental projects will be attracted, it is hoped.

If the plan succeeds, it could make Consett, which lived for so long with the pollution of a 19th century industry, into a centre of excellence for the environmental concerns of the 21st.

The idea is seen in the town as a way of keeping faith with its young. Many steelworkers used redundancy payments to buy their council houses - they wanted to stay in Consett. This meant a future had to be found for their children.

Large numbers of these children had a difficult time in the 1980s, with parents unemployed or on low incomes. Julie Swinburne, Kay Poulter, Emma Fail and Debra Wilkinson, teenagers at Moorside Comprehensive, have grown up in a town dominated by the economic and social impact of unem-ployment. Their song is about the steelworks closure which caused this. But it is not a message of despair.

The red dust has blown away,
A new start has begun;
This is the beginning of a brand new day.

I retired from BSC on 1 April 1989 after thirteen years there. It has become a legend of patient, hard, successful work, of which I have told only a part. BSC was denational-ized in 1988, for a second time. Its labour costs had been reduced by a half, its operating costs were lower than those in America, France, Germany and even Japan. Its annual profits were approaching £400 million.

BSI still had a lot to do to regenerate the steel communities and to help them become centres of excellence in the modern industrial Britain. Bob found Harry Ford, director of BSC Tubes at Corby, to succeed me, and Vernon Smith in Sheffield took over from Roger.

At a heart warming farewell dinner I quoted Churchill after the battle of Egypt in 1942. 'This is not the end, not even the beginning of the end, but it is perhaps the end of the beginning.' What surprised me most on that occasion was the speech of Roy Evans, who had succeeded Bill Sirs at the ISTC. He said: 'We used to call you a murderer when you were closing steel works, but now we see you were right. Trade Union members and steel workers in particular don't like working in businesses where there is no profit, where they can see nothing to go for. You started the turnaround in BSC and you have repaired the damage you did to steel towns and communities. Eddie Linton and I have come here, on behalf of the Trade Union movement, to thank you for what you have done.'

INDEX

British Motor Corporation, 111, 112.
British Steel (Industry), 178, 225.
British Steel (Overseas), 172.
British Steel Corporation, 98, 201.
Broinowski, John, 101.
Broken Hill Proprietary, 101.
Brooke, Roger, 117.
Broom and Wade, 113.
Brown Bayley, 121, 122.
Brown Boveri, 118.
Brown, George, 107, 111.
Brown, Professor Jonathan, 120.
Brynmawr, 246.
Buchman, Dr Frank, 40, 44, 57.
Buckingham, 1st Duke of, 19.
Buckley, Sir John, 163, 172.
Bullock, John, 240.
Burge, Rupert, 101.
Burghley, Lord (later Marquess of Exeter, 60.
Burns, Sheila, 158.
Butler, Adam, 193.
Butler, R A, 90, 91.
Buxton, Joe, 54, 60.
Buxton, Maj. Toby, 58.
Buxton, Phyllis, 58.

C

Cairncross, Sir Alec, 132.
Callaghan, (later Lord), James, 151, 152, 166, 175, 185, 193, 223.
Cambrai, 1.
Cambridge Instruments, 115, 116.
Campbell, Sir Nigel, 88.
Candover, 117.
Cannon, Sir Leslie, 127, 160.
Cant, Ben, 107.
Capel, James, 1.
Capital Steels, 166.
Cardiff, 225.

Carey, Sir Peter, 176, 177, 179, 180, 181, 195, 218.
Carrington, Peter, 71, 195.
Caspari, Fritz, 45, 46.
Castle, (later Baroness) Barbara, 128.
CBI, 124.
Cecil, Lord Robert, 10.
Cecil, Robert (later Marquess of Salisbury), 71.
Central Bank of Italy, 143.
Chamberlain, Neville, 53, 54, 62.
Chandos, Lord, 93.
Channel Tunnel, 141.
Château de Ferrières, 99.
Cheetham, Barry, 158.
Cherry Orchard, 2, 3, 5, 7, 12, 177.
Churchill, 34, 53, 54, 67, 68, 69, 71.
Clapham, Sir Michael, 127.
Clarendon, Lord, 52, 86.
Clarke, Sir Otto, 122, 153.
Clayton, 'Tubby', 31, 32, 34, 35, 37, 38, 39, 40, 41, 43, 44.
Cleveland, 222.
Cliveden, 54.
Clyde, 170.
Clyde Iron, 166, 225, 230.
Cobbold, Kim (later Lord), 88, 97.
Coe, Seb, 193.
Colvin, Maj. Dick, 63, 64.
Commercial Union, 137.
Consett, 189, 195, 209, 212, 213, 219, 222, 225, 247, 254, 255, 257.
Coopers and Lybrand, 168.
Corby, 183, 186, 187, 190, 195, 213, 219, 222, 225.
Cork Gully, 135.
Cork, Sir Kenneth, 135.
Cornish, Francis, 246.
Cornish, Lt Col 'Billikin', 63.

INDEX

Coulter, Ian, 158.
Counsell, John, 242.
Courtaulds, 109, 114, 134.
Croda, 94.
Cromer, Lord, 98, 100.
Crosland, Anthony, 119.
Crossman, Dick, 44, 47, 48, 51.

D

d'Ursel, Count Michel, 147.
Darling and Company, 101, 102.
Darling, John, 101.
Davies, John, 124.
Davies, Pat, 240.
Davignon, Vicomte 'Steevie,' 179, 184, 185, 186, 190.
Davis, John, 115, 117.
Davis, William, 118.
Davy, 172.
Davy International, 163.
Daw, Nick, 239.
Day, Robin, 214.
de Bellaigue, Toinon, 84.
de la Barre d'Erquelinnes, Count Henri, 85.
de Rothschild, Baron Guy, 99.
Dean, Sir Maurice, 108.
Deeside Industrial Park, 229.
Defraigne, M, 185.
Denning, Lord, 211.
Department of Economic Affairs, 107.
Desborough, Lord, 54.
Deutsche Bank, 98.
Dix, Peter, 137.
Douglas Home, Sir Alec, 107.
Douglas Home, William, 45, 50, 51.
Drayton Corporation, 131.
du Parc, le Marquis, 85.
Duffy, 204.
Dunbar, John, 242, 245, 249, 251, 252.

Duncan, George, 131.

E

East Moors, 166, 170.
Ebbw Vale, 171, 225, 245, 246.
Economists Advisory Group, 233.
Edwardes, Michael, 190, 195, 214.
Edwards, Nicholas, 208.
Electoral Reform Society, 214.
Emmitt, Ray, 168.
English Electric Company, 119.
Equity Corp, 140.
Esperanza Trade and Transport, 136.
Eurofer, 179, 185, 186.
Eurotunnel, 114.
Evans, Moss, 152, 174.
Evans, Roy, 258.
Everitt, Harry, 130.
Ewart, David, 117, 122, 130, 131, 137.
Ezra, (later Lord) Derek, 172, 173.

F

Fairfax, Vincent, 101.
Faulkner, Brian, 132.
Feather, Vic, 127.
Federal Trust, 143.
Fenchurch Insurance, 136, 139.
Finacor SA, 142.
Finniston, Sir Monty, 153, 157, 158, 159, 225.
Fisher, Edwin, 6.
Fisher, Rt Hon HAL, 42, 46, 51.
Fleck, Lord, 115.
Fleming, Peter, 60.
Flower, Maj. John, 58.
Flower, Pamela Constance, 57.
Foot, Michael, 152, 171.
Ford, Harry, 257.
Forest Row, 6.

261

Holloway, Frank, 173, 183, 187, 219.
Holman Bros, 113.
Howard de Walden, Lord, 67.
Howard, Miles (later Major General the Duke of Norfolk), 72.
Howe, Sir Geoffrey, 195, 214.
Humphreys, Bill, 244.
Hunsdon, Lord, 15.
Hunterston, 190, 222, 225.

I
ICI, 115.
Industrial Reorganisation Corporation, 97, 105, 107, 115, 117, 119, 121, 149, 153, 210.
Institut Bancaire, 97, 116, 141.
International Compressed Air Corporation, 113.
International Distillers and Vintners, 131.
International Institute for European Banking Studies, 97.
International Monetary Fund, 153.
Iron and Steel Trades Confederation, 160.
ISTC, 184, 199, 202, 203, 212, 216, 217, 223.

J
J. Henry Schroder, 103.
James, Dr Monty, 28.
Jeffreys, Christopher, 64.
Jenkins, Roy, 124, 128, 210.
Jenks, Brian, 233, 239.
Joad, Professor, 38.
Johnson, Cliff, 249.
Johnson, Neil, 255.
Johnston, Brian, 45, 47, 51, 71, 84.
Jones, Barry, 187.
Jones, Jack, 127, 150, 152.

Jones, John Broadbent, 226.
José, 85, 86, 94, 95, 102, 116, 154, 196, 212, 229.
Joseph, (later Lord) Keith, 118, 153, 176, 177, 178, 180, 181, 182, 184, 188, 191, 192, 195, 197, 199, 201, 202, 208, 209, 210, 212, 214, 215, 218, 222.
Joseph, Maxwell, 131.
Junor, John, 214.
Jurbise, 85.

K
Kaufman, Gerald, 153, 166, 168, 170, 174, 206.
Kearton, Sir Frank (later Lord), 105, 108, 112, 115, 124, 129, 210.
Keightley, General, 81.
Keith, Kenneth (later Lord), 149.
Kent, Rodney, 115.
Kerry, 'Cyrus', 28.
Keynes, Maynard, 10, 49.
Keys, Bill, 216.
Kiam, Victor, 240.
Kindersley, Lord, 97.
King, John (later Lord), 122, 123, 141.
Kinnock, Neil, 168.
Kissin, Harry (later Lord), 136, 137, 138, 139, 150.
Knight, Bob, 221.
Knight, Mike, 114.

L
Lambert, Baron, 137.
Lane Fox, Jimmy, 45.
Lazards, 97, 119.
Legal and General Assurance, 103.
Leith-Ross, Sir Frederick, 94, 97.
Leopold of Belgium, King, 64.
Lever, Harold, 216.